1

THE SUM OF HISTORY

René Grousset

THE SUM OF HISTORY

ENGLISH VERSION BY
A. and H. Temple Patterson

HYPERION PRESS, INC.
Westport, Connecticut

Published in 1951 by Tower Bridge Publications, Hadleigh, Essex
Hyperion reprint edition 1979
Library of Congress Catalog Number 78-59024
ISBN 0-88355-697-9
Printed in the United States of America

Library of Congress Cataloging in Publication Data
Grousset, René, 1885-1952.
   The sum of history.

   Translation of Bilan de l'histoire.
   Reprint of the 1951 ed. published by Tower
Bridge Publications, Hadleigh, Essex.
   1. Civilization—History.   I. Title.
CB73.G713   1979   901   78-59024
ISBN 0-88355-697-9

CONTENTS

PAGE

TRANSLATORS' FOREWORD

English-speaking readers are reminded that this brilliant and timely survey, by one of the most distinguished living Orientalists, is written primarily from a French (and Catholic) standpoint. But the writer's analyses and vital conclusions are of universal interest and will command the attention of all ' civilised ' people.

Footnotes are the Author's unless marked T.P., when they are the translators'.

I

ESTIMATE OF CIVILIZATION

Man's Origin

MAN has no longer any illusions about the wild beast lurking within him. Recent events, war, and concentration camps, have reminded him of the lowliness of his origin—about which theories of evolution and the Christian dogma of original sin are in complete agreement. Totalitarian doctrines gave the beast its chance to break loose from the chains and destroy, over vast areas, a civilization which had believed itself immortal. Faced with such a spectacle, to what heights might not Pascal have risen! Since his day all human progress has but served to make our periodical relapse into barbarism immeasurably more deadly. Henceforth, once a war has broken out, the whole urban civilization of a country can be razed to the ground in a few hours.

We need but recall our illusions of 1900, or even of 1918:— History, interpreted as the story of peoples in conflict, had (we imagined) 'come to a full stop'. In just the same way, forgetful of the earth's past, do we persuade ourselves that its crust is definitely stabilized and that eruptions, such as those of the tertiary era which lifted up the Alps and the Himalayas from the beds of the first mediterranean seas, will never be seen again. What an awakening it has been, after the last political lull and after tasting the full sweetness of peaceful life, to find our planet once more in the throes of violent upheavals—to find society still so very near to primitive man.

This grim realization makes a retrospective survey imperative. The time seems ripe for stocktaking, for a review of history which must also be some sort of self-examination on the part of mankind. What, then, is the Sum of History?

*　　　*　　　*　　　*

First, what does human history amount to in proportion to that of the earth? Our past, prodigious though it may seem in itself, is only a speck in the vastness of planetary time. A comparison of figures speaks eloquently. Geologists estimate at

a thousand million years the duration of the primary era in which
the development of the lower forms of life took place; at 150
million years the length of the secondary era with its giant
dinosaurs; at 40 or 50 millions the tertiary era with the reign of
the great mammals, the mastodon and the machairodus; and
'only' at 600,000 or at the most 1,300,000 years the distance
which separates us from our most remote hominoid ancestor,
at the dawn of the quaternary era.

Even so, human progress has been remarkably slow. According to the evidence hitherto generally accepted, it took mankind
no less than five hundred thousand years to pass through the
various phases of the lower palæolithic age. It must therefore
have been some five hundred thousand years ago that there
lived the famous 'Sinanthropus' of Pekin, who was the contemporary of our Chellean Man in Europe and possessed the
ability not only to shape stone, but also to make and use fire.
On any interpretation, it was at least 120,000 years before our
era that there appeared the Neanderthal Man (represented to-
day, e.g., by the skeleton found at La Chapelle-aux-Saints)—a
creature as yet unable to stand fully erect, heavy-jawed, with
little cerebral development; and yet already capable of 'religious'
ideas, since he buried his dead.

At last there emerged our direct ancestor, *Homo Sapiens*, as
we are pleased to call him. He made his appearance with the
Aurignacian and Solutrean cultures, which we place together
approximately between 45000 and 25000 B.C. This time there
was decisive progress—suddenly and excitingly revealed in art.
Horses' heads from the Mas d'Azil, carved out of reindeer horn,
have been compared to those on the Parthenon frieze. With the
Magdalenian frescoes and rock-carvings (between 25000 and
13000 B.C.) beauty had found expression: the grace of the deer,
the headlong flight of the wild horses, the furious charge of
the bison, which leap to view in the caves of Altamira or
of the Dordogne, bear witness to such realism, such a sense of
movement and of life, that not until the time of the great
Egyptian animal-painters and sculptors were such masterpieces equalled. But, of course, there was no question here
of 'art for art's sake'. The portrayal of animals was true to
nature precisely because it was connected with the most utili-

tarian practices; the life which the artist breathed into the creatures thus summoned up was indispensable to the ceremonies of imitative magic on which success in hunting depended.

The masked sorcerer who dances on the walls of the *Grotte des Trois Frères* affords us a glimpse of the nature of these gloomy prehistoric religions. More bluntly, the 'Aurignacian Venuses' and the statuettes of the *Tuc d'Audubert* tell us of the fertility-cults which were afterwards practised throughout the whole of the ancient world, from the Astartes and Mother-Goddesses of the classical East to the *lingas* of Hindu Shivaism. As for human sacrifice, another legacy from primitive man, this is repeatedly found in the infancy of our most brilliant civilizations, in the earliest tombs at Ur, in the first Chinese burial-places at Ngan-Yang, to say nothing of the slaughter of captives on the altars of all the Assyrian or Aztec, Scythian or Polynesian, Central African or Germanic gods. All the moral depravity which we can discern in that field from the earliest times is connected with that mass of appalling mental complexes which constitute primitive man's reasoning, and with the obscure labyrinthine wanderings of pre-logical thinking.

Thus, at the very moment when man was emerging from the animal world, his progress, in some respects at least, served only to provide him with new pretexts for lust and murder. The original bestiality that sprang from the reproductive instinct, and the behaviour of the carnivore striking down its prey in obedience to the instinct of self-preservation, were followed in thinking man by the promotion, through ' religious' sanction, of lechery and homicide to the rank of innocent and sacred actions. It is in this sense (and if we restrict the 'religious' act to the incomplete definitions of some sociologists) that the Christian can subscribe to Lucretius: *Tantum religio potuit suadere malorum* (To so much of evil has superstition persuaded men).

This congenital perversion is one of the most disturbing facts that emerge from our investigation. Furthermore, over all primitive religions there hovers the idea of an Unknowable who is conceived as a god of terror, a god thirsting for blood. A fearsome conception, it is true, but not unrelated (let us fearlessly admit) to a whole aspect of our everyday experience

under the pitiless pressure of natural forces and of the laws
of life. In its most elaborate form, the Threat thus dimly felt at
the dawn of the human conscience will one day take on the
shape of the Hindu Shiva, the cosmic god beneath whose dance
the generations groan. This concept we should scarcely be entitled to dismiss off hand, that is on *a priori* grounds alone, if the
world and life were merely what they seem to be.

The East

To resume our rapid survey of human evolution:—

At about 1300 B.C. we can record in Europe one of the most
remarkable revolutions of all time:—The reindeer civilization
suddenly disappeared and was replaced soon afterwards by a
culture clearly more advanced than the Old Stone Age had been,
a culture marked not only by the much more skilful fashion-
ing of tools in polished stone, but presently by the invention
of pottery, the taming of animals, and the cultivation of crops.
These were immense advances, destined to improve the conditions of human life out of all recognition; they have been
paralleled only by the industrial revolution of the nineteenth
century. But these decisive improvements in the field of technical achievement were accompanied by a complete artistic relapse.
This eclipse lasted some ten thousand years, until the eve of the
Ancient Egyptian Empire! Here we have hit upon a historical
law which we shall meet again and again: in human societies
progress is generally made, at any given point, only at the price
of more costly recession in other sectors.

Hither Asia and Egypt were, in the period that we are about
to consider, in fact much more the ancestors of our European
civilization than Europe itself. After a fairly long period of
gestation,[1] there suddenly appeared (do the laws of Vries and
Morgan concerning biological mutation apply also to human
societies?) the *miracle of Egypt* and the *miracle of Sumer*. They
were comparable—in their own field— to what would later be
the *miracle of Greece*. As in the Magdalenian epoch, a strong religious impulse was again responsible for aesthetic development.
This was particularly so in Egyptian sculpture, which reached
its climax under the Fourth Dynasty of Memphis when the

---

[1] As witness the elegant stylizations of wader-birds and ibexes on the vases
of 'Susa I', before 3400 B.C., and the realistic portrayal of animals on the pre-
thinite palette of Narmer, about 3200 B.C.

Great Pyramids were built—(2723-2563 B.C.); the necessity of ensuring the survival of the 'double' by making it as like the deceased as possible gave rise to those 'statue-portraits' whose haunting look still pursues us to-day after four and a half thousand years in the silence of our museums. Writing too—which was associated through 'pictography' with primitive magic and which enabled mankind to create a collective memory that has functioned uninterruptedly since then—appeared simultaneously in Egypt and Mesopotamia as early as about 3000 B.C., though it was only much later, in the fourteenth century B.C., that it was simplified by the Phœnicians through the introduction of an alphabet.

This was a period of intense creative activity. Memphis and Sumer each evolved in a relatively short time[1] a whole world of institutions, beliefs and original values, which were long to sustain future ages. Thus, until Cyrus captured Babylon in 539 B.C., Assyro-Babylonian art and literature lived upon an accumulated capital of Sumerian art, as we know it, e.g., from the tomb of Queen Shoubad at Ur (about 3000 B.C.), and of Sumerian literature, as revealed to us by the first version of the epic of Gilgamesh (at the end of the third millenium B.C.). It was the same in Egypt: the Theban epoch (2160-1085 B.C.) certainly added considerably to the previous stock of ideas. The conception of the survival of the soul, hitherto limited to the aristocracy alone, spread to the whole people; the cults of Ammon and Aton prepared the way for monotheism. But these ideas already existed in germ in the beliefs of Memphis. Many biblical ideas, including some of the most elevated, are undoubtedly old Egyptian conceptions.

Here we encounter another law which we shall meet throughout history:—After a short period of triumph during which civilization conquers new domains, and a long quiet period in which it is content to exploit these conquests, there comes a period of deterioration which sometimes sets in quite early. In the history of art, for example, the decline of the creative faculty, and the tendency to repetition and academism, are (despite some remarkable leaps and recoveries) almost continuous in Egypt from the Fourth Dynasty to the Saïte epoch, and in Mesopotamia from the Sumerian period to the age of the Sargonids.

[1] 2778-2443 B.C. in the case of the Memphite Empire in Egypt; 2950-2584 B.C. in that of the first Sumerian hegemony in Mesopotamia.

Above all, in the matter of civilized ways of living, there seems already to be a decline from the old Sumerian society to that of Babylon, as the Code of Hammurabi describes it about 1750 B.C., and a more distinct falling-off thereafter to the harsh Assyrian society of the ninth to the seventh centuries.

The chief cause of this moral and material retrogression was undoubtedly the constant wars which the Assyrians, 'the Prussians of ancient Asia', imposed on the world for three centuries. The annals of the Sargonid dynasty (722–612) are nothing but a sinister account of cities razed to the ground, populations deported, captives flayed alive or impaled with every refinement of outrageous cruelty. Each successive Assyrian conquest was the murder of a civilization. It is because the prophets of Israel uttered the protest of the human spirit against so much bestiality in man that they are such great figures. But there was worse still. In the wars the Assyrians waged they killed not only the most flourishing urban societies but also, in the regions upon which they fell most heavily, the very land itself. The admissions of the kings of Assur on that point are strangely like the descriptions which Arab annalists give us, twenty centuries later, of the ravages of the Mongols—wells choked, irrigation canals blocked, rivers turned into marshes, orchards and tilth left naked to the inroads of the sand, trees slaughtered like men, and the conquerors making themselves everywhere accessories to that 'death of the earth' which, in dry steppe countries, always dogs the footsteps of cultivation. And the capacity of civilization for resistance is not infinite. Even Xenophon, in the course of his *Anabasis*, could no longer recognize in those permanently devastated regions the once-fertile territory of Nineveh. How much, then, was likely to remain ultimately of the numerous garden-cities of Iran and Irak, when to the destruction made by the Assyrians in ancient days there were added the ravages of the Arabs, Turks, and Tartars in the Middle Ages?

Mankind can be justly congratulated on the Achæmenian Peace which, from 539 to 334, followed the Assyro-Babylonian wars in the East. Such a peace was absolutely necessary for that cockpit of Hither Asia in which all the combatants had slaughtered each other. After so many massacres and ravages, it marked a pause for the ancient world. Moreover, Achæmenian art, that happy combination of Babylonian and Ionian, had an undeniable charm, even a grandeur, thanks to the background against which it was set. What traveller has been untouched by solemn thought on the terrace of Persepolis, at the spectacle of the vast ring of mountains whence the Great King seemed to stretch out his rule to the utmost bounds of the universe? In addition, the Achæmenian Empire represented the extension of Assyro-Babylonian material civilization to the whole of Hither Asia, from the Bosphorus to the Indus. In the same way, the Roman Empire would one day represent the extension of Greek civilization from Brittany to Armenia. Yet we observe in both cases a new historical law of decisive importance: by diffusing itself in this way, a civilization loses in depth part of what it gains in breadth. This law—as we shall see—indicates the heavy price paid for progress.

Despite the benefits of the Achæmenian unification, 'the power to guide the course of history' had in truth tended—even before the Median Wars—to pass from Hither Asia to the Greek world.

The Miracle of Greece

To-day we can no longer forget that the way was paved for the 'miracle of Greece', over a long period, first by the dazzling pre-Hellenic civilizations of Crete (which reached their zenith between 2400 and 1400), next by the rich Mycenæan civilization (1600–1200), and finally, after the 'Dorian Middle Ages' (12th–8th centuries B.C.), by the 'Hellenic Renaissance' of the seventh and sixth centuries. Nevertheless, it remains indeed a *miracle*, in the sense that the thousand years of Græco-Roman classicism, to say nothing of our own renaissance, our own classicism, and finally the whole of western civilization and modern science, have lived on the values created by Hellenism between the beginning of the Median Wars and the establishment of the Roman hegemony (480–200 B.C.). During those three centuries all that was latent in the Greek genius was realized; all the potentialities of the human spirit were foreshadowed or indeed proclaimed.

Nevertheless, the Greeks themselves were pleased to call themselves the pupils of the old civilizations of Egypt and Mesopotamia. What, then, distinguished them from their teachers? This—that the Greek genius represented the liberation of the human spirit in every field and for the first time. Out of the rule-of-thumb devices of Egypt and Babylon it extricated pure science, even in the days of the first Ionian philosophers; out of the hoary secrets handed down by colleges of priests for purposes that were always more or less magical, it produced disinterested speculation; out of the rustic choruses of Dionysus, the rebellious cries of *Promethus Bound*, the rigid Achaean *xoana*, came the free and lovely bodies exulting in the full light of day, and the cult of pure art. As to science, we need only recall that Copernicus, who in the sixteenth century established the laws of motion of the heavenly bodies, merely revived the teachings of Aristarchus of Samos, who died about 230 B.C.[1] In the political field—despite the fetters with which the Greek state loaded its members—Greek society created the free citizen and the free government of the city. Speaking more generally, Hellenism established the dignity of the human personality, and the concept of those 'unwritten laws' which bind the *Antigone* of Sophocles for the same reason as the Socrates of the *Criton*. So high indeed was this conception of human worth that artists like Phidias and Praxiteles believed the greatest honour they could confer upon their gods was to raise them to the dignity of men: the serene majesty of the Olympians whom they carved in marble is based above all on a perfect balance of human faculties. In the field of art as of religion, the universe (in Renan's phrase) has been thus humanized because the Hellenes reduced it to human proportions. We must add that Greek man humanized himself first of all: in the general trend towards civilized life, even the slave found himself treated with more consideration in Athens that was the free man in most other countries.

For three centuries these exceptional qualities assured the spirit of Hellas, brimming over with spontaneous creative power, of a perpetual youthfulness. The Greek of that day moved with the assurance of a young god who knew no rivals, either in the contests of the mind or—after Marathon and Salamis—in the grimmer games of war.

---

[1] 'There are only the Greeks and ourselves,' Paul Valéry once said to me, perhaps summing up in this striking formula the whole account of human adventure.

However, after the death of Pericles (429 B.C.) disturbing symptoms appeared. Richly endowed with mental gifts, the Greek began to abuse them. Increasingly he used his brilliant intellect for the sheer pleasure of using it—and his virtuosity seduced him into losing sight of fundamentals. The same dilettantism spread to politics; at the gravest moment in the life of Athens, it made Alcibiades an adventurer. Moreover this people, so gifted and so conscious of their cultural superiority over the rest of the world, could never—incredible though it seems—rise to the notion of a united country. Their 'country' remained limited to their own city-state, and the three chief cities, Athens, Sparta and Thebes, spent their time in internecine wars. Sparta, the principal military power of Hellas, ended by playing in the Greek world the rôle of Germany in twentieth-century Europe: being unable to impose her dominion on the remainder of the Greeks in any other way, she did not hesitate, by the Treaty of Antalcidas, to make a pact with the Asiatics and to deliver to them Outer Greece (387). To these fratricidal wars we may add a frightful voluntary sterility, the suicide of the Greek race, at the very time when the Greeks were about to be called on to defend themselves against the attacks of first the Macedonians, and afterwards the Romans.

The Macedonian conquest gave Hellenic civilization, as a priceless compensation, at least the domination of Asia; and we know what a stimulus to the Greek spirit was this encounter, in the Alexandrian syncretism, with the genius of the East. Unhappily, after a hundred years of splendid progress, the Alexandrianism which, in the third century, had presided over the hellenization of the East, suffered a reversal: the Greek spirit was in turn invaded by oriental ideas. Euclid and Aristarchus had lived at Alexandria, but it was also at Alexandria that the neo-Platonists and gnostics lived. Lucian's outbursts of laughter (in the second century A.D.) were the last protest of the critical spirit against the return of the murkiest pagan mysticism.

Furthermore, when Alexander had made the Greeks masters of the East, they transferred to it their own inability to unite. The Macedonia of the Antigonids, the Syria of the Seleucids and the Egypt of the Ptolemies, like Athens, Sparta and Thebes before them, wore themselves out in an inconclusive struggle

which made them fall, one by one, an easy prey to the foreigner
—in this case to the Romans. Not with impunity had the
Græco-Macedonian dynasties assumed the mantle of the old
oriental despots. The Greek spirit, which in the days of Marathon and Salamis had been synonymous with the very idea
of liberty, learned servile ways in the courts of Alexandria,
Antioch and Pergamus. Callimachus succeeded Æschylus. The
Hellene of the Median Wars began to shrink into the 'Little
Greek'. And this lowering of Hellenic dignity coincided with
the breakdown of the creative faculty among the Greeks. From
the second century B.C. onwards, there were still innumerable
Greek artists and savants; but Greek art and science ceased to
make progress. Hellenism, henceforth, was only a cosmopoli-
tan civilization that lived on its capital, even if it continued to
render humanity inestimable service by undertaking the education of the Romans.

Rome Viewed from Greece

Looked at from East or West, Rome's achievement presents
two very different aspects. In the East the Romans, conscious
of being both heirs and custodians of Hellenism, completed the
task begun by the Macedonians. One might say that it was
under the Cæsars that Alexander completed the conquest of
Asia! In fact, at the very moment when the Hellenistic monarch-
ies were tottering and Asia seemed on the point of taking her
revenge through Mithridates and the Parthians, it was thanks
to the might of Rome and the *Pax Romana* that Syria and Egypt
remained under the spell of Hellenism for seven centuries
more, and Asia Minor even for about twelve centuries. The
Roman Empire, in that part of the world, never really ceased
to be a Greek Empire. The partition of the Roman world
between two capital cities did not date, as commonly held, from
the foundation of Constantinople; it began with the reign of
Augustus when Rome and Alexandria assumed different rôles
in the Empire. Even in the West Latin thought from the third
century B.C. onwards was dependent on Greek thought; hence
every advance the legions made over the Spanish table-lands or
through the forests of Gaul meant a corresponding extension

of the zone of influence of the Greek spirit. Once the entire West had been latinized, one common Græco-Latin civilization —presided over by a single central power—stretched from the Euphrates to the coasts of Brittany.

This was an immense blessing, a fundamental advantage which the Mediterranean world had not known before, and was never to recover. We may look with envy upon that Age of the Antonines when emperors born in Spain or Gaul ruled as far as the boundaries of Armenia; when Rome's greatest captains could at the same time be Alexandrian dilettantes with a cosmopolitanism as eclectic as Hadrian's, or Greek philosophers as saintly as was Marcus Aurelius. If Europe has ever existed, in the sense which we should like to give to that geographical expression—namely as a common fatherland and a common civilization—it was then, during these four centuries between the accession of Augustus and the death of Theodosius. Has not the whole European drama of the subsequent fifteen hundred years sprung from the fact that we allowed ourselves to break that Roman Peace?

At first sight, then, it would seem that the Roman Empire represented only the fortunate extension to the whole Mediterranean basin, and then to the whole West, of the benefits of Hellenic civilization. But in truth civilization had lost in depth and content what it had gained in breadth and continents. To be sure, the contribution of the Roman genius to the arts included works remarkable for their vigour (such as the statue-portraits of the imperial era) which were often worthy of the sculptors of Memphis; or again, in the realm of thought, the astonishing poem of Lucretius, that pagan Pascal whose profound scientific poetry, with its virile pessimism, had no counterpart among the Greeks. But we cannot deny that in the Latin (or Græco-Latin) civilization as a whole, the creative faculty became sterile. Lucretius notwithstanding, the scientific spirit disappeared; from the standpoint of the history of science the 'Middle Ages', in the pejorative sense of the term, began with the Roman conquest. The same held true of the humane virtues. While the Athenian had spent his leisure listening spellbound to Socrates, the Roman mob demanded the blood of gladiators and the spectacle of tortured wretches thrown to wild beasts. Despite the sententious oratory of rhetoricians like the elder Seneca, the decline was obvious. The Coliseum had replaced Olympia. Already we were on the road to the Dark Ages.

Rome Viewed from Gaul

Thus Rome appeared when seen from the Parthenon; but it would look different if we took our stand in a clearing in Gaul or the forests of Germany. It is true that distinguished scholars have cast doubt on the advantage of the Roman conquest in the West, and especially in Gaul, contending that in Druidism the Gauls possessed a noble religion, capable of rich development; and that this development, which would certainly have taken place under the influence of Hellenism coming from Marseilles, was completely arrested by the Roman conquest.

In reality, this issue goes beyond the relation of the Celtic and Latin civilizations. It raises the question whether the Indo-European peoples who were the primitive inhabitants of northern Europe could have attained to any high level of civilization if they had not been profoundly influenced, either as conquering or as conquered peoples, by the old cultured races of the south. No doubt primitive Indo-European society was full of promise from an intellectual and moral point of view. But—whatever the upholders of the 'Aryan Myth' may have pretended—the Indo-Europeans were only able to fulfil this promise when their genius was fertilized by contact with the old empires of the south. This was the case with the Latins, the Greeks, and the ancient Persians, who were civilized respectively by the Etruscans, the Minoans and the Assyro-Babylonians. On the other hand, the Indo-European peoples who remained in their native environment—Germans, Balts and Slavs—continued barbarians till the day when they came, directly or through some intermediary, under Mediterranean influence.

It is true, some consider that the Gauls might have received this from the Greeks of Marseilles by a peaceful radiation which would not, as did the Roman tutelage, have suppressed Celtic originality. But the establishment of the Phocæans in Provence coincided pretty closely in time with the spread of the Celts throughout Gaul. The two peoples lived together for five centuries. Now, during the whole of this time, this Græco-

Celtic association produced nothing but a crude coinage.[1] More-over, was Hellenism really capable of making an impact on the barbarians of the North? It is too often forgotten that it only made itself felt in countries where civilization was already long-established—in Asia Minor, Syria, Egypt, Italy, Iran, and Buddhist India. But with the northern peoples the imprint of Greek civilization amounted to very little; the experience of the Scythians, Illyrians, and Thracians was typical.

Finally we are faced by the fundamental question: would Gaul have had sufficient cohesion to resist the pressure of the Germans without the support of the legions? Certainly, the stirring and epic resistance of Vercingetorix proved that a real 'national' feeling existed among the Gauls. But that patriotism had the same limitations as the pan-Hellenic sentiment in the fifth century B.C. The general assembly of the Gauls reminds us of the Amphictyonic[2] councils. And neither Olympia nor Delphi succeeded in stopping the Greeks on the road to national suicide. Were the Gauls more capable than the Greeks of achieving a national consciousness, no longer diffused and inter-mittent, but clear and permanent, such as creates unitary states? The Arvernian hegemony of Vercingetorix was a dictatorship similar to that of Athens after Salamis, and in the event of victory it would hardly have lasted longer than that Athenian hegemony did in Greece. The Aedui and the Arverni, the Remi and the Belgae showed themselves as incapable of a lasting association as had Athens, Sparta, Thebes, and Corinth. The Greeks had scarcely been able to unite for a few weeks against the Barbarians. They broke apart again so quickly that in the end it was the Barbarians who, as we have seen, gained the advantage by bringing the Median Wars to an end by the Treaty of Antalcidas; and Ionia could only be freed from them by the intervention of the Macedonian. Similarly, the Gauls failed to make a confederation against either the Cimbri or Ariovistus. Indeed, like the Greeks of the fourth century B.C., they themselves invited the Barbarians to intervene in their quarrels: it was the Helvetii who opened the crossing of the Rhine to the Cimbri, and the Sequani who called in Ariovistus, with the result that twice in one century Gaul came within

---

[1] Recent excavations in Provence suggest that this view may need some modification.

[2] The Amphictyonic leagues of Ancient Greece, the most famous of which con-trolled the international oracular shrine of Apollo at Delphi. T.P.

measurable distance of being conquered by the Germanic tribes, and owed its salvation only to a double Roman intervention, first by Marius and later by Cæsar.

Now the peril here was not only political, but also racial. There were already in Belgium a number of Belgo-German tribes; and a kind of tidal movement periodically brought new waves of invasion from beyond the Rhine. After the Cimbri there would have come the Suevi, the Sicambri, and all the hordes of the German forests. What of the future of France if Clovis had followed immediately upon Ariovistus? The whole country would to-day be a *Westerreich*, a western Germany. To break down the bridges across the Rhine by which Teutons could threaten Celts, the axes of the Roman legionaries were needed.

It was the Romans who brought out the best that was latent in the Gauls, and poured that noble metal into the mould of an indestructible unity. We may regret, with certain Celtic scholars, that the Gallic genius lost something of its suppleness and originality in the process, and that Gaul even forgot its mother-tongue: regret it, because the Celtic languages which survived are so full of dreams, idealism, and subtle poetry! But on the other hand it is no mean advantage to have a share in the logical genius of the Latin tongues, those great architects of intellectual order. And above all, from a political standpoint, Romanized Gaul fared better than Ireland, where the Roman discipline has been so sadly lacking. If Ireland only became a political entity in 1922, a thousand years after France, is it not because she was never romanized? Irish Celticism remained throughout the Middle Ages what Hellenism was in ancient Greece, a pleasing way of life, a focus of sentiment, indeed everything except the basis of a viable State. Everywhere else in Europe the mark of the Roman master-builders can be seen at the foundation of every achievement.

In the East, ancient Greece, despite the superiority of its civilization, had never been able to rise above the city-state. The imperial framework which Alexander had vainly striven to give it had been bestowed upon it by Rome. The Byzantine Empire was Panhellenism finally achieved for the Greeks by the last of the Romans. In Central Europe, the Germans remained at the tribal level until a new Cæsar Augustus—Charlemagne—forcibly imposed upon them the Roman idea of the State. Further East, even the Slav peoples received the elements of political organization, some through the Holy Roman Empire, others through Byzantium. In either case it came from Rome; whatever the intermediary, we find in the origins of all European states the mark of Rome.

France's immense advantage was that she was romanized by direct contact, and eight centuries earlier than the Germanies. No belated material progress could enable Teutons to overtake her after that eight centuries' start down the road of Roman order which Gaul had given her. Let us remember the chaos into which Gaul almost fell when the Roman barrier on the Rhine and the Roman order in the interior of the country both broke down. Only the discipline of Catholicism—that is, of the new Rome, heir of the old—arrested anarchy and maintained Latin civilization and the moral unity of the Gauls through all the Merovingian and Carolingian partitions, until the Capetian kings, emperors within their own realm, undertook their great work of territorial reconstruction.

Finally, if the character of French thought is considered, who can fail to see what France would have lost if she had not passed through the Latin school? The Roman genius was the basis of intellectual order, judicial security, and doctrinal unity. From old writers about the Gauls and from the Celtic peoples of to-day, we know that the Celtic spirit, on the other hand, is characterized by sensibility and by a penchant for dreams and soaring fantasies. Now, the secret of the French spirit lies precisely in the close association and perfect balance of these two tendencies. Cut off from either of these sources, the current of French history would have run a very different course. How true this is may be gauged by the fact that France's two great centuries, the thirteenth and the seventeenth, were those which bore the strongest imprint of Latin discipline.

Christianity

Bossuet depicted Roman history as converging upon Christianity. It is certainly true that the *Pax Romana*, the political unification of the Mediterranean world by Rome, furthered the spread of the Gospel westwards. In the same way (and more or less in the same period) the Chinese Peace which the Han dynasty established as far as the Pamir plateau favoured the expansion of Buddhism towards the Far East. Although both religions were clearly universal in their appeal, historical circumstance brought it about that Christianity soon assumed all the characteristics of a Roman creation, while Buddhism preserved the aspect of an Asiatic (or, to be more exact, Far Eastern) creed. But we must not forget that this simplification is somewhat arbitrary as far as Christianity is concerned, because it neglects a whole side of its history. The Christian apostolate was so far from confining itself to the Roman world that it founded in the Persian Empire of the Sassanids a flourishing church, extended to the coasts of India, and even established itself in China in the seventh century. Christianity cannot, therefore, without historical injustice be accused of having forgotten the principle of universality proclaimed in the Gospel (Matthew xviii. 10).

The transcendency of the Gospel is obvious. It reigns supreme over race and time, and would be equally valid for the inhabitants of other planets. It is only from the human standpoint that it can be included in the great movement of ideas which, in the first four centuries A.D., led oriental thought to the conquest of Greece and Rome. This movement illustrates the historical law of ebb and flow, which pursues the victorious expansion of races and doctrines with strange sequels. From Alexander's day to Hadrian's, Hellenism had claimed to impose on Asia its standards, its concepts, its arts, even its gods. Antiochus Epiphanes had tried to enthrone Zeus in the temples of the Jews. The Ptolemies had occupied the throne of the Pharaohs, and the Indo-Greek kings that of the rajahs. But there is no victory which remains for ever unavenged, no conquest which does not in the long run make captive the conqueror: the Ptolemies soon became as degenerate as the worst of the Pharaohs. The Indo-Greek kings indianized themselves even to the point of becoming Buddhists, and under the Roman Emperor Heliogabalus the most disreputable of the Syrian priests were installed in the palace of the Cæsars. Because the old Græco-Roman cults proved emotionally inadequate, the world ransacked the East for religions of salvation or, as the Indians say, of refuge. If Christianity had not triumphed, it would have been Mithras or Serapis, *Sol Invictus* or the Great Goddess. From the third century A.D. the old Græco-Latin paganism—as Christians would call Hellenism—was dead, and its last defenders were unaware how far they were themselves speaking the language of their opponents. The Emperor Julian, for example, was more imbued with oriental mysticism, and further removed from the old classical spirit, than many Fathers of the Church.

Whence came so general a defection from the spirit of Pallas Athene? That is a question to which Renan, at the end of his *Prayer on the Acropolis*, has given a succinct answer: 'the world, O Goddess, is greater than thou deemest.' The human heart, in particular, can reach to profounder depths than could the wisdom of the ancients. Hellenism seemed so perfect only because it had arbitrarily limited man's vision of things. How much greater was the appeal of the boundless horizons envisaged by the prophets of Israel, or by the philosophers of India! Despite some poignant sayings of Æschylus or Sophocles, Hellenism fell because it could not give human suffering its rightful place—the first. After seeking, with the Olympians, to lose itself in a dream of beauty, the world has had to realize that suffering is the very law of life; that from the agony of the soul rises the dignity of thinking man. The Zeus of Phidias has given place to the Man of Sorrows of Mathias Grünewald, a change which represents the greatest revolution of all time.

Christianity, it will be said, is merely akin to the Indian philosophies which—and this applies equally to Buddhism and Hinduism—are all religions of suffering. But it has gone far beyond them. Buddhist pessimism was content with a disillusioned and negative wisdom; and Shivaïte Hinduism with a dark acceptance of the cruelty of life, a positive acquiescence in evil. On the other hand, though Christianity unshrinkingly faces the problem of evil, it remains (in contrast to Buddhism) a creed of faith and action, and (in contrast to Shivaism) the religion of pity itself.

Modern man was born of the Christian revolution; he was separated from the generations that went before him by a gulf

—the ditch that was dug ere a cross could be raised upon the rock of Golgotha. And yet, in another way, the Christian belief in the existence of the spirit descends from the wisdom of the ancients, and in particular from the Platonic philosophy of which it can claim to be the culmination. Henceforward, every civilization was to find itself necessarily restored in Christ, and Christianity (as those ages and countries which denied Him again were to find to their cost) proved to be, in the words of Taine, 'the great pair of wings on which alone man could rise above his nature.'

Rome's Suicide

Christianity was sorely needed to save what could still be saved of ancient civilization. For the old world was growing dark.

In general, no civilization is destroyed from without unless it has first brought about its own ruin; no empire is conquered by a foreign foe unless it has first committed suicide. And a society or civilization perishes by its own hand only when it has ceased to understand its own *raison d'être*, when it has, as it were, become a stranger to the dominant idea around which it formerly grew up. Such was the fate of the ancient world. Augustus, Horace, and Virgil already appear before us in the guise of archæologists who, with much brandishing of laws or official poems, seek painstakingly to bring home again to the Romans the meaning of Romanism. After the death of Marcus Aurelius, the old attachment to the city of Rome finally disappeared, killed by the régime of the *pronunciamentos*. Even 'Italian patriotism' was absorbed in provincial cosmopolitanism. Admittedly, to the very last there were still splendid exceptions, men for whom the Latin fatherland was no mere empty word—a Julian, defender of Strasburg and conqueror of the Alamanni, an Ammianus Marcellinus, intrepid soldier and faithful historian, a Claudian, the last poet-patriot, singing the Roman valour in pitched battle against the Germans on the eve of the final, fatal invasion. But their voices did not carry. The Roman world was already sinking, under its own weight, into the Middle Ages. Even if that last onrush of the Germans, which broke down the frontier defences, had not been made, Gallo-Roman society was moving of itself towards the conditions of the Merovingian age. Social classes were finally hardening into a hierarchy. The *coloni* (husbandmen) were on the road to serfdom. Money was disappearing; the shocking financial system of the Lower Empire was killing trade, ruining agriculture, and bringing about depopulation. In face of the growing paralysis of all administrative machinery, provinces, cities, and even the large estates themselves were being organized on the basis of a closed economy.

In the political field there was a similar degeneration. The State which Constantine had erected, omnipotent and yet powerless, entrusted with the direction of everything, collapsed beneath its burden. The position of the emperor had developed from the principate of Augustus into an absolute monarchy, deified under Diocletian and considered, since Constantine's day, to rest on divine right, but in either case copied from the Persian model.

All the while the Barbarian was pressing on the frontiers. But worse even than the Barbarian at the city gates was the Barbarian within the city itself. To keep pace with the depopulation of the countryside and to provide labour for agriculture, the imperial government had perforce settled whole bands of immigrants or German prisoners *en masse* as tillers of the soil in all the frontier provinces such as Gaul, Illyria, Moesia; the Rhine valley and the Danubian lands swarmed with them. This peaceful penetration even reached the steps of the throne itself, since the commanders of the 'Roman' army were Vandals or Franks. The great invasion of 406 merely hastened the process. When the Western Empire crumbled under the German onslaught it was already to a considerable extent germanized.

As for the Eastern Empire, it was Asiatic from birth. Persians and Parthians, Achæmenians, Arsacids and Sassanids, all the vanquished of the old wars, who had each in turn been routed by the phalanx or the legions, now took a posthumous and insulting revenge in the Sacred Palace at Constantinople. Their spirit it was which, beneath the imperial purple, now kinged it over the grand-nephews of Pericles and Augustus. The heir of Augustus was now nothing more than a 'Great King' of the

Persian sort, once so despised: the Greeks knew why they themselves gave him the title of *basileus*!

The Latin world germanized, the Greek world turned Asiatic;
Hellenic liberty and Greek science replaced by Byzantine ceremonial, and Roman order and civic pride by the massacres of
Teutonic tribesmen. Between the two, what remained of Mediterranean civilization, the sacred heritage of a thousand years
and the fountain-head of all our modern Europe? Its remnants
had taken refuge in the Church, where the treasure of Greek
and Latin learning was still handed down, and whence came the
only opposition that human conscience could now muster
against the despotism of the *basileis* or the bloodthirsty whims
of the German kings.

This loss of its European character, suffered by our continent,
can be very precisely measured in the realm of art. The world of
aesthetics had known for centuries two great and distinct zones,
divided according to latitude; they became practically strangers
to each other. In the Mediterranean world there ruled the
plastic arts, naturalism, and anthropomorphism. In the steppes
and forests of the north, from Siberia to the Rhine, we find a
geometrical stylization, where even the depiction of animals
was turned into a tangle of floral or linear decoration, frequently
offset by coloured stones or enamels. Around the Mediterranean
there was the art of civilized men who lived in marble cities,
where goddesses stood at the threshold of their temples, their
gaze directed towards the sea that had given them birth. In the
Nordic zone, on the Mongolian steppes over which the Huns
then roamed, on the Russian steppes where Scythians, Sarmatians, Goths, and Huns followed upon each others' heels,
and also on the heaths and in the forests of Germany, it was a
riot of barbaric jewellery, trappings for the armour of horse and
man, the only luxury of nomadic hordes for ever on the move.
As long as the legions held their ground, the Rhine and the
Danube also marked the border-line of the rival aesthetics. But
on the morrow of the Great Invasions the barbarian art of Hun
and German in its turn invaded Gaul and Spain. Aesthetically,
our old western lands were joined in forced wedlock with
Siberia.

There was yet a third zone of aesthetics, that of Sassanid Iran.

Although it had borrowed its models from the naturalistic art of the Assyro-Babylonian world, it distorted them by stylizing them with an obstinate insistence upon a symmetry which was more rigorous than that of the art of the steppes, and which ultimately led to heraldry. This Sassanid Persian art, rigid and dessicated in tendency, in due course invaded Byzantium, and Byzantine art is largely derived from it.

Thus, whether we consider the West, into which the art of the steppes was introduced by the Germans, or Byzantium, where Sassanid art was directly imitated, we see on both sides the dispossession of the European genius. Now that the invaders had occupied its soil and soul alike, Europe was well and truly conquered.

The Dark Ages

German scholarship did not wait for Hitler before trying to persuade the world that the great invasions of the fifth century rejuvenated and revived civilization. The historian looks in vain for these alleged services. To be sure, he recognizes the moral defects of the Lower Empire, but fails to see that the German invaders effected any cure. On the contrary, they immediately acquired these defects and added nothing to them except their native barbarism. All the vices of the Sacred Palace can be found in Merovingian Gaul, with the only difference that their setting was not the Golden Horn but some royal manor in a remote clearing of the Neustrian forests—for the first effect of the German occupation had been a widespread abandonment of urban life. Let us ponder the death-agony of civilization that followed, the slow mental torture of the disciples of Ausonius or Sidonius Apollinaris, steeped in Græco-Latin culture and refinement, yet compelled during the long winters of occupation to endure the society of these guzzling Goths. And then the descendants of the last Gallo-Romans themselves became barbarians. As we read Gregory of Tours and Fredegar we see that contact with the conquerors no longer irks them. They have got used to it. Civilization does not resist for ever. . . .

For four whole centuries the West, as we know it, ceased to exist. The German tribes . . . what a tragic destiny was theirs! At their every onrush upon the world they have brought darkness in their train. Whence did they draw the fatal power to leave such a wrack behind each time they passed across the stage of history?' *'How did ye spite the gods to earn that curse?'*

Their very origins are uncertain. Their protagonists have striven to present them as the supreme expression of the Indo-European race. They have even spoken of the 'Indo-Germanic' race, or else (by an even stranger misuse of terms) of the 'Aryan' race.[1] Now, analysis of consonantal mutations has led eminent linguists to declare the Germanic tribes not to have been originally members of the Indo-European family, but people who at some point adopted wholesale an Indo-European dialect! So that, by a glorious coincidence, out of all the races who speak or have spoken Indo-European languages the Germans alone would have no right to that title of 'Indo-Europeans' or (to use their own political terminology) 'Aryans', in whose name they have aspired to the overthrow of the world. At all events, they appeared in and around 'Denmark' in the sixth century B.C., whereas the Indo-European centre is rather to be sought in the neighbourhood of the Ukraine. Neighbours of the Celts (who originally occupied the greater part of western and southern 'Germany'), they borrowed from them the first elements of civilization. Then, while the Celts were gradually withdrawing from 'Germany' to populate the British Isles and Gaul, the Germanic tribes stepped into their place, but still remained for long dependent on Celtic culture.

Could the unhappy destiny of the Germanic tribes spring from the character of the land itself? In that vast plain of Northern Germany, with its monotonous arid heaths unbroken by any natural boundary, environment does not automatically restrain activities; the people are not tethered to the soil, as they are in the Mediterranean peninsulas, the British Isles, even in France. But German propagandists have made extraordinary efforts to call that initial disadvantage a distinction by proclaiming that Germany's destiny is to be for ever on the march. In reality the Germanic tribes, without ever having been true nomads like the Turco-Mongols, constituted for neighbouring civilizations a danger of the same kind; whenever they might be expected to have thoroughly settled down, off they set once more, at the bidding of some war-leader, across the Rhine, the

---

[1] The term 'Aryan' could properly be applied only to the Asiatic branch of the Indo-European linguistic family; that is, to the Persians and Indians.

Alps, or the Vistula, to conquer fresh lands. This basic instability has condemned the German peoples to the most paradoxical of fates. At times, they have been moulded by their leaders into a colossal Germania grinding Europe underfoot (as in the Migrations, the *Völkerwanderung*, or under the Hohenstaufen, the Bismarckian Empire and the Third Reich). At others, they have withdrawn and collapsed, leaving in central Europe a mighty chaos (as during the Great Interregnum, after the Treaties of Westphalia and in 1945). The whole German drama lies in these contrasts.

German expansion was originally directed towards the southeast. Between A.D. 200 and 375, the Goths made themselves masters of the Ukraine, from the Vistula to the Crimea. Like all German conquests, this was short-lived. In A.D. 375, driven back before the advance of the Huns, the Goths were hurled upon the frontiers of the Roman Empire, thus giving the signal for the Great Invasions. Teuton expansion soon seemed to have reached its zenith. Although it had lost the Ukraine, it now held Gaul, Spain, Italy, and North Africa. But this expansion, which had ruined the West and put European civilization back some ten centuries, began almost immediately to work to the prejudice of the Teutons themselves. In order to occupy the Roman West, the German tribes had, in effect, been obliged to leave vacant a good half—all the eastern part—of their old ground; and this had been at once taken over by the Slavs.

It is essential for the understanding of Germany's destiny to appreciate this primary catastrophe. Historical maps speak very eloquently here. About A.D. 300, the Teutons had expanded as far east as the Crimea. About A.D. 600, when the Great Invasions had come to an end, they were retreating so far to the west that their eastern frontier was henceforward marked by the lower Elbe and the Saale. It took the German princes, from the Ascanian margraves to King Frederick II of Prussia, six hundred years to recover a part of this territory. And even then, theirs was labour lost! Under our very eyes the same causes are producing the same results. Hitler, by taking Germany back to its origins, has also brought it back to the disasters of the seventh century. By attempting to repeat the Great Invasions of the past, as far as the Pyrenees and even Tunisia, he has in the end only succeeded in reproducing the advance of the Slavs to the basin of the Elbe. The dreamer of Berchtesgaden had forgotten the law of German history—which Bismarck understood and always dreaded—that every German onslaught upon the heritage of the Latin world ends in handing over half the German fatherland to the Slavs.

The Carolingian Renaissance

Were the Teutons then, having lost all their possessions in the East after the seventh century, destined at least to keep their new gains in the west? Not even that. After four dark centuries of occupation, the first rays of light cast by history show us that Gaul and Italy had remained Romance lands. At the taking of the Oath of Strasburg in 842, no Neustrian could understand the speech of the men from beyond the Rhine. At the most, the Great Invasions can be credited with the establishment of Germanic dialects in Flanders, the Rhineland, part of Switzerland, Vindelicia and Noricum (southern Bavaria and Austria). An achievement which, though considerable in itself, becomes merely secondary if we consider the area which at one time had been covered.

The great historical merit of Charlemagne is his realization of this fact (hence the abuse heaped upon him by the disciples of Hilter). Charlemagne sought, if not to de-germanize 'Germany', at least to romanize her. His achievement, above and beyond the brief 'Carolingian Renaissance', was a Germano-Latin civilization with the stress deliberately laid on the Latin contribution. In the absence of the firm geographical framework which it could never have, the German world had at last found its political and social mould in the Roman setting. Two great creations resulted: the Holy Roman Empire and German scholarship.

From the point of view of civilization, their rôle was to be very different. From the monks of Fulda to the humanists of the Renaissance, and from these to the learned editors of the Teubner collections, the acceptance of Latin learning in Germany resulted in an enormous output, thanks to the prodigious patience and industry of the Germans. A Latin growth had been successfully grafted on the rude trunk of the German forest, thereby limiting the consequences of the disaster to Varus (perhaps the greatest misfortune in European history). No doubt, like all grafting, this was an artificial operation. German humanism, despite its industry, always wore an air of apprenticeship. Even in its heyday, it gave the impression of Greek beauty and Latin order appreciated intellectually, not loved heart and soul. Only in Goethe do we really find beyond the Rhine the classical zest of a Ronsard. But this development was certainly a move in the right direction, and it is best to do justice to an effort through which the Germans have become—for ever, we would hope— an integral part of the West. Unhappily, the foundation of the Holy Roman Empire had made them the dominant part of that West, a rôle for which nothing had prepared them.

Chance in History

The Carolingian empire had been a well-balanced compromise. From its centre at Aix-la-Chapelle, half-way between the Rhine and Wallonia, it could bring Gaul and Germany into agreement. We may even speculate on what the fate of Europe would have been if the future France, the future Germany, and in the background the future Italy, had been able to develop peacefully grouped around that middle zone constituted by the future Belgian lands. But the Carolingians, much as they tried to be neo-Romans, were only German chieftains after all. As such, they regarded the Empire simply as a family patrimony to be partitioned according to the established customs of inheritance. The results of such an outlook were the otherwise incredible Carolingian partitions, the best-known of which, the Treaty of Verdun in 843, cut the Empire into three long and artificial strips—France in the west, Lotharingia with Italy, and Germany—each allocated without any kind of historical sense or geographical basis.

Now, this haphazard treaty decided the whole destiny of Europe. Through the weakness of the last Carolingians and the first Capetians, the kings of Germany managed to annex with little difficulty the whole of the famous 'middle zone', namely 'Lotharingia' (Lorraine and Brabant) in A.D. 880, then in A.D. 1034 the 'Kingdom of Arles' (that is, almost the whole

Rhône basin, from Besançon to Marseilles), to say nothing of Italy, which they received legally through their accession to the imperial throne.

'France' was therefore robbed at birth of at least a third of her inheritance. A good part of her energies, throughout nine and a half centuries of history, were directed towards recovering the formerly Romance-speaking lands to the east, French in spirit, of which the Carolingian partitions had deprived her. And these partitions had equally perverted the destiny of the future Belgium; at the same time as they gave the Romance people of Wallonia to Germanic rule, they bestowed on the future France a population with a Netherlandish dialect, namely the Flemings. A good part of Belgian history was to be taken up by the latent revolt of the Flemish spirit against such an allegiance.

We should be introducing into history the doctrine of final causes if we attributed to the men of the Middle Ages ideas which they never had, at least not in any clear form—the conception of nationality, for example. Something like it was, however, latent in them. That is why, in the course of the Crusades and during the whole lifetime of the Latin East, we find those French barons who held their lands from the Empire spontaneously associating with the barons of France proper, and turning their backs on the German nobility. But the drama of European history springs from the fact that at certain decisive cross-roads it has been diverted from its previous direction to wander at random down by-paths. We stand amazed before the chain of conflicts and disasters brought about by the pure chance of the Treaty of Verdun being followed by the marriages of the Plantagenets, and these in turn—pure chance again!—by the Austro-Burgundian marriage. The cardinal misfortune of the Middle Ages was that, thanks to the bad example of the Merovingian and Carolingian chieftains in partitioning their kingdoms among their sons, the Roman idea of the state as a unity was constantly displaced by the Teutonic view of it as the heritable property of a royal family. Or rather, the two conceptions existed side by side and constantly got in each other's way. Twentieth-century historians of the 'Capetian School' have shown how eager were the French lawyers of the Middle Ages, steeped in Roman law, to group around the King of Paris firstly the baronies which were in feudal dependence upon that city, and afterwards the lands of the ancient kingdoms of Arles and Lorraine. But it must be admitted that this task, like Penelope's web, was undone as often and as soon as it was completed. Whenever the reunion of the land of France was set on foot, in some great reign like those of Philip Augustus and Charles V, the fatal system of appanages (the territorial provision for younger sons) jeopardized the results soon afterwards. The essential step towards French unity, the junction of the northern lands which spoke the *langue d'oïl* with the southern lands which spoke the *langue d'oc*, was largely made possible by the crown's acquisition, after Louis VIII's reign, of the County of Toulouse. And this great fief was actually acquired only through the completely fortuitous circumstance that Alphonse of Poitiers, the first and last Capetian Count of Toulouse, was incapable of having children!

The evil effects of the system of appanages were seen at their worst when the Burgundian cadet branch of the royal House of Valois set up that 'grand-duchy of the West', stretching from Dijon to Brussels, which attempted even as late as the fifteenth century to revive the kingdom of Lotharingia. 'We Portuguese', Charles the Bold used to say in his desire to repudiate French nationality, revealing thereby an outlook more in keeping with the time of the Treaty of Verdun. All the activities of Louis XI and Francis I, Richelieu, Mazarin, Louis XIV and Fleury were needed to remove the effects of that Burgundian nightmare.[1]

The establishment of the Teutonic Holy Roman Empire had therefore, from the outset, loaded the destiny of France with a heavy burden which it required eight centuries to shake off. It handicapped still more the future of Italy. Paul Valéry's revolt against the doctrine of 'historic rights' and the dreadful misdeeds committed in their name finds its complete justification here. The transfer of the heritage of Augustus to Teutonic Cæsars gave a pretext in Latin Law for the periodical raids of the Barbarians southward over the Alps. From the time of Otto the Great to that of Frederick II of Swabia, Italy ceased to be master in its own house; and even when, after the fall of the Hohenstaufen, the emperors remained within their own boun-

---

[1] The 'prohibited zone' which Hitler's Germany reserved for itself in France after the 1940 armistice actually corresponded to this self-styled 'Burgundian mortgage'. It followed in practice the French frontier of 1610.

daries, their theoretical rights served to prevent the formation of any national kingdom of Italy. The peninsula, so clearly intended by nature as a political unit, was thus condemned in its most active region, the north, to be split up into a number of petty city-states, while the south formed a separate kingdom, always ruled by foreign dynasties; and the centre was occupied by the States of the Church.

Eminent members of the regular clergy have strongly deplored the establishment of the temporal power of the Church for more than a thousand years. By becoming a temporal sovereign the Pope was inevitably entangled in the politics of the day, especially in Italian quarrels, and ran the risk of compromising his spiritual authority. It was, indeed, immediately after the pontificates of Alexander VI and Julius II that the Reformation took place. On the other hand, it may be argued that in that iron age the Papacy needed a territorial foothold to ensure that independence without which even its religious freedom would have been lost. The example of the patriarchate of Constantinople, utterly subordinated to the Byzantine court, may be quoted, to say nothing of the Avignon popes ('mere chaplains of the kings of France', as those who urged them to return to Rome used to say) at the beginning of the fifteenth century.

Christian Civilization

Men of to-day are beginning to realize that it is easier to destroy civilization than to rebuild it. It took the people of the Middle Ages six centuries, after the disaster of the Invasions, to recover the creative impulse of Greece and Rome.

This European renaissance, of which the Church was the prime mover, began in the eleventh century. Like all such movements, it showed itself in every field at once: in the Cluniac reformation, Romanesque art, the reconquest of Spain from the Moors, in the Crusades. The Church returned, of its own accord, to the austerity of its early days and set to work, at the same time, in a broad human spirit, to organize a world whose whole future henceforth depended upon it alone. To this world, divided by feudalism into a vast number of small and almost water-tight compartments, exhausted by endless dynastic wars, and ruled by the law of the mailed fist, not by classical justice, the Church restored Roman unity, Roman peace, and Latin intellectual order. From Gregory VII's day to Innocent IV's it challenged the Teutonic hegemony—and broke it. Confronting the threat from Asia, Rome constituted during the whole era of the Crusades (and until the Battle of Lepanto) the very conscience of Europe. Within its peaceful cloisters, true philosophy appeared once more. Once more human reason rose up to take stock of the universe. If St. Thomas Aquinas dominated his age, it is not only because he offered a synthesis of the knowledge of his own time, reconciled Aristotle's philosophy with Christianity, and indissolubly joined reason and faith, but also because, unlike so many modern thinkers, he trusted in human reason and so postulated, as a preliminary to all enquiry, the universal validity and cosmic range of the laws of the mind, leaving nothing outside their scope.

This soaring metaphysical achievement was matched by the upspringing of the great cathedrals. First of all, there developed that Romanesque which might equally well be called the French style and which is indeed so very French in its restraint and its balance between lofty inspiration and solid construction. The master-masons who, in the West, thus virtually re-discovered the arch went on to handle it with growing sureness. The Romanesque sculptors, for their part, though they lacked the naturalism of classical artists, recaptured the sense of movement and of life—as witness the intense animation of the bold stone frescoes of Moissac, Autun, and Vézelay. These owe something, moreover, to illuminated manuscripts and even, as regards the detail of ornament, to oriental or barbarian influence. Hence the Romanesque cathedral is a synthesis in which the great Latin tradition allots due place to the ornamental arts of the Invasion era. The religion of Christ had at last met an aesthetic worthy of it, for this is the first time that in a country which had been subjected to Latin influence we find an adequate rendering of what was for the Middle Ages the Christian conception of the world and of life. But bear in mind the passage of time: the victorious Church had needed seven centuries before it could thus put its seal on the art of the West; for in the history of art no less than in that of ideas the 'penetration in depth' of even the greatest revolutions is very slow.

But the Cathedral aspired yet further heavenwards. Gothic architecture, sprung from that upward urge, is still no less French in its logic and idealism—an upthrusting logic, intent on lightening the whole edifice, seeming to make sport of the laws of gravity, but from which emerge the great aerial shrines of Notre-Dame and Rheims, Chartres, and Amiens. 'Music in stone,' these cathedrals have been called. But while admiring their loftiness and slender elegance, let us not overlook the fact that these daughters of French soil are as solidly planted in it as the peasant-women of Péguy, and as much at home there; that they proclaim themselves French not only by their idealism, but also by a fullness of harmony, a classic purity, which correspond as closely as a Racinien tragedy to what is permanent in French taste. Add that this imprint of origin does not prevent them (so much does the bent of French thought incline to the universal) from being—above all considerations of race or time and in spite of their dimensions and their boldness—as satisfying to the spirit as a Greek temple.

And this time sculptor as well as architect re-discovered the eternal springs. Effortlessly and unconsciously (hence their superiority to more erudite renaissances) the unknown French image-carvers rivalled the work of Phidias. At Amiens and at Rheims there arose a host of statues breathing, as in Greece, nobility and harmony; just as idealized as the Greek gods, but in a more spiritual way, and, for all that, never untrue to their native idiom. In that golden age of the thirteenth century, the miracle of Greece was reproduced in France, but more than a thousand years of Christian exhortation had enriched artistic inspiration with moral values of which the Greeks had never dreamed. Purity of form had here no other purpose than to express this spiritual beauty—the mild tenderness of Virgins, the smile of angels, the goodness of saints, the doctrinal certainty of pontiffs—but it did so with a human touch that moves us all the more because in these apostles or virgins we recognize the old men and maidens of our own village. Human and vivid and familiar also are the mischievousness and verve depicted in the scenes that show devils or the common people, scenes that are full of the salt of the medieval *fabliaux*.

The folk who filled these cathedrals were not unworthy of them. Their ideal of high courtesy or, as they said, of the *prud'homme* (the *prud'homme* of the thirteenth century has something of the perfect 'honnête homme' of the seventeenth) was embodied for the era we are considering in two great figures: St. Louis of France and Jean d'Ibelin, lord of Beyrouth and leader of the barons of the Holy Land (+ 1236). Both are well known to us, since their lives have been described by two of the best prose-writers of the time, Joinville and Philip of Novara respectively, racy and shrewd story-tellers, full of good-hearted sly humour. The two portraits are very much alike: perfect dignity of life, high sense of honour and justice, sincere piety which nevertheless did not prevent even the saint from a prudent use of reason, chivalrous and uncompromising courage, yet very sound political judgement, profound goodness of heart beneath a majestic bearing, deep wisdom, veiled when necessary in a subtle bantering which is altogether French. Nor have the two biographers merely taken a conventional type and drawn their respective heroes to correspond to it. The abundance of picturesque episodes and traits of character obviously drawn from life proves the sincerity of the two pictures, but Jean d'Ibelin and St. Louis had both modelled themselves so closely on this thirteenth century Christian and French ideal that it had become second nature to them and they lived it without giving it a thought.

Scarcely any higher ideal is known to history, nor any more finished type of humanity than that which the Church held up as a pattern. It stands comparison with the classical ideal personified by a Marcus Aurelius. A society which has produced such men has fulfilled its mission.

But on these heights it can never remain. The theory that there are certain Great Ages is no mere literary fiction. Put another way, the old Indian conception of the *kalpa* corresponds to reality. Humanity, after a vast deal of groping in the dark, periodically sees its way clear towards some new ideal. This it eventually attains, with brilliant though brief success; then, instead of holding fast, it makes a fresh start in some other direction, apparently at random, until it distantly envisages the plan of some other Perfect Society which it eagerly constructs. Thus, from the second half of the fourteenth century throughout the fifteenth, one might say that French royal and feudal society ceased to understand its true *raison d'être*, the mission which had given it greatness and even its soul. It disintegrated. On the throne, the spirit of the 'pré carré',[1] the spirit of the direct Capetian line, gave place to the spirit of the Valois, of the magnificent follies of Crécy and Agincourt—which was also later to be the spirit that led to the Italian Wars. The nobility, which in the thirteenth century had for the most part become sobered and disciplined as it closed its ranks around the throne, reverted to its old disorderly anarchy. The country, devastated by feudal strife, began to despair of recovering political and social order. The worst of these conflicts was the struggle for the crown between the first Valois and their cousins the Plantagenets of Bordeaux and London. This rivalry rapidly degenerated into a national Anglo-French Hundred Years War and turned 'the fairest realm under Heaven' into the country of 'the Great Misery', a land as devastated and depopulated as was to be the Germany of the Thirty Years War two centuries later.

Art too forsook the peaceful thirteenth century. Architecture, abusing virtuosity, gave itself over to the *tours de force* of Flamboyant Gothic, which led nowhere. Sculptors, weary of the peaceful classicism of Amiens and Reims, sought new effects in realism, even in the most moving expression of grief— a fitting theme for these nightmare centuries. True, the realistic sculpture of the fifteenth century often displayed remarkable power, notably in rich, robust Burgundy, whose Dukes had linked its destiny with that of Flanders and had sheltered it, along with Flanders, from the general distress. But long before this time, in view of the troubled state of French society, the leadership of the Renaissance had passed from France to Italy.

Italy and the Renaissance

As in the Roman period, Italy became once more the chief centre of western civilization. The first manifestation of her re-awakening was a great Christian revival. St. Francis of Assisi

---

[1] *Faire son pré carré* = to round off one's domain, used more particularly of the royal domain, the *pré du roi*. T.P.

led back man's soul to the very fount of Christianity, the joy of the first disciples on the shores of Lake Tiberias, the divine tenderness of the Sermon on the Mount. Francis walked in the footsteps of Christ; moreover, he was poet no less than saint. A sensitive affinity with all beauty, all created things, with our brethren the animals, revealed to the West a spiritual climate which only Buddhist India had known hitherto. The painting of the fourteenth and fifteenth centuries received lasting inspiration from this refreshing Franciscan poetry.

In a very different field—so rich was the land of Italy in creative energy—the old conception of the State reappeared. Its pathfinder was none other than the complex and extraordinary Frederick II, at once the last of the great Germanic Emperors of the Middle Ages and the first of the Italian princes of the Renaissance. Nevertheless, it was against him, against his anachronistic Cæsarism (which was either too late or too early!) that there rose up in Lombardy and Tuscany, just as once before they had risen up against his ancestor Barbarossa, the communes and leagues which restored to Italy the glory of free institutions, unknown there since the fall of the Roman Republic. Actually, it is rather of the ancient Greek cities that we are reminded by the Italian communes with their long rivalries and their inability to extend the idea of a common fatherland beyond the immediate territory of their own town. We are reminded of them, too, by the integrity of this limited patriotism, and by the civic sense and love of liberty which went with it.

But the great Italian communes were remarkably ahead of their time and already quite modern by virtue of the economic basis of their institutions. Florence, before her liberties were filched from her by the Medici bankers, offered an example of a republic run by the large employers with the co-operation of the commercial middle-class. Venice remained to the end an oligarchy of great ship-owners. But both were industrial and commercial communities whose political power rested upon their wealth. Now these great Florentine cloth-merchants and these patricians of Venice passionately loved their cities. After making them rich and prosperous, they aspired to adorn them with all the beauty of contemporary art and letters. The pride of each was to commemorate his share in government by some immortal monument. Such an outlook provided, as once in Athens, an incomparable and personal stimulus for artists and poets.

Moreover, Italy had been less affected by the Teutons. The Romance speech of the peninsula had remained so close to Latin that Latin was still understood by whole urban populations when the genius of Dante made its appearance in this setting. His profound Latin culture, which he boldly translated into the 'vulgar' dialect, the ardour of his Christian faith, as well as his bitterly partisan passions, transformed Tuscan overnight into one of the great literary languages of mankind: it was thus destined to become the 'Neo-Latin' of the Renaissance. Thus gloriously consecrated, Italian, from the Petrarchan era, was to rival the tongue of Virgil as a vehicle of humanism.

The appearance of humanism in Italy as early as the middle of the fourteenth century, at the moment when France was sinking, a victim of the disasters of the Hundred Years War, constituted a major event in the history of the European spirit. True, the taste for Roman antiquity still remained purely literary, but in the fifteenth century the humanists were to pass from language to ideas, while at the same time the sudden revelation of Hellenism reinforced Latin literature. The imitation of antiquity was to become a cult and a passion; Plato was studied in the household of the Medici and even in the palace of the Popes. Together with the wisdom of Hellas, Greek beauty was to undertake once more the conquest of the world.

No more was art anonymous, as it had been among the Gothic sculptors of France. Peerless personalities arose on every hand, beginning with Giotto, who created the great Italian painting just as Dante had created great poetry; he was in many ways comparable to Dante: in authority of accent, breadth of composition, and the sense of pathos. Brunelleschi brought fresh life to architecture, but his Palazzo Pitti remained faithful to the typical Florentine palace, sober and strong, elegant yet rugged; in it there lived again the indomitable soul of the city. With the equestrian statues chiselled by Donatello or Verocchio, sculpture recovered epic feeling and Roman grandeur. Nor did this strength preclude grace. Indeed, Fra Angelico, the disciple of St. Dominic, seemed rather to have been commissioned in Heaven by St. Francis to express, upon wall or panel, the joyousness of the *Fioretti*. For, in intimate union with beauty rediscovered, Christian tenderness was present everywhere; and in this harmonious blending lies the charm of so many Florentine masters, all through the *Quattrocento*.

Note, however, that we have reached the moment when behind the painter may be seen the humanist with his science, his doubts, and his complexity. Such was already the case with Botticelli, whose Venus rising from the foam, touched by the same languor as his Madonnas, revealed at the same time the neo-paganism of the age and the artist's precocious disillusionment. It was even more so with Leonardo da Vinci, undoubtedly the greatest figure of the Renaissance, with whom humanism amounted to an instinctive anticipation of modern science and whose acute psychology concealed so many secrets. And it was also the case with Michael Angelo, the only man of his day to venture, from the top of his scaffolding in the Sistine Chapel, to portray the God of the Bible—without being struck dead! To find his equal we must travel far in time and space—to the eighth-century Hindu sculptors and the grottos of Elephanta or Ellora.

To all these men, even to the restless Botticelli and to the gloomy Michael Angelo, their work was pure joy. They were inspired, as Phidias and Praxitiles had been long before them, by a mighty afflatus, and lifted up by a great pride: that of belonging to a privileged race at a unique moment in history. They were borne aloft by the Spirit of which they represented one aspect and one moment. That Spirit even uplifted all their fellow-citizens, for here, as at Athens, a whole people shared a common worship of art. From the more moderate wielders of personal power—Cosimo dei Medici or Lorenzo the Magnificent—to the worst tyrants, such as Gian Galeazzo Visconti, there was not one of the rulers of the day whose very enemies were not ready to forgive him much if he had built much, protected artists and scholars, and held high the spiritual prestige of his city. Patronage was the justification of power. At Rome, Julius II and Leo X won thereby imperishable renown. Amid the lagoons of Venice, the whole aristocracy of the republic watched with deferential admiration the prodigious work of Titian.

For more than two centuries, Italy thus remained the favourite abode of that god who dwells in peoples at their apogee (whatever they may then undertake, they find themselves crowned with success in every field). Afterwards, he withdraws without warning (whereupon, at a stroke, they are stripped of everything!) The florin of Florence and the Venetian ducat dominated the markets of Europe. The colonial empires of Venice and Genoa reigned over the Levant. Against the Turk, the captains of St. Mark gloriously took up the rôle of defenders of Christendom, and the heroism of Bragadino reminded the world how a patrician, whose name was written in the Golden Book, could die in the service of Our Lord. What the Hellene had been in his great days, what the Anglo-Saxon would one day be, the Italian was then;—a being of a superior essence, a superman or demi-god, striding freely over land and sea with the inward pride of one who knows no equal. It was not only Venice or Florence which felt themselves superior to other lands. It was the Venetian or Florentine citizen who amounted to something in himself, over and above his city. The *Quattrocento* saw the development and liberation of the individual to a degree which ancient Greece itself had not been able to attain. Of that intrinsic worth of individual personalities, the Italian of the Renaissance was fully conscious. It allowed him to carve out his own destiny like an artist, and to play out like a virtuoso the game of life.

Of this game, like the Athenian of yore, he failed to make the best use. By the sixteenth century we meet him energetically squandering his talents, as the contemporaries of Alcibiades had done. In the delight of knowledge and of action—a delight which had become pagan again beneath a veneer of Christianity —he ended by forgetting all that was most solid in the old free republics, even the sentiment of liberty and patriotism. Liberty was dead. After the fall of Soderini, there were no more republicans in Florence. At Venice, the oligarchy was transformed into a police dictatorship. Everywhere the militia of the communes were replaced by the *condottieri*. In literature, Aretino reigned in Dante's stead. It may be said that Italy, like so many other nations in the course of their existence, had become the opposite of her true self.

Then, as always in such cases, came invasion. The inability of the Italian states to unite, their mortal feuds under the very eyes of the 'barbarians', ended by delivering them over to Spanish rule. For three centuries the Italian lost his 'fatherland'. To this loss he adapted himself fairly well, content with his own personal survival by virtue of his superior culture, which made him indispensable in courts and academies. Like Hellenism after the fall of Greece, Italianism had really become an international culture, 'the mould of fashion and the glass of form,' sought after from Paris to Vienna and from Warsaw to Madrid. But such a fall is bound to involve deterioration in the character of a country's citizens. In the courts of Europe the Italian cosmopolite cut the same figure as the Graeculus (the 'Little Greek') had done in the Roman Empire. The subjection of Italy, moreover, led to general impoverishment. The commercial and financial centre moved from Tuscany and the Lombard towns towards the markets of the Rhine and the Low Countries.

At length, like so many other conquered countries, Italy became a battlefield on which for more than three hundred years the great powers fought out their quarrels. She who had been queen of the age and leader of civilization tasted the bitterness of seeing the gravest questions of Europe settled upon her soil,—but without her participation.

The Flemish and German Towns

The greatness of Flanders had the same economic and social causes as the greatness of Italy. At Ghent and Bruges the cloth industry played the rôle of the *Arte della Lana* at Florence. An eager bourgeoisie of merchants organized the cities into practically autonomous communes where patriotism was born of the defence of liberties. Just as the Italian communes had checked the Emperor in the twelfth century, so in the fourteenth the men of Flanders repulsed the French at the Battle of the Golden Spurs. Forty years later Jacques van Artevelde, the leader of the cloth-merchants of Ghent, made the Flemish democracy momentarily a great power, and the arbiter between France and England. Then, just as in Italy, the towns came once

more under the authority of the princes, in this case the Dukes
of Burgundy. But the court of Burgundy, like that of the Medici,
justified its power by its splendid patronage of art and learning.
In this period the towns of Flanders and Brabant blossomed
with delicate carvings in stone, and the *Retable de l'Agneau* set up
a new landmark in the history of painting. The art of Flanders
was a great power which established its primacy over both the
France of the *Riches Heures* and the Rhineland of Memlinc.

*   *   *   *

The Teutonic world, when unified, has all too often emerged
as a menace to civilization; but when divided and politically
quiet, it had lent invaluable aid to the common task. Once the
German threat has been dispelled, there remains the German
capacity for work which has repeatedly made Germany great.
Such was the case in the middle of the fifteenth century when,
thanks to the weakening of the central power, so many Rhenish,
Franconian or Hanseatic towns had in practice organized themselves as Free Cities after the fashion of the Flemish or Italian
communes. Once more, economic activity was the foundation
of municipal liberty. The Hansa, which represented the most
remarkable commercial expansion that the German world has
ever known (although the Germanic Empire was virtually non-
existent at that period), was covering the coasts and even the
hinterland of the North Sea and the Baltic, from London to
Novgorod, with what were in effect its colonies. At Augsburg,
at the beginning of the sixteenth century, the Fuggers' bank was
about to become a power capable of financing the election of
Charles V to the Empire and the colonization of America! As
in Italy and Flanders, this prosperity had favoured the arts.
Engraving—a technique then exclusively German—and great
painting came together in Albrecht Dürer—an artist, moreover,
very characteristic of his time and setting, because in the full tide
of the Italian Renaissance the fantastic character of one whole
side of his inspiration, as well as the intricacy of his *décor*, showed
him to have been still a prisoner of the 'Teutonic forest'. On the
other hand, his junior Hans Holbein proved himself, under
Lombard influence, so completely free of it as to become, with
Goethe, one of those Germans with whom Mediterranean minds
can unhesitatingly claim kinship.

The triumph of this latinization of the Teutonic world seemed to be the accession of Charles V to the Empire. For was not the new Cæsar as much a Spaniard as an Austrian, to say nothing of his Burgundian ancestry, his Italian possessions, and his Roman faith? Hitler's propagandists made no mistake when they pursued him with the same vindictiveness—and for the same reasons—as they rejected Charlemagne. For the second time a demi-Latin had become the emperor of the West. But unhappily, since Charlemagne's death, this empire had lost a province of some magnitude: France. To recover it, or at least to win back his ancestral Burgundy, Charles V entered into a rivalry with Francis I and Henry VIII that proved both premature and inconclusive; from time immemorial the German Empire (even when supported by Spain) has only been able to act effectively in the West when its hands have been free in the East. But in the East, Charles V was struggling with the Turkish invasion which surged to the very gates of Vienna.

Confronted by the impossibility of being everywhere at once, Charles V resigned himself to a partition of his lands, leaving his Austrian possessions to his brother, and to his son his Spanish territories together with occupied Italy and the Netherlands.

The Greatness of Spain

Such was the apparent origin of the Spanish hegemony in Europe. In reality, the greatness of Spain went even further back. Before her abrupt rise, Spain had deserved her elevation by the bitter struggle which she had had to maintain single-handed, isolated in her peninsula, for five hundred years when she drove the Moors from her soil. This arduous *Reconquista*, a 'crusade at home' which was waged relentlessly for so many centuries (the only crusade which succeeded!) had tempered the Spanish character like a Toledo blade. Furthermore, the expulsion of the Moors had coincided with the unification of the Spanish kingdoms. Thus, well before the kings of France had brought all the French peoples of Gaul together under their rule, Spain was the first European nation to have achieved complete unity. This was so clearly dictated by physical and human geography that one may say: if Africa ends at the Straits of Gibraltar, Europe stops at the Pyrenees.[1] Spain has even been

---

[1] The ancient Iberians (from whom the Basques may be descended) do not seem to speak an Indo-European language.

called 'the Africa of Europe', on the argument that it has given its own brand of Catholicism so peculiar a flavour as to make it almost 'a Christian Islam'. But we must take account of a certain literary exaggeration in these epigrammatic phrases, for the characteristics of Spanish Catholicism existed before the Moslems set their stamp on Spain; they were already strangely distinct in the councils of the Visigoths.

To find too much fault with the Spanish spirit for standing aloof from the rest of Europe, in haughty isolation, 'encased in its armour', is to forget how that armour had been imposed by destiny. No sooner had Spain driven the last of the Moors from Andalusia than a double chance—the Austrian marriage and the discovery of America—assigned to her in Europe and in the New World a task which proved to be beyond her powers. For two centuries, alone against the world, she was compelled to pour out the blood of her sons in every clime: against the Turks at Lepanto; against the Berbers in the African *presidios*; against the Indians on the Anahuac plateau or in the scaling of the Andes; against the Tagals in the Philippine Islands,—to say nothing of the exhausting struggles in the Netherlands which the Burgundian inheritance forced upon her. Here was the first epic on a planetary scale.

Along with so much greatness, there went spiritual wealth. To Spanish Catholicism the West owes the writings of St. Theresa and the Canticle of St. John of the Cross. And, strange as it may seem, these Catholic voices responded—sometimes word for word—to the appeal launched nine centuries earlier, from the heart of Buddhist Asia, by the Indian mystic Çântidêva in his *March towards the Light*; so much do the needs of the human heart in quest of the Saviour prove to be everywhere alike!

Above all, we must remember the major service which Spain rendered to the Latin world by winning for it two of the three Americas, South and Central America. The Roman 'New World' thus created still remains one of the great spiritual reserves of the future.

The German Reformation

Against Spain there rose up the Reformation, a multiple movement, if ever there was one. In it the most diverse elements were allied or opposed to each other: Latin logic, the rather arid classicism of French reason as seen in Calvin;—and, with Luther, the still medieval (or already romantic) tumult of the German temperament at fever-pitch; dynastic self-interest on the part of certain German princes tempted by the secularization of church lands—and, in the German peasantry, the one and only attempt at social revolution which that people, schooled to passive obedience, ever permitted itself; the freest humanism, the keenest critical spirit in the circle of Melanchthon, that rival of Erasmus;—and finally, among the partisans of the Reformation equally with those of the Counter-Reformation (*cujus regio ejus religio!*) the most colossal religious intolerance. In the minds of those who began the movement, it was meant to be a return to the teaching of Christ and to the peace of the Gospel. Yet, the result—for thus does some god of irony seem to sport with the plans of men—was more than a century of religious strife, ending in the cataclysm of the Thirty Years War.

We shall return later to the Reformation in Holland and England. The fact which matters here is that the German peoples found in this great spiritual movement an opportunity to reject seven centuries of foreign tutelage. Since Charlemagne's day, the German spirit had been permeated by the Latin culture which the Roman Church disseminated. By shaking off this influence, and claiming the right to preach the Gospel in his mother-tongue, Luther not only freed German literature as the *Divine Comedy* had freed Italian literature; he liberated the German genius at one stroke, and revealed Germany to herself. His revolt against the second Rome renewed the revolt of Arminius. The Reformation thus became in Germany the re-awakening of 'Teutonism', just as the Renaissance had been in Italy the re-awakening of 'Latinism'. It was the earliest of the great German revolutions.[1]

But, as we know only too well, upheavals in Germany always end disastrously. After the eruption of the volcano nothing remains but the empty gulf of the crater. The boiling over of the German Reformation and the devastating lava of the Thirty Years War left the earth scorched. Germany, by the time of the Treaties of Westphalia, lay prostrate for a century. The loss in

[1] In what is said here I am not claiming to judge in any way the merits either of the Reformation as a whole or of the part it played in other countries. Moreover, the resistance which in Germany itself leaders of the Lutheran Church offered to Hitlerian paganism is well known.

population had been frightful; the countryside was deserted,
the towns ruined, trade destroyed, the overflowing wealth of
the age of the Fuggers reduced to nothing. The Baltic, once
the maritime empire of the Hansa, had become a Swedish lake.
Since Spain too, exhausted by her effort, was on the verge of
collapse, the leading rôles reverted to a new power, Holland,
and a revived power, France.

John de Witt, Spinoza, Rembrandt

No country ever deserved its greatness more thoroughly than
the Republic of the United Provinces. We might call it a country
greater than itself, if we compare its contribution to civilization
with the size of its territory. It was a self-created land, which
had wrenched itself with a mighty effort from the womb of the
sea—a triumph of the human will. Similarly, by dint of sheer
heroism, its people had wrested their freedom from the iron
hand of the Duke of Alva, in defiance of all the headsmen at his
command. What an epic story, from the Sea-Beggars to William
the Silent, of a nation united in one resolve:—to resist, strong
in faith and freedom, the empire on which the sun never set.
And this tiny people forced in the end that huge empire to
yield! Never, since Marathon and Salamis, has a purer victory
been won by free men.

And what wisdom was shown, after the victory, in organizing
the liberty thus gained! What respect for the autonomy of provinces, cities and corporations! As with the English parliamen-
tarians a little later, what a wise distrust of *a priori* definitions
and all verbal logic, what supple empiricism in the harmonious
juxtaposition of powers! Not that the United Provinces lacked
legal minds; for this was the country of Grotius. But, despite
periods of full-blooded parliamentary republicanism during the
rule of Oldenbarneveldt (1586–1618) and John de Witt (1653–
1672), parliamentarism in Holland, as later in England, was recorded less in documents than in a way of life. It was a republic
of unwritten law, whose bourgeoisie ran it like a prudent business house.

Indeed, it really *was* a business house. Its foundations were a
powerful cloth industry, inherited, along with the love of
liberty, from neighbouring Flanders; and naval shipyards from

which were launched the most powerful merchant fleets of the day. It was to these yards that Peter the Great came to serve his apprenticeship to his own trade of empire-building. The wealth thus drawn from all the oceans was afterwards centralized by a system of credit which governed the European market. To the rôle which had been played in turn by Florence with the banks of the Bardi and the Medici, then by Augsburg and Frankfurt with the banks of the Fuggers and the Welsers (and which the City of London and Wall Street were one day to play), the bankers of Amsterdam now succeeded. And the capital steadily accumulated by this commercial development was re-invested by Amsterdam in even greater enterprises after the foundation of the East Indian Company. A century before, the Portuguese, by accomplishing the circumnavigation of Africa, had wrested from the Venetians the monopoly of the spice trade. Now the Dutch, by establishing themselves in the Indian Archipelago, dispossessed the Portuguese in their turn. The foundation of Batavia proclaimed the success of this great design (1619). At the outset a purely commercial enterprise, it expanded progressively into one of the richest colonial empires Europe could boast.

The rich merchants who ran the state became versed—through these enterprises—in the conduct of affairs. Yet, despite their ever-growing wealth, they remained spartan and industrious. No social class has ever been less intoxicated by its own success. At the peak of his power, John de Witt did not cease to show himself the unostentatious model of all the ancient virtues, by the simplicity of his life, his disinterestedness, his feeling for liberty, his high culture. As sparing of the public funds as of their private fortunes, these merchants could take bold risks when the flag of Holland had to be defended. They could also spend magnificently upon the products of the mind. Throughout the seventeenth century, they undoubtedly represented the most liberal and enlightened part of Europe. Holland was then the refuge of liberty of thought and expression, the home of what was one day to be the liberty of the press; Spinoza was able there to elaborate his system of philosophy.

In the field of art, the whole world—from France to far Japan —is indebted to Dutch genius. The Dutch School would have deserved well enough of posterity if it had done nothing more than produce Rembrandt, undoubtedly the greatest painter of all time, whose interplay of light and shade translates the whole human drama, and whose message is particularly moving for the Christian, for his *Pilgrims on the Road to Emmaus* will never fail to inspire in us, more intensely perhaps than any other work of art in any other country, hope and faith. Moreover, if elsewhere, in the Italian *Quattrocento* and among the French primitives, painting had already shown awareness of landscape, it had been only landscape glimpsed in fragments, serving as the accessory and background. The Dutch, however, depicted it for its own sake, as the Chinese landscape-painters had been doing for some nine centuries. And lastly the whole existence, the whole daily life of this shrewd, quiet and active Netherlandish people is conjured up for us by the so-called secondary masters, with their honest, healthy realism, and their delight in lovingly depicting the truth of things.

This merchant people could at need afford most magnificent proof of courage. Such, Ruyter gave upon the sea. When Louis XIV invaded Holland, the inhabitants did not hesitate to break down the dykes to check the enemy. But in the storm of this war the purely parliamentary rule of John de Witt was overthrown by the stadtholderate. Moreover, to repulse the French invasion, Holland was obliged to accept a close association with England which involved some sacrifice of independence. England delivered her likewise from the domination of Napoleon, taking the Cape and Ceylon as the price of that service. But if Holland has ceased to be the moving spirit of the West, she has not ceased to be herself and to play a rôle which is still far from negligible.

The Age of France

In the course of this Sum of History, we have repeatedly met a historical law:—that the development of a society seems always to operate around an idea, which is at once the animating impulse and the goal of that society, since every human group (like every individual) sets its course more or less consciously

'towards the invisible star that shines within.'

Such had been the rôle played in the thirteenth century by the Capetian and Christian idea of which St. Louis had been the purest incarnation. Around this sovereign idea, jurists had begun to build up the State of France. Through it, France had once already won a primacy in the West which was recognized in far distant lands; in 1253, on the banks of the Volga, one of the grandsons of Genghis Khan remarked upon it in conversation with the Franciscan Rubrouck. This pre-eminence, moreover, owed as much to spiritual forces as to military glory. It was because of his moral stature, as well as his victories, that the royal saint was appealed to as arbiter between the Pope and the Emperor, and then again between the Court of London and the English barons. The prestige of the Capetian monarch could be judged when in the course of his crusade in Egypt all the princes of the Latin East, from the Villehardouins of the Morea to the Lusignans of Cyprus and the Ibelins of Jaffa, ranged themselves around him of their own accord. Overflowing the narrow bounds of the French realm, the Capetian idea was already serving as a rallying-point for 'Greater France'.

But this first greatness did not last. If we embark on a rapid flight across the history of France, we receive the impression that for two and a half centuries—from the Battle of Crécy to the accession of Henry IV—the face of the country is shrouded in mist. This is a false impression and an over-simplification, since such a judgment takes no account of the recovery effected by Charles V, nor of the miracle of Joan of Arc and the French revival under Charles VII, nor of the great reign of Louis XI. Nevertheless, it is true that the Hundred Years War, the Austro-Burgundian marriage, the straying of French policy towards the mirage of the Italian Wars, and finally the Wars of Religion did incessantly frustrate both the external consolidation of the country and the internal development of French society.

With the Bourbons the Capetian idea reappeared, incarnate in an almost uninterrupted succession of great ministers from Sully to Vergennes. The feudal lords, who fancied that they were still living in the days of the Valois, bowed their heads upon Richelieu's scaffolds. The great departmental chiefs who were Louis XIV's ministers resumed the task laid down by the jurists of Philip the Fair; once more they levelled and made square the *pré du roi*.[1] The theory of the sovereign state which corresponded to the revived Roman law, the view of the king as 'emperor within his own realm', was further reinforced by the Catholic doctrine of Divine Right; and this in turn was interpreted by the Gallican clergy—and cast in bronze by Bossuet. The French spirit was disciplined on the same principles. After welcoming indiscriminately all the contributions of the Renaissance—Rabelais as well as Ronsard—France regrouped them in good order according to an ideal of greatness and a desire for clarity which were to be the hall-marks of the age. The châteaux of the Loire were surpassed by the glory of Versailles, and the Hellenism of Ronsard by that of Racine. The classicism thus created corresponded so perfectly to the inherent tendencies of the rational French mind that in spite of the later Romantic confusion it was never to be entirely cast aside.

Under this strict discipline, however, there was perceptible an upward surge of energy, a physical vigour, and an intellectual vitality which made France the mistress of the hour. Her demographic position in relation to the rest of Europe had never been—and will never be again—so strong. With her 20 or 21 million inhabitants France left all the other Great Powers far behind (Austria had 12 to 13 millions; Britain 8 to 9 millions; Russia scarcely 10 millions). If Frenchmen imposed their ascendancy on Europe, this was due in the first place to their numbers. They imposed it, too, by their all-pervading intellectual influence. What Italy had been in the sixteenth century, France was in the seventeenth. The whole of European higher society, and every court, spoke her tongue, read her literature, and imitated her fashions. There was not the minutest German principality which did not dream of having its own Versailles in miniature.

This supremacy of the French mind was matched by the upsurge of French power. The hour of the great revenge had struck. To appreciate how fully the French of that day were conscious of it, we should read Mme. de Sévigné's account of the crossing of the Rhine or the Yssel, throbbing as it is with excitement at the triumph of French arms, and also at the sacrifices with which the flower of the nobility had bought those

---

[1] See note 1 on p. 32. T.P.

triumphs. 'From Alsace to Canada'; such was history's epigraph upon the great reign. For the French once more crossed the seas, calling New France into being upon the shores of the St. Lawrence and Louisiana on the Mississippi. The seventeenth century, Barrès would have said, is French Energy schooling itself to be worthy of its destiny.

Did the eighteenth century really break that impetus and shatter that discipline? If the other states of Europe grew appreciably (20 million inhabitants for Austria in 1789; 25 for Russia; 12 for Britain; 5.6 for Prussia), France maintained first place: in that same year 1789 she had 26 millions. If Canada was lost in 1763, the 60,000 Norman, Angevin and Poitevin peasants who remained there clung so tenaciously to the soil that their descendants were one day to constitute a magnificent nation of 3.5 million souls (5 millions, if we count the emigrants in the United States), an indestructible witness to their vitality. In Europe, even in the dark days of Rossbach, the French language, the French intellect, and French art preserved an incontestable hegemony. As for the rationalism of the *Encyclopædia*, what was it but Latin logic and French clarity of the seventeenth century, directed against the seventeenth century, but obeying the same intellectual rules, with the same qualities and shortcomings? The analysis which Taine made (and to which we must always return) has not aged at all: whether in Bossuet or Voltaire, the French classical spirit, following the Cartesian practice which constitutes its inward essence, always simplifies in order to understand better, and, so as to be sure of grasping reality, automatically reduces it to its most general aspect. From the *Discourse on Method*, which may be called the declaration of the rights of reason, to the *Declaration of the Rights of Man*, which is in some degree the political application of Cartesianism, the French mind seeks after laws of universal application. Such an attitude, of simplifying to the extreme, undoubtedly has grave drawbacks when it is a question of penetrating the psychology of neighbouring peoples (some of France's most notorious errors in foreign policy have had no other cause than this). Yet the French should beware of substituting for it an empiricism or a Machiavellism for which they are not made. In a world in which they count for less and less as far as mere

numbers go, it is at once their distinction and their *raison d'être*
to represent these great universal principles.

The Revolution and the Imperial Epic represented, like the
seventeenth century, and in many ways even more so, a triumph
of French Energy. They were also a triumph of the same
internal logic. All that Richelieu and Louis XIV with their
administrators had begun to do in order to centralize and streng-
then the country, was achieved by the Convention and by Bona-
parte with their representatives on mission or their prefects.
Saint Simon, with his clear-sighted hatred of what the monarchy
had accomplished, had distinctly foreseen the distant outcome
of that achievement, and had condemned it for that reason. The
Revolution and the Empire, covering the flags of France with
imperishable glory, also carried out Louvois' programme of
territorial expansion. Indeed, they went far beyond it, and beyond all prudence. But here again, the men of the Convention
and the Emperor were victims of their classical outlook, a
legacy from the whole eighteenth century. They sought to pour
Frenchman and German, Italian and Spaniard, into the same
mould.

Yet they conferred real benefits upon their neighbours. The
prefects of the Empire, for example, gave the Rhineland an
administration that was honest, active, vigilant, tolerant, and
anxious for the public weal—a model administration, infinitely
superior to the previous régime. Revolution and Empire carried
everywhere the ideas of political liberty and civic equality which
had been enshrined in the French constitutions or codes. The
French Epic was thus invested with a spiritual value which it
would be wrong not to mention. We know into what darkness
other conquerors, before our very eyes, have plunged the
world. If, on the contrary, we recall how much of Napoleon's
legacy there was in the movement which swept Europe between
1830 and 1848, we shall agree with Heinrich Heine that the sun
of Austerlitz had really marked for many peoples the dawn of
liberty.

But the nations, unmindful of benefits received, soon turned
French principles against France herself. By sowing the *Declaration of the Rights of Man* in the tracks of their victorious armies,
the generals of the Year II reaped, after thirteen years, Fichte's

Addresses to the German Nation. French domination, despite the immense services which it had rendered and which it might still have rendered, was thus destroyed by the revolt of the very principles which it had helped to spread. But the German call to liberty in 1813, like the so-called liberalism of Alexander I at the Congress of Vienna, proved sheer deception of the peoples concerned. In most European countries Napoleonic administration was replaced by governments decidedly less efficient.

Germany and Prussia

Germany's hour had struck: the nineteenth century was to be largely a German century. Since 1648, Germany had achieved much. The Treaties of Westphalia, by breaking her will to power, by delivering her for two centuries from herself, that is, from the evil dreams which surge up periodically from her semi-barbarous temperament to overwhelm her civilized brain, had done her immense service. Despite Napoleon's mistake in starting to bring order out of the German chaos, despite the Treaties of Vienna which had followed the same path, the balance established in 1815 between Prussia, Austria, and the secondary German states kept the German Confederation in a condition of political inertia from which the German spirit and civilization benefited as much as did the peace of Europe. A Germany so chastened that throughout the nineteenth century she was regarded as a model of calm, honesty and hard work, commanded the world's respect. In the field of scholarship, of exegesis and of science, her work was vast and conscientious. The German word was law for European scholars, by the same token as the Greek word for Rome, the Italian word for the sixteenth century, and the French for the eighteenth. From Oxford to the Sorbonne, all the universities paid tribute to Leipzig. From Kant to Schopenhauer a chain of legendary metaphysical works gave the West the equivalent not, as has been thought, of Greek philosophy, but of Indian philosophy. It was in effect the same trend which in both Germany and India led through criticism of the most radical sort to Monism, and indeed to Pantheism rampant.

A Cartesian, clearly, is born, not made, since the equivalent of the Cartesian idea in Germany, namely Kant's thought, led to

Fichte, Schelling and Hegel. Can we go so far as to say that the trend of German thought is non-European? It remains secretly governed by an undercurrent of intellectual myth and of vast lyrical conceptions which are as far removed from that pure reason claimed by its most illustrious philosopher, as they are from the spiritual climate of the Mediterranean.

That all this German thought flowed from an unacknowledged undercurrent of collective sensibility, is clear from the supremacy won by music. Indeed, it was a new world, mighty and this time without known equivalent, which the German genius now opened up. At most one might compare the message of Beethoven to that of Rembrandt; but the musical revolution inaugurated by the master from Bonn was to win a far wider audience, for it was to reach a whole people, and then the whole of cultured Europe. Germany, whose literature has not always met with due appreciation outside her own frontiers, found in these great musical poems the expression of her best self, in an international language which presently established her cultural hegemony over the West.

In this rich and deep culture disquieting symptoms could, however, still be glimpsed. With Hegel, German philosophy apparently arrived at the apotheosis of the State; with Nietzsche, at the repudiation of all pity, Buddhist or Christian, and at the exaltation of all harshness and violence: the fact that Nietzsche afterwards heaped sarcasm upon German imperialism (which, he said, was murdering the German spirit) was of little avail if his theory of the Superman furnished a philosophical justification for that self-same imperialism. With Wagner likewise, musical lyricism led to an outburst of epic power, the harbinger of imminent cataclysm. Finally, with Treitschke, German historiography ceased to be a science and became an apology for nationalism. Prussia, it seemed, had invaded the German spirit.

*   *   *   *

It appears to be a historical law that in many countries the frontier provinces, the march lands, are often called upon to play a preponderant rôle politically. Their peoples and their dynasties, war-hardened by constant battle, win a military superiority which in the end establishes them as rulers over their own compatriots. Without going for examples to the Far

East, where a borderland gave its name to China and founded the Chinese Empire, we may point to Macedonia in relation to ancient Greece, and to Prussia or Piedmont in relation to modern Germany or Italy.

Historians recall the wholly military origin of the Prussian monarchy. On the one hand, in the middle of the twelfth century, there was the conquest by the Ascanian margrave, Albert the Bear, of the Slav land of Brannibor, which became the Germanic Mark (or march land) of Brandenburg. On the other hand, in 1230, there was the installation of the Teutonic Order in East Prussia, a country then inhabited by pagan Balts whose conversion was desired—and who were submerged. Once installed as conquerors, the Teutonic Knights had to remain encamped and armed, confronted as they were by the hatred of all the neighbouring Baltic and Slavonic tribes. From the outset the Prussian state was unique, an offspring of that massacre of Borussians, at once a monastery and a barracks, marked with the double seal of strict military discipline and still more severe monastic rule. Its character was scarcely changed when, in 1525, it was secularized by the Grand Master Albert of Brandenburg: the monasteries disappeared, but the barracks remained. Nor did it change when, in 1618, it fused with the Electorate of Brandenburg. At Berlin, as at Königsberg, the Hohenzollerns were poor princes who in 1640, on their Brandenburg lands and in their East Prussian forests, could still muster no more than 2.4 million subjects all told. But they hastened to reclaim heaths and marshes, and promoted the immigration of colonists from other countries. After the Revocation of the Edict of Nantes, e.g., the arrival in Brandenburg of 20,000 French refugees, 6,000 of whom settled in Berlin alone, was regarded by the Great Elector as an unexpected stroke of good luck.

With others, the State has been the product of the land. Here it was the Prussian State which, out of nothing at all, created arable land, cultivation, settlements, and towns. The very universities were a creation of the dynasty, often serving a political purpose. Interior colonization was indispensable to increase the number of the petty gentry who supplied the hereditary officer caste for the army, as well as the number of peasant serfs who constituted the 'other ranks'. The universities became no less useful in spreading the doctrine of the State and establishing militarism in the intellectual world. Lutheran pietism supplied the cement which held the whole edifice together. Nothing changed when the Elector became a king in 1700: his son, the 'Sergeant-King', saw to that. Nor did these features change when Frederick II made Prussia a great Power, nor when the Treaties of Vienna, through Talleyrand's (to a Frenchman) inexpiable blunder, installed her in the Rhineland.

Thus were added to the barren lands of Prussia and Brandenburg the rich soils of the Rhineland, and the Junker society of the East was linked to the prosperous bourgeoisie of the West. This might have merged Prussia into Germany. But so strong was the Prussian edifice that, on the contrary, it was Germany which was prussianized. The country of Leibnitz—one of the men who have best understood Christianity—and of Schopenhauer—one of the Europeans who have penetrated deepest into Buddhism—agreed to enter the barracks which were opened to it by the grandsons of the Sergeant-King. It is true, the barracks was buttressed by the university. But Hegel's teaching was interpreted as envisaging the Prussian State as God incarnate upon earth, and German historians viewed the history of the universe as leading up to Bismarck. Prussia was the only one of the great European Powers which attempted to mobilize the intellect permanently in the service of the State.

When Bismarck had achieved the proclamation of the Second Reich at Versailles, there was ground for fresh hope that the Prussian spirit might be disarmed by the old German civilization. In fact, however, they marched closer together than ever. At first Germany seemed to have good cause to congratulate herself on this partnership. German diligence had always commanded respect. Stimulated by victory, stiffened and directed by Prussian discipline, it obtained between 1880 and 1914 prodigious results. In this period the last stage of the Industrial Revolution was changing the face of the earth. And in this, Germany started with unforeseen advantages. Destiny had favoured her. She, whose soil had hitherto appeared so poor, found that hidden underneath it lay the treasures of the coal age. Could heavy industry only be established in the neighbourhood of raw materials? It was precisely in Westphalia, Saxony and Silesia that coal abounded. Did industrialization demand a whole General Staff of specialists? The laboratories of Saxony and the Rhineland turned them out by the thousand. The very methods of the Prussian State, resolutely applied to industrial production and commercial expansion, resulted in making Germany a formidable rival to England, which still clung to its empiricism and liberalism.

Germany's rapid progress, around 1900, could be compared only to that of the United States. She seemed to be the America of Europe. This ancient people, having become a young nation, almost a new country, worked in a fever of activity, an intoxication of success, a vertigo of transformation, which reminded the observer of the New World. What did its erstwhile rivalries matter now? Germans could view them with complacency. Germany's population, which in 1872 still numbered only 40 millions as against 36 million Frenchmen, had risen by 1914 to 70 millions as against 40. In order to complete the elimination of France, to beat even the English, to 'win the war', all Germany needed was—not to make war.

Then why did she? Because to the old-type Hohenzollern, mediocre but prudent, had succeeded an impulsive *Kaiser*, of freakish intelligence, incapable of keeping peace even though he grasped all its advantages? Or because in transforming herself within a few decades from an agricultural country into a manufacturing one, Germany had exceeded the speed-limit, so that, her over-production lacking outlets, in order to break into the markets monopolized by her rivals she was driven on into aggression by her own achievements? There was also the old pernicious dream of Pan-Germanism, a term, however, singularly inappropriate henceforward, since the object was no longer merely to unite all the lands claimed as Teutonic, but also to ensure colonization-rights over the neighbouring Slav or French-speaking 'marches'. Saxon professor and East Prussian Junker thus joined hands with Westphalian forge-master in the war of 1914–18.

If we read history aright, we see that, most commonly, an empire, state, civilization, or society, is destroyed by a foreign foe only insomuch as it has previously committed suicide. This is never likely to be more evident than in the case of

Germany in 1914. Who would have dared attack her? In Africa, she was obtaining by threats all her territorial demands. On the seas, the English were avowedly unwilling to stop her commercial progress. When lo!; deliberately and by an act of collective madnesss she stumbled into that war-on-two-fronts which had been the nightmare of Bismarck and Bülow alike; she herself welded into hostile coalition Anglo-Saxons, Latins, and Slavs. If ever anything was suicide, this was. But, alas, it became suicide likewise for the Europe of which Germany was the geographical centre and had been the directing power since 1871. Suicide, too, for the western civilization which would never completely recover from the catastrophe of 1914, but run straight into that of 1939.

The End of a World

The second Thirty Years War had begun. At the time, most people failed to grasp this fact, since to them the Treaty of Versailles seemed to have completed the ruin of German imperialism. What aberration led the Anglo-Saxon allies at Versailles actually to leave untouched the work of Bismarck and to preserve German unity intact—or rather to allow it further increase, since the suppression of provincial autonomy could have no other result? And to this Germany, more unified than that of the Iron Chancellor had ever been, they served up Danubian states, appetizingly chopped up, unprotected by any federal bond, and already exposed to the call for an *Anchluss* of Austria. The great voice of Marshal Foch was raised in vain against these errors, which have led to so much bloodshed. And furthermore, on the east of the Reich, the builders of the new Europe had overlooked the existence of Russia.

True, it was quite reasonable to expect that Germany, once freed from Prussian tight-lacing, would transform herself after 1918 into a commercial democracy on the lines of the United States. Her industrial plant, which had been left intact, rendered such an adaptation easy. But the Prussian spirit, far from disappearing, remained more indomitable than ever. Pan-Germanism, exasperated by defeat, plunged into dark dreams from which emerged the cult of Hitler.

The sheer blindness of the Anglo-Saxons is staggering. Great religions were born beneath their eyes (a religion, in the sociological sense of the term, is not necessarily spiritual) and they failed to see them, or at least they became aware of them only when they were already being threatened with the brandished sword. Their own pertinent criticism of Nazi ideology sufficed to reassure them. And indeed, from a rational standpoint, the Hitlerian doctrine was a poor affair; the allegedly historical 'Aryanism' on which its dogmas were based would strike any scientific mind as false. On the other hand, in the field of mass emotion, National Socialism, as a combination of myths capable of stirring the German subconscious, represented undreamt-of power. A materialistic and pagan religion, but yet a religion in the affective sense of the word, it went straight to the depths of the German soul because it aimed at freeing it from all 'foreign' accretions. Thus at a single stroke, it tried to sweep away eleven centuries of Christian civilization and humanism, all the gains of German scholarship, everything which had made the country of Leibnitz and Goethe a land of rich culture, beloved of scholars. And such were the intoxication of that coarse mysticism and the mass dementia into which it plunged an entire people, that National Socialists did not even perceive how they were being impoverished. They harked back beyond the Gospels to the old religion of Odin, the faith of the Saxon chiefs whom Charlemagne had conquered, and to a whole pre-history which, from the aesthetic and moral point of view, was utterly barren. Never had there been such a backsliding, not even in the fifth century when the Barbarians established themselves in the Roman Empire; for they, at least, showed good will and some inclination towards Latin culture and Christianity, whilst Hitler's Germany deliberately turned its back on both. To such regression there was no limit short of the brute barbarity of Dachau and Buchenwald.

National Socialism has been compared to primitive Islam, which was likewise a religion of the sword. But the Arab conquerors allowed a share of their plunder and their paradise to any people—Persian, Turk, or Berber—who believed in the Koran. The 'racial religion', on the contrary, was exclusive to the 'Aryans'. Moreover, despite her proud boast of 67 million inhabitants, Hitler's Germany had in fact a demographic basis much too narrow for the world domination at which she aimed. Whatever the grip imposed on her people, she could not cope simultaneously with Christianity, Judaism and the two Internationals, the interests of the Anglo-Saxon countries and the working-class of the West, and particularly with those two other worlds, as inaccessible to her bombing planes as if they had been separate planets: trans-Uralian Russia and America. Then came the hour when the Nazi chiefs had nothing left to offer their people but mass suicide; but so furious was the madness into which the belief in Hitler had plunged the Germans that they accepted even this. In a cosmic cataclysm the ruins of Germany came crashing down upon the corpse of the Third Reich.

English Liberty

Twice in a quarter of a century England saved the West. It is the privilege of her insular position that she is the zealous guardian of liberal traditions. It is thanks to the same geographical isolation that she had been able, secure from foreign threats and invasions, slowly to hammer out that prototype of parliamentary democracy and local self-government which other peoples have subsequently sought to borrow. The same insular conditions have made the British temperament so profoundly different as to confer upon it a combination of incommunicable characteristics—defects as well as qualities—to which it owes its greatness: a cool, determined energy, a tenacity, a stubbornness which, in the darkest hours of the Napoleonic Wars or of the German Wars, made every Englishman imitate the example of the Iron Duke or of Winston Churchill; a steadiness of nerve, a phlegm to which a certain sluggishness of intellect, a certain lack of imagination, undoubtedly contribute, but which make possible 'extensive hopes and expansive thoughts'; a historical sense, and the continuity of action needed to found the empire which is at once the mightiest and the most liberal that the world has ever known; an instinctive empiricism, sprung from experience in the conduct of affairs and from a fundamental indifference to abstract schemes—a state of mind which, although it greatly offends the Latin logic of a Frenchman, has allowed the juxtaposition of powers instead of their opposition, even to the point of reconciling (as if it were the most natural thing in the world) a royal pomp most jealously preserved and the social privileges of the most brilliant aristocracy in Europe with a parliamentary democracy so radical as to usher in government by the Labour Party.

What to a Latin mind would seem illogical is not so in the eyes of an Englishman. In this fortunate land which, thanks to an uninterrupted evolution, has been spared revolutions such as France has known, social classes have never been as sharply divided as on the Continent. Since Tudor times, the 'gentry' have assimilated the rich merchant as readily as the descendant of a knight; moreover, between the squires (who comprise this class) and the peers of the realm no hard-and-fast division is apparent. Under our very eyes, the British aristocracy continues to renew itself by opening its ranks first to the business world and then to trade unionists and workers: from factory to manorhouse the path is clear.

The Englishman's aversion from abstract formulae has had other happy consequences. Whilst the Latin nations periodically proclaimed the advent of liberty in sounding tenets more honoured in the breach than in the observance, England translated it not into constitutional phrases but into deeds. She talked less about it, but practised it, breathed it, lived it. For her, liberty was not an invisible idol, a magic formula in a more or less unknown tongue, but a natural way of life, the true and very climate of the mind.

Such liberalism is all the more deep-rooted for being the product of an imperceptible evolution. The English have never assembled on a particular day or hour, to set up representative government in a whirlwind of enthusiasm. They have built it up during seven centuries, almost without noticing what they were doing. The barons who in 1215 proclaimed Magna Carta, that is, the obligation upon the King not to impose extraordinary 'aids' without previously consulting the baronage and the City of London, had no inkling of the fact that they were laying the foundations of the rule of parliament. Later, the opening of the parish juries to yeoman smallholders was likewise not perceived to be what it really was: the first step towards democracy. Henry VIII, in founding the Anglican Church in 1533, aimed at no more than the organization of what has been called a 'national Catholicism'; but after the breach with Rome there sprang up and multiplied all those sects whose very number, after a furious outburst of intolerance, was to lead one day to complete religious toleration. The Bible, it is true—read with the fanaticism of a Koran—went at first to the heads of the Puritans. Since the Stuart king attempted to revive absolute monarchy against them, they dragged him in 1649 to the scaffold. But neither the Puritan dictatorship of Cromwell, nor the royal absolutism subsequently restored, corresponded to the British temperament. It could be satisfied only with the bloodless revolution of 1688, that is, with the final advent of the parliamentary monarchy to which England has clung ever since, yet without ceasing to adapt it periodically to the needs of new situations.

Pride in this great liberal tradition burst forth in Tennyson's poem on his country:

> It is the land that freemen till,
>   That sober-suited freedom chose,
>   The land, where girt with friends or foes
> A man may speak the thing he will ;
> A land of settled government,
>   A land of just and old renown,
>   Where freedom broadens slowly down
> From precedent to precedent.

This is the cry of legitimate pride which called forth a sigh of envy from Paul Valéry (it was in the very year 1945 which deprived France of that great light)—a jealous admiration of so much innate liberalism, so much political maturity, 'such an art of national *savoir-vivre*.'

Inspired by these ideals, so universally accepted in his homeland, Kipling's countryman remains one of the finest products of humanity which history can boast. By his 'sporting' character, his happy physical and moral balance, his absence of complications (I am speaking of the pre-Huxleyan era) he reminds us at first sight of the Hellene of the great age of Greece, the young god in a glorious human animal. His 'fair play', the word which is his bond, the straightness of his dealings, all bear witness moreover to the strong imprint upon him of Christianity and the chivalrous ideal. But beneath the coldness of the island temperament, beneath the reserve and humour of an Oxford education, there is the ill-disguised pride at belonging to the island-empire; and the Empire, for him, is to some extent the whole planet. For we know that the *civis britannicus* cherishes in relation to other peoples the same sentiment of legitimate pride as did once the Roman citizen. The latter, from Hadrian's Wall to Doura-Europos, felt himself everywhere at home. Kipling's heroes, too, were at home from Calcutta to Ottawa, from the Cape to Sydney. *Facta est insula orbis.*

It is understandable that England dominated the world in the nineteenth century. 'A mass of coal and iron,' she was, like Germany, and much more than Germany, predestined to continue to take the lead of the Industrial Revolution. Her sailor people, brothers of the Dutch and the Scandinavians, but having the advantage of insularity, had in the course of the eighteenth century finally wrested the empire of the seas from France and Holland. Not only did they strew the surface of the planet with British colonies, but they peopled with new Englands all such colonies whose climate did not make residence there too suicidal for Europeans. And as soon as these Canadian, South African, and Australian lands were sufficiently advanced, the British people endowed them, within the framework of the Commonwealth, with the status of free dominions. Their imperialism had formerly subjugated other European colonists in these lands—Frenchmen in Canada, Dutchmen in the Transvaal; but their liberalism (which constitutes the other aspect of their policy) lost little time in restoring to these captives their full linguistic, cultural and even administrative autonomy. This policy was as skilful as it was noble, since it sowed among former enemies the seeds of a loyalty that proved its value in the hour of danger. An imperialism that can set itself such limits may well succeed in getting itself accepted, and can conquer not only the lands, but the minds of men. In this, precisely, lies the fundamental difference between the English and the German method, to the undying honour of Great Britain. Even to the Indian Empire, which Disraeli romantically revived in 1877, the charter of dyarchy granted in 1919 gradually restored the prerogatives of self-government, fully acquired by India, Pakistan, and Ceylon in 1947.

Never since the Rome of Trajan's day has a spirit more tolerant and respectful of all races, creeds and cultures, and an administration more liberal and beneficent, presided over the government of the world. Never was greatness justified by services so great. The British Empire was certainly not Carthage; it was the Roman Empire of the time of the good emperors, enlarged to world dimensions. This community of over 500 million souls represented humanity's first attempt to form, without distinction of origin, a federation of free peoples and of those just about to be freed, a league of nations without interior frontiers, governed by those amongst them who were best fitted.

And Europeans should not forget that this empire was also the best guarantee of Europe's primacy over the other continents. To attack it meant, willy-nilly, to threaten Europe. All the more, then, was it a crime of *lèse-Europe* to invoke against it the revolt of Islam, as was childishly attempted by William II's Germany, or the revengeful spirit of the Far East, as Hitler did.

Twenty Years of Errors and their Consequences

But the respect for tradition, the relative slowness of ideas, the absence of imagination and the day-to-day empiricism which had contributed so much to the formation of English liberties, as also to the building of the British Empire, almost turned traitor to that Empire and jeopardized liberty's very existence.

Louis XIV's duel with William of Orange, and later the wars against Napoleon, had left the average Englishman obsessed by the 'French peril'. In 1870, Victorian society scarcely disguised its satisfaction at seeing French hegemony on the Continent replaced by that of Germany, whose piety, respectability and industry it found estimable. It required the extravagant boasts of William II, threatening the English even in their own element ('The future of Germany lies on the water!'), and, on the English side, the personal intervention of a king whose common sense bordered on genius, to bring the London Cabinet to the point of making the *Entente Cordiale* of 1904. Even after his death Edward VII's spirit led the Allies during the Great War, and it was he—with Foch—who was the victor of 1918, for the greatest victories are often posthumous, as had been seen in the case of Richelieu dictating the Treaties of Westphalia, and as we were to see ourselves in the case of Roosevelt receiving at Rheims the surrender of the Third Reich! But after the Treaty of Versailles English mistrust of France reappeared once more. To some, Foch and Poincaré on the Rhine seemed to be Louis XIV and Napoleon reincarnate. Promptly the British Foreign Office re-sighted its batteries with the single objective (whether at international conferences or at Geneva) of containing French influence in Europe and Syria, and for that purpose striving after a disarmament which, in the nature of things, would be in particular disarmament of France. Lloyd George, the self-constituted champion of that policy, failed to grasp that Foch's armies—so long as they were not whittled down to nothingness—were the defence of London.

To redress the balance of power on the Continent, to lay the resurrected ghost of Napoleon, certain British leaders even contemplated without misgiving the restoration of Germany. If the most far-sighted British statesmen—Churchill, Vansittart—perceived the danger, this return, even though only partial, to the *germanophilism* of the Victorian Age won the support of too many sentimental elements, and also of too many vested interests, not to be fraught with incalculable consequences. Notwithstanding Anglo-Saxon realism, the Puritan ideology often falls into the same facile generalizations as the Latin classicism of the French. There are general truths which may nevertheless be errors in particular cases. In the abstract, what could be more legitimate than *Gleichberechtigung*, equality of treatment between a France and a Germany mutually reconciled and both members of the League of Nations, under the impartial arbitration of Great Britain? In practice, and in view of Germany's potential resources, her birth-rate, her industrial plant, and the militarism of the Prussian spirit, merely to recognize equality would have been to give the Reich an immense economic and military superiority. By the time the English political parties had grasped the truth of this, it was too late. The *Luftwaffe* was already over Paris—that is to say over London also.

As was once said by a British friend of mine, who has always shared the French point of view, 'the jungle is the jungle, and any one entering it unarmed is as much responsible for his own death as the wild beast that devours him.' How many million human lives would have been spared if those who lived on the fringe of the German jungle had partaken in time of that elementary wisdom! But it would be cruel to labour the point, when the free peoples have paid so dearly in blood and tears for their noble confidence in the goodness of man. Besides, the British bulldog spirit did prevail. The countrymen of Churchill saved not only their own island, but civilization itself.

But if, by and large, the victory of 1945 was much more complete than that of 1918, the situation of Great Britain is no longer the same. However great the glory of the country which, in the darkest hours of 1940, held its own for a time against an enemy commanding all the resources of Europe, it could only win the final victory with the aid of two other continental giants: America and Russia. Certainly the indomitable heroism of old England—'the lion-hearted kingdom'—together with that providential island-situation which shielded her from German invasion, are guarantees that she would never have surrendered. But it is none the less true to say that she was relieved by the arrival of first the Russians and then the Americans. Now, such services as these demand reward. Duly, Britain granted the Russians the control of half Europe, as far as Magdeburg, Vienna, and the Adriatic; and this, it must be admitted, is a far cry from the policy of Disraeli. As for the United States, the English people to-day stand to them in the same relation as France to England in 1919—in the position of a debtor nation. That is a particularly delicate situation in a world where financial considerations are of some weight. Like France under the banner of Foch in November 1918, England has never been, and may never be again, so morally great as in the spring of 1945 under the banner of Montgomery. But in the shape of things to come, is it not to be feared that the direction of the world has passed from her hand to the two 'Greater Powers' at Washington and Moscow?

From Port Arthur to Pearl Harbour

At the root of these troubles, according to a distinguished Englishman, was the mistake made by his fellow-countrymen in 1919 'in taking the French for Germans and the Germans for Frenchmen'. An error no less momentous had been committed by the Anglo-Saxons seventeen years earlier, when they helped to create Japanese imperialism. English policy—this is to the credit of its realism—has never hesitated in Asia to form the boldest temporary alliances in order to get the better of the enemy of the moment, even though it might soon become apparent that a more formidable adversary of the future had been strengthened thereby. At the beginning of the twentieth century the Anglo-Indian empire had just been carried to its greatest expansion by a Viceroy of tremendous prestige, Lord Curzon (1899–1905), who had drawn Tibet into its orbit, but who was disturbed at meeting there the advancing Russian influence. To check this infiltration, and at the same time to ward off the Muscovite menace from the rich lands of Manchuria and the approaches of Peking, the London Cabinet decided to ally itself with Japan. On January 30th, 1902, Lord Lansdowne, the British Foreign Secretary, signed with the Japanese ambassador Hayashi a pact of mutual guarantee against Russian encroachments.

It was an act fraught with incalculable consequences, for it may be said that the whole history of the Far East until the actual outbreak of the Japanese War proceeded from it. What had Japan been until then? Despite her victory over China, she had been a very secondary state which could be compelled by mere pressure from Europe to give up in 1895 the greater part of her conquests from the Chinese. Overnight, the English alliance transformed her into a Great Power, the only Great Power native to the continent of Asia and therefore an object of passionate interest to all colonial peoples who suffered from an inferiority complex with regard to their white rulers. And over India, Burma, and a score of other territories from Alexandria to Hong Kong, England held dominion.

The English alliance, it is true, could have restrained Japanese ambition. That, we know, is how Edward VII saw it. Unhappily the result was the opposite. The Hayashi-Lansdowne Treaty gave the Japanese the assurance that henceforward they would never again find themselves alone, as in 1895, in face of the coalition of Russia and her allies; the intervention of the latter would be rendered impossible by Britain's veto. It amounted to leaving the Cabinet of Tokyo free to attack the Russians. Though the profound wisdom of King Edward strove to the last to dissuade it from making this attack, it is more than doubtful whether all the English in India followed the royal example. The result was the Manchurian War; or rather, prior to any declaration of war, the Japanese attack of February 8th, 1904, on the Russian fleet at Tchemulpo and Port Arthur, which foreshadowed the onslaught launched thirty-seven years later against the American fleet at Pearl Harbour. There followed the succession of resounding victories which went ringing through Asia—Liao-Yang, the capture of Port Arthur, Mukden, Tsushima. The legend of white invincibility was shattered, and Japanese pride uplifted to heights unknown before; while all the China Seas were recognized as Nippon's sphere of influence. Every plotter against the Union Jack or the Star-Spangled Banner, from Hong Kong to Singapore, and from Manila to Calcutta, began to direct his gaze towards the armies of Oyama and the fleets of Togo.

In the Japanese victory the Anglo-Saxon powers had played a large part. The British had enjoyed the satisfaction of beating Russia by proxy. America, for her part, had lent the Japanese financial support and had ranged public opinion on her side. Rudely awakened by the repercussions of the Russian disaster, London and Washington pulled themselves together. Discreet pressure on their part induced the Tokyo government to sign the Treaty of Portsmouth (5 September 1905). But it was too late. Both in Europe and Asia the mischief had been done.

In Europe, the Russian defeats in Manchuria had tipped the scales in Germany's favour and destroyed, to her advantage, the European balance of power. William II, with his hands freed at last in the East, could now turn against the West. His 'warlike evolution' dates precisely from this moment. The war of 1914 stands thus in direct line with the Russo-Japanese war of 1904. In Asia, the Manchurian War was to have consequences no less remarkable. In vain did Britain strive to keep victorious

Japan within her orbit by renewing an alliance which flattered and yet temporarily fettered her. The moment came, in 1921, when Britain was obliged at the Washington Congress to renounce that alliance—which had in any case grown increasingly nominal—in deference to the objections raised by the United States and the Dominions. The fears of the Americans and the Australians were only too well founded. Weary of following in Britain's wake not only as regards foreign policy but also in the liberalism of their domestic government, the rulers of Nippon went back to school at the *Kriegsakademie*. The advent of Hitler was to turn them definitely towards war and to lead them to the signature of the Tripartite Pact with Germany and Italy in 1937.

There is at least some intellectual satisfaction in seeing how the Prussian and Japanese military castes, originally separated from each other by many centuries and the entire width of the world, came together. On the one side there were the descendants of those Teutonic Knights whose real religion was war—miscalled a holy war. On the other there were those famous clans of Chôshû and Satsuma whose religion was that of the sword, to such a degree that they even managed to turn into a Samurai code the doctrine of all-pity of the Buddha Çâkya-mouni. Between these two fedual societies, born of war and maintaining even in the twentieth century a fanatical worship of military prowess, there was a kind of pre-ordained harmony. Across all differences of race and surroundings they recognized each other as brethren.

When, taking advantage of the absorption of the British forces in their European struggle against the Third Reich, the Japanese fleet surprised and destroyed the American First Squadron in the waters of Pearl Harbour on December 7th, 1941, the future of the white races seemed momentarily imperilled. Despite the effect of surprise, Hawaii held out, but the Philippines, Hong Kong, Singapore, and Java fell. Even Burma was occupied, and the armies of the *tennô* arrived at the gates of India. Here, as in Europe, the British bulldog spirit won through. But, again as in Europe, it did so only by virtue of decisive help given by the American forces. It was MacArthur who, when all hung in the balance in April and May, 1942,

saved Australia by the great aero-naval battles of the Coral Sea.
In the South Seas, as shortly afterwards in so many other parts
of the world, the Star-Spangled Banner protected the British
Empire and the western world.

The Epic of America

The story of the United States, relatively brief (for it goes
back only to the seventeenth century) is perhaps the most thrilling of all, because it allows us to see in the full light of day
what is normally hidden in the chiaroscuro of pre-history: how
a people, a civilization, a nation comes into being. Can we speak
of the American race? Obviously not, if we stick to the so-called
'racial' theories. But if we are guided by the latest scientific
investigations, we may regard it as a race in process of taking
shape before our eyes. The theory of 'pure' races (at least as
far as civilized peoples are concerned) is a myth, but a myth
which it seemed difficult to track down and destroy amid
the mists of the past wherein its defenders took refuge. Such
was notably the case with the famous 'Aryan race' which the
Hitlerian atlases declared to have arisen miraculously in the
Urheimat of Jutland in the course of the third millenium B.C.
But of late the 'red ochre' burial places of south Russia have
yielded up to us skeletons of that very period, representing undoubtedly the oldest traces of the Europeans. And what do we
find? A most unexpected mixture of dolichocephalic and
brachycephalic types. The future 'Aryan race', the chosen race,
was even before its dispersion, even in its cradle, an ethnic
mixture! The same is true of that other 'People of God', the
self-styled Jewish race which, beneath the uniformity of its
Semitic culture and its monotheism, still presents to-day a most
varied collection of fair people and dark.

Races, in reality, far from being starting-points, ultimates
which have come down from the heaven of Indra, are nothing
but relatively late products of environment, social conditions
and economic organization. It is likely, as Meillet thought, that
the 'Indo-European aristocracy' which, in the course of pre-
history, merged on the steppes of south Russia the various
peoples on whom it imposed its language, owed its supremacy
and even its existence to its way of life: its members were, in the

phrase of the Iliad, 'horse-breakers', who were enabled by the possession of chariots—a new weapon—to subdue in turn so many ancient civilizations. Similarly the Mongolian Turks, despite the differences between their dialects, have since time immemorial constituted a relatively homogeneous race, thanks to the climate of their steppes, the requirements of their pastoral life, and the nomadism resulting from the periodical movement of their flocks between summer and winter pastures. These are phenomena, deduced by science but not hitherto verifiable by experience, which the formation of the American nation allows us to examine with our own eyes. We can witness these developments, formerly relegated to prehistory, taking place in our own day in the western hemisphere.

To produce a race, history demands first of all a markedly distinct geographical environment. Such we have seen in the Russo-Polish plains which gave birth to the Indo-European horse-tamers, and in the Turco-Mongolian steppes which brought forth the Tartar herdsmen. But North America supplied an environment still more favourable, for that vast continent had the benefit of a geographical independence equivalent to that conferred by insularity. Endowed with all the riches of the soil and every form of mineral wealth, it was practically empty before European immigration. A virgin land, almost a new planet—waiting for Man.

He came in the shape of the Anglo-Saxon, that is, of one already well fitted both for economic effort and for political life. Moreover, many of these first immigrants had been already finely tempered by the very circumstances of their departure from Europe—they were Puritans and other non-conformists who, seeking refuge from the intolerance of the Anglican Church, landed with no intention of returning and brought with them not only a steadfast faith but a zest for hard work. Their story is an epic of strong and simple pioneers, which opens with their arrival in the woods of Massachusetts and moves ever onward to the farthest confines of the Great West. With the Bible and the woodsman's axe they saved their souls and cleared the ground. These 'rude forefathers' stamped American democracy with their indelible imprint. To them it owes its background of unquestioning Christianity and its sense of the concrete, a quasi-religious idealism in political or social problems, and, in economic life, its stark realism. Speaking of a case which is superficially similar, that of the German masses, Alfred Fouillée pointed out the lack of harmony between their love of music and metaphysics and their temperamental addiction to the use of the mailed fist, between their *Gemütlichkeit* and their *Faustrecht*. Indeed, German duplicity springs in part from that fundamental dualism. In America nothing of the sort exists, for dualism there is only apparent. Idealism and realism —an idealism which never loses sight of reality, and a bold constructive realism uplifted and exalted by the joy of action—are only complementary aspects of the same force, that American energy destined, three centuries after the arrival of the *Mayflower*, to become mistress of the world.

The ethnic and cultural bedrock of New England has been the crucible in which gradually all the races poured in by immigration have been melted down and fused together. First of all, the Swedes of Delaware and the Dutch of New Amsterdam, elements easily assimilated, because they were very close to the Anglo-Saxon in physical appearance, mentality, and religion. But the French of Louisiana after 1803 and the Irish who arrived, 'a whole nation at once,' after the middle of the nineteenth century were also assimilated, notwithstanding the obstacles offered by their religion and temperament. The sons of Ireland, at one and the same time English-speaking and English-hating, devoted themselves to their new country all the more passionately because they were creating, on the shores of New England and in its heartland, what had been refused them in their mother country: a free and republican New Ireland. Furthermore, the vivacity of the Celtic spirit, a complement of Anglo-Saxon gravity, enabled the Irish-American to play the most brilliant rôle in the politics of the young democracy. On the other hand, it was by their diligence, the regularity and solidarity of their work, that the Germans made themselves accepted. They too came ashore in great numbers, especially after the revolution of 1848 and again in the 1880's, and showed a tendency to group themselves around Chicago, in the 'North Center'. In spite of this concentration, they yielded with surprising speed to the Anglo-Saxon 'melting-pot'. Having arrived before the Prussianization of Germany, or having escaped it by emigration, they proved excellent people. In their own way, they repeated in the New World the adventure of those Angles, Saxons and Jutes of the fifth century who, by crossing the North Sea, broke with Teuton tribal life once and for all and became Anglo-Saxons. This time, too, the severance was final. It was the descendant of one of those German-Americans, General Eisenhower, who in 1944 led the United Nations to the destruction of the Reich.

In the twentieth century, Nordic immigration gave place to elements still further removed from the Anglo-Americans in psychology and temperament:—Italians, Jews from Eastern Europe, and Slavs. New York to-day (1946) contains more Italians than Rome and also constitutes the largest Jewish city in the world. On all of these, however, even when they have remained massed together in town or country, the American way of life has imposed itself irresistibly; and they have become by no means the least patriotic Americans. The most that can be said is that racial differences are revealed in choice of profession. The various elements among recent immigrants tend to form a social hierarchy based on the degree of their spiritual affinity with the Anglo-Americans. Possibly this example may serve to explain the laws which governed the formation of social classes in many ancient or medieval nations. Likewise, the existence in the United States of more than ten million negroes helps us to understand how in ancient India the Aryan society reacted by setting up a caste barrier. But if American society regards assimilation of its negroes as out of the question, it has, on the whole, already done much for them by giving them its language, its Christianity, its ideals, and by admitting them, in no small degree, to share its prodigious prosperity.

These varied elements, thus deposited in the course of three centuries by immigration (with the exception of the black element), have been subjected to a powerful mixing-process:— American geographical unity. American physical environment and conditions of life, have for the most part transformed them, even physically. According to Boutmy, the uniformity of an extreme and violent climate, from one end of the United States to the other, has created a new physical type, which is becoming

less like the Anglo-Saxon European and more like the Indian—
a tendency all the stranger since there can have been scarcely
any interbreeding with the latter. 'The dry air and the wide
range of temperature make the skin turn grey and the bones
stand out, increase nervous activity and produce a capacity for
endurance superior to that of other peoples.' Upon all the
immigrants, moreover, the mere fact of transplantation has had
an effect of renewal and rejuvenation. Here we encounter a law
which biologists declare holds good both in zoology and in
botany: a plant transferred to new soil resumes its growth
apace; the first horses imported into Canada or Australia produced species of an almost savage vigour.

This example brings us to a biological law complementary to
the previous one: it is the sudden impetus which a species gains
when it is abruptly transported from a limited territory—where
its activity was cramped and hindered—to boundless space
where it encounters neither obstacle nor enemy. As soon as it
becomes aware of this widening of its field of action and of this
infinite enlargement of its familiar horizon, as soon as its organism experiences this feeling of limitlessness and becomes intoxicated with the sense of space, everything changes. Its energy is
increased enormously. Its breast swells with the breath of freedom. Whether animal species or human race, it leaps to begin a
new existence.

So it was with the American farmers when, behind the Appa-
lachians, they discovered the endless expanse of the Prairie, and
beyond the Prairie the infinite Great West. However matter-of-
fact these men might have been, they felt the call of the ocean.
There began what has been called the 'American nomadism'.
The descendants of old peoples had become a young race because they were re-living the very youth of the race. In their
virgin continent they resumed the trek which in the dawn
of history had led their remote ancestors, the primitive Indo-
Europeans, to the discovery of Eurasia. Indeed, the American
achievement represented the first really massive and lasting conquest made by the European races for more than two thousand
years. Certainly, Europe had never ceased to send out colon-
izers on every side, from the ancient Greeks to the thirteenth-
century Venetians, and from the Portuguese to the modern

Anglo-Indians. But these colonizations did not people the land. Even in Spanish America, the *conquistadors* left only a thin top-dressing of population, spread out over vast spaces. The American farmer would have none of that. Obedient to the teachings of the Bible which, as far as the Quakers and Mormons were concerned, was interpreted in its most literal and primitive sense, he grew and multiplied his seed indefatigably. And the unremitting stream of fresh settlers from New England or Europe did the rest.

It was a mighty increase: 3.9 million inhabitants in 1790; 12.9 millions in 1830; 23.2 millions in 1850; 50.2 millions in 1880; 63 millions in 1890; 76.3 millions in 1900; 92 millions in 1910; 113 millions in 1925; 129 millions in 1939... America has thus done more for the white race than Europe with all its colonies! For colonies without settlement pass away, but the New Europe of the western empire abides.

In this demographic increase, industrial development, especially from 1865 onwards, played an ever-growing part. Here was made manifest, as readers of the Bible would put it, the blessing vouchsafed by the Almighty to His people. This earth, so fabulously rich in its boundless fields of wheat and cotton, concealed within it colossal hoards of coal, iron, and oil—to say nothing of the gold-mines of California. But the gold rush was the affair of a day. Industrial expansion, on the other hand, rushed on continuously, also at a dizzy speed. Born of a farm, the United States now became a gigantic factory, working zestfully, in an ever bolder and fuller rhythm, with that willingness to take risks without which nothing great can be accomplished and which had been handed down from the first settlers to their descendants, the twentieth-century captains of industry. The nomadism of the early stock-raisers was reflected again in the cheerful readiness with which the industrialist scrapped factories still new, in order to replace them by plant ever more up to date. A race of vikings, always on the crest of a wave, and reckless of the backwash! Groundswells which would have swamped others, colossal crises and crashes, served only to nerve their energies. In 1937 the United States produced more than 447 million tons of coal against 245 million from England, the next largest producer; 173 million tons of oil against 27 million from

the Soviet Union; 37 million tons of iron against 28 from the
Soviet Union; more than 51 million tons of steel against about
20 from Germany. The value of its exports amounted to 1.9
million gold dollars, against England's 1.5 million; and its cash
in hand to seven thousand and fifty-four million gold dollars,
while England's totalled one thousand and fifty-nine millions.
There is 'poetry' in these figures. American toil, American production, and the American conquest of the world's markets
form one of the most thrilling epics of the twentieth century, the
epic of human effort at its (so far) fullest possible stretch.

America's Hour

But the markets were shrinking. The autarchy of Germany,
Soviet Russia, and Japan—the last of which was striving to
annex the 450 million Chinese—to say nothing of the British
Empire's movement towards protection, presented America too
with the gravest of problems. Its President in those pre-war
years 1933–41 (for he had been elected just when Hitler came
to power) happened by fortunate coincidence to be one of the
greatest men of his age. It is rare that under a purely democratic
régime the party game allows a political leader the continuity
of action necessary to bring all his programme to fruition. For
the twelve years of a Presidency three times renewed, Franklin
Roosevelt was to receive at the hands of God and his people
that exceptional favour. No one could have deserved it more.
He represented the synthesis of all that was best in America, and
combined in his strong and versatile personality its many
aspects and even its contrasts. A descendant of one of those
Anglo-Dutch families of New Amsterdam who have always
headed the patricians of the East, he had nevertheless not hesitated, in the days of the New Deal, to launch forth upon the
experiment of a planned economy in order to rescue his country
from an unprecedented crisis. Profoundly Christian, after the
fashion of the old seventeenth-century immigrants, he did not
hesitate to go hand-in-hand with the Soviet Union in order to
break the Axis Powers. But then, from his observatory at the
White House, he had long seen the storm approaching. The
American press and public opinion, less well informed than he,

were not ready for it. Discreetly but firmly he laboured to inform them. To complete that process, he was assisted by an unexpected stroke of fate: the Japanese attacked the Hawaiian bases, and Germany (*quos vult perdere!*) herself declared war on America.

Samurai or *Junker*, the two military castes of the old world had never been able to see beyond the barracks. If they had these at their command, they presumed themselves competent, by dividing their robbers' task, to overcome all nations. Such was the monstrous dream of a few frenzied men, who were, moreover, ignorant of all the laws of contemporary economics. The barracks of to-day is useless without the factory which feeds it, and the briefest survey of world-production statistics should have revealed that neither the American factory nor the American laboratory could be defied with impunity. The damage done by the *Luftwaffe* faded into insignificance before the devastation wrought by the Flying Fortresses, Nor could all the suicide-fliers in the country of the *Samurai* prevail against the atomic bomb.

By the resources at her disposal (in comparison, the industrial plant of Germany seemed obsolete and inconsiderable), by the cataclysmic character which the science of her chemists conferred upon her bombing, and by the invulnerability of her bases of attack, America turned the tables. The intervention of the New World was really like that of another world, of another planet pouring upon ours robots with fabulous powers. The invasion of Normandy and the pulverization of German and Japanese towns were like so many 'anticipations' worthy of H. G. Wells. In fact, this *War of the Worlds*, like his, was a matter of applied science. When the hour of Liberation struck at last, the peoples of the West looked on astonished as the Germans were put to rout, not so much by another army in the traditional sense of that word, as by a factory on the march.

The American eagle, winging its way over the Rocky Mountains, high above the secret laboratories where the atom was split, had conquered the German eagle and cast its shadow over the Rising Sun. The barracks had been destroyed by the American factory. Over against this, though associated in the same work, was rising up the Soviet factory.

Basic Facts of Russian History

Behind the scenes of history there lurks a mocking demiurge, who delights in drawing from men's actions the consequences least foreseen. If some hard-pressed author of the year 4000 should one day try to sum up in a single line the work of the two Napoleons, he will doubtless simply observe that theirs was the responsibility for the nineteenth-century unification of Germany and for her subsequent hegemony. And to sum up in the same brief fashion the work of William II and Hitler, our future brother of the pen can be content to credit them with Anglo-Saxon hegemony over one half of the planet and, perhaps, the triumph of Slav Communism over the other.

There is good reason why the Soviet Union and America should to-day appear to be the two rulers of mankind. Despite appearances, despite the most obvious contrasts, they have more than one common characteristic. Russian expansion resembles American expansion, with this difference, amongst others, that instead of requiring a mere three hundred years, it was spread over twelve centuries: Russian patience is indefatigable; that is why the Russian race believes it has eternity on its side.

'In the beginning . . .' (that is, towards the end of the Merovingian period—at the end of the seventh century A.D.—in France) the future Russian people may be seen separating itself from other Slav nations in the Kiev region, on the border of that zone of *tchernoziom* or black earth which their descendants were one day to make the richest wheatland in Europe. A little later, other clans ventured into the clearings of the Muscovite forests, where they immediately set about the work of russification. The clearings grew, the forest shrank, the Finnish tribes withdrew to avoid being submerged. Thus was born Great Russia, which was to double the original Ukraine and, when its time came, to supplant it.

The Slavic soul—as the example of the Poles proves only too well—may, if left to itself, show some tendency to anarchy. The Slav mass had hitherto been shapeless. To make the dough rise, Russia needed the Varangian leaven—the coming of the Vikings (862). What a strange rôle has been played in history by these sea-kings who, either directly or through their descendants, founded Russia with Rurik (and gave it its name) and laid the foundations of English greatness with William the Conqueror. From them the Slavs of Russia took their first ideas of the State, a purely military State it is true, based on a wholly personal allegiance to a war-leader, after the fashion of the Teutonic kingship. On the other hand, the Roman conception of the State in its historic completeness, preserved by Byzantium, was handed on, together with Greek Orthodox Christianity, to the Russia whose capital was still Kiev (about the year 1000). True, the Byzantine theory and its Russian application were more sharply contrasted than the Cæsars of Old Rome and their Carolingian imitators. But even with these reservations, and in spite of feudal divisions and family partitions, such as repeatedly delayed the course of history here as well as in the West, the Slavs of Russia were henceforth endowed with a principle of political unity and continuity which their Polish and Yugoslav brethren sometimes lacked.

Despite all appearances, the Tartar yoke which for nearly two and a half centuries (from 1237 to 1480) lay heavy upon Russia did not break up the Russian State. Quite the reverse: the princes of Moscow modelled their political régime on that of the Khan, their suzerain. The *yassaq*, the barrack-room discipline which, with knout and scimitar, ruled the Mongol hordes, was also employed to rule the land of Russia for the benefit of the *kniaz* of Moscow. Tsarism thus sprang directly from the Mongol régime. The great princes of the Russian Renaissance, Ivan III and Ivan IV, the Terrible, were in their own fashion the heirs of Genghis Khan. The autocratic Tsar was a Christian Khan. The Golden Horde, surrounded by its Muscovite vassals, had formed a Mongol-Russian empire. The Tsars of Moscow, surrounded by their Tartar vassals, headed from the days of Ivan the Terrible onward a Russo-Mongolian Empire. The relationship was reversed; the factors remained the same. The Mongolian rule, then, had in the long run only strengthened and toughened the Russian State, and endowed it with a central power compared to which that of contemporary western princes such as Louis XI or Henry VIII seemed mild.

Before the Mongolian invasion Russia had begun to look

towards the West. In the eleventh century King Henry I of France and Emperor Henry VI of Germany had married the daughter of Yaroslav the Great and the daughter of Vsévolod of Kiev respectively. The Mongols drove the Russian soul back into Asia. While the West was passing from the Gothic Renaissance to the Italian Renaissance, the Russian *kniaz*, in succession from father to son, had been obliged to go and knock their foreheads on the ground, at Karakoram or Saraï, in front of the felt tent of some descendant of Genghis Khan, in order to obtain from him the indispensable *yarligh* of investiture or sometimes, as a special favour, the hand of one of his nieces. But the Mongol yoke had no sooner been cast off than the Russian princes turned again towards the West and Ivan III brought Russia into contact with the Italian Renaissance. However, the Mongolian experience had not been lost upon the Russian spirit. The Mongols had tried to deport it to Asia. It had escaped, but was never to forget its sojourn. Or rather, it remained at the cross-roads of the civilizations. It remained Eurasian, a state of mind which implied in this case a complex culture, drawn from both Europe and Asia, capable of understanding Asia as well as Europe, and presently dominating both while still remaining unshakably itself. Between Asia and Europe, Russia was to be Eurasia—a third continent.

Thus tempered, having passed through the most terrible melting-pot into which a nation has ever been plunged, Russia was preparing for high destiny. Irresistibly, the Russian expansion (which Mongol rule had halted for more than two centuries) began again. In the twelfth century the old *kniaz* of Souzdal and Vladimir had already penetrated the enormous forest mass, the home of the Finno-Ugrian tribes, which stretched from north of Kazan to the Arctic tundra. Ivan III conquered it as far as the Arctic Ocean (1472–1489). Similarly, from the beginning of the tenth century, the Olegs and Igors, by making their way down the Russian rivers, had reached the Black Sea and pushed to the very suburbs of Tsargrad (Constantinople), the fabulous Rome of the Bosphorus, the city of pure gold which the prophets foretold that their race should rule. They had failed to storm the gates of the city; but when the Mongols came in 1220, the steppes to the north of the Black

Sea, then inhabited by the Coman hordes, acknowledged Russian protection. From the day of the Liberation, Russia resumed this march towards the Euxine, at the expense of the Tartars. By the conquest of the Khanate of Kazan in 1552 and the Khanate of Astrakhan in 1554, Ivan the Terrible annexed almost the whole of 'European Mongolia', that vast zone of black earth, grey steppe and white steppe, which stretched from Kharkov to the mouth of the Volga and from Kazan to the mouth of the Don and to Terek.

After the unification of Russia came her abrupt entrance upon the stage of European politics. Stalin has good reason to look upon Peter the Great as one of his predecessors! Like the Soviet rulers in recent days, the great Romanov wished above all to modernize his empire and develop its industries. What interested him in the West was not the pomp of Versailles, but the naval dockyards of Britain and of Amsterdam where he worked as a common carpenter, the cloth-mills and the blast-furnaces, the craftsmen's secrets and their technical skill. Travellers from the West who visited Russia at the time of his death described it as one vast dockyard 'ringing with the noise of axe and hammer', with mushroom-towns like St. Petersburg and Petrogradovsk, busy rope-walks, great steel-mills served by the rising state-mining industry of Perm and the Urals. As for the methods used to turn the peasantry into the working-class needed for this modernization, the Tsar showed himself the direct precursor of the Soviet rulers. The first 'five year plan' dated from Peter's return from Holland.

To become part of Europe, Russia had to acquire a part of Europe. In 1721, after twenty-two years of war, Peter the Great, by the Treaty of Nystad, burst the bars behind which Sweden had 'imprisoned his country', subjugated Estonians and Letts, and opened wide a window on the Baltic. Catherine II—the only one of his successors who was of his calibre—completed his work by annexing the remainder of Latvia and Lithuania and half of Poland. It must be admitted that, in spite of her effrontery, the old Empress was the only one of the three rulers who partitioned Poland to have at her disposal a valid excuse: the region she appropriated had a partly Russian population. But this Russia in Europe—more than half the continent—was only the 'visible Russia'. Behind it lay a Russia as yet unnoticed because the West did not yet suspect its economic importance: Russia in Asia.

Another Continent: Eurasia

'Russia in Asia' corresponds to a geographical reality: neither physically nor ethnically do the Ural Mountains form a barrier. On that soil which so much resembles European Russia —the same tundra, the same taïga, the same steppes, the same climate—Russian territory finds its natural continuation. The first Cossacks to venture there felt quite at home. Led by Ermak Timofevitch—that Russian rival of Cortez and Pizarro—they penetrated in 1581 to the heart of the Khanate of Sibir; six years later the first Russo-Siberian colony, Tobolsk, was established there. What a prodigious ride they made, those Cossacks, along the northern 'verge' of the globe! Beyond the Turkestans and Mongolias which had been the previous limit of man's knowledge, they galloped ever onwards into the rising sun and found an unknown Asia bordering on the Sea of Okhotsk. The track of their raid was marked by the foundation of Siberian towns: in 1604, they were at Tomsk in the heart of Siberia, between steppe and taïga; in 1652, at Irkutsk to the west of Lake Baïkal; in 1658, at Nertchinsk in that district of the Onon and the Kerulen which had been the very cradle of the power of Genghis Khan. In fact, they repeated the raid of Genghis Khan, but in the opposite direction, retracing the route of the Mongol invasion to its starting-point. When they had reached the summit of the Saïan and Yablonovy Mountains, from which the whole Mongolian country can be seen stretching into the distance, they could measure the extent of their conquest: the empire of the steppes was at their feet. And like the companions of Balboa, who found the 'Pacific Sea' on the far side of the Isthmus of Darien, they saw, when they reached Okhotsk in 1638, the vastness of that Ocean spread out before them.

It is not, however, of the *Conquistadors* that we are reminded by Ermak's successors, but rather of the pioneers of the American or Canadian prairies, who like them were prospectors, trappers, settlers and woodsmen. As in the United States and Canada, the colonists here met only thinly scattered populations, incapable of stopping their advance. Palæo-Asiatics, Tartars, Buriats, Yakuts or Tongus passively allowed the Muscovite adventurers and immigrants to occupy the clearings best stocked with game and the watercourses richest in fish. Like the French-Canadians in the Great North, the Siberian Cossacks felt no repugnance about marrying the native women; they produced a race of 'half-breeds' as sturdy and hard-working as the Canadian *Bois-Brûlés*. The Siberian won general esteem by the same qualities of endurance and courage, and the same spirit of enterprise, as were displayed in America by the pioneers of the Far West or the St. Lawrence. From the beginning of the nineteenth century the name once given to Alaska, then part of the Tsar's dominions—the 'Russian America'—could have been applied to Siberia. The extent of cultivable land (nearly ten times the area of France) and the mineral wealth it revealed would have justified the comparison.

Soviet Industry

Lenin has said that the basic Slav element, left to itself, is sometimes a little fluid and slippery. The successive masters of the Russian State set themselves to cast it into an indestructible metal. For this purpose these primitive iron-smiths never hesitated, when the need arose, to borrow hammer and anvil from their neighbours. In the tenth century the Russian State was first of all a *droujina*, a band of Varangar adventurers who, on the model of the Scandinavian war-bands, had come to bring order out of the immemorial anarchy of the Slavs; then in the eleventh century the Christian court of the *kniaz* imitated after a fashion the Sacred Palace of Constantinople; from the sixteenth century onwards the Tsars reigned as a Muscovite translation of the Mongolian *yassaq*; and in the eighteenth and nineteenth centuries there ruled that same Tsardom, reshaped in Western style by Peter the Great, with a military cadre and a bureaucracy of the German type, and sometimes even with a General Staff of Teutonic race in the persons of the Baltic barons. Similarly, the Soviet State had under our very eyes borrowed its ideology from Marxism, and drawn its directing personnel not only from Slavonic elements, but also from all sorts of non-Russian 'maximalists', Caucasians, Armenians, Jews, and Tartars.

Russian Communism represents a strange convergence of factors. Western inspiration is obvious in it. In addition to the Marxism which inspired its pseudo-Hegelian theory of the State, how many of its founders had come, 'to learn revolution', to Paris or Geneva? But at the same time Lenin considered the Soviet movement as a 'return to the sources', a restoration of the oldest Russian institutions. And it is true that from the very beginnings of Russia around Kiev collective property occupied a prominent position in the *mir*, the village community whose lands were held in common by all the inhabitants. It was only in the sixteenth century that the peasant communities were dispossessed of their lands for the benefit of the princes or the boyars and that, at the same stroke, the peasants were made serfs. This *de facto* enslavement was officially legalized by the code of 1649, the effects of which were by no means completely undone by the manifesto of Alexander II in 1861. If the Bolshevist revolution of October (November) 1917 succeeded, it was doubtless because, beneath the doctrines borrowed by the intelligentsia from Western socialism, the Russian soul thought to find in it very old or familiar native tendencies. Moreover, despite appearances, continuity between Tsarism and the Soviets is greater than one might think. We have already noticed a similar continuity between Richelieu's work and that of the Convention. The like may be seen in Russia, provided we compare the Soviet rulers, not with the nineteenth-century Romanovs (who, notwithstanding their nominal autocracy, exercised little real power), but with the only two really absolute Tsars that Russia has ever known: Ivan the Terrible and Peter the Great.

The 'Legacy of Peter the Great' consisted less in the advance towards the open seas than in the industrialization of Russia. This is the programme which (since 1928) the Soviets have resumed with their succession of Five Year Plans. To bring this mighty industrialization to success, Russia has become a dictatorship of engineers and technicians. The boldest part of the programme, although inspired by the ancient institutions of the *mir*, was the brigading, from 1930 onwards, of 110 million Russian peasants in 242,000 *kolkhozes* or collective farms handing over 35 per cent of their crops to the State. The 'battle for wheat', the production of which, between 1925 and 1929, had risen from 215 to 308 million quintals, had to be won. But the chief effort was directed towards the creation of industrial man-power. Millions of Russian, Tartar or Uzbek peasants, and even Kirghiz, Mongolian or Yakut nomads, were officially transformed into factory-hands. The effective strength of the industrial population thus rose from 11.5 million souls in 1928 to nearly 23 millions in 1932. As a result of this colossal effort, production shot up like an arrow from a bow: the output of iron ore, between 1913 and 1938, rose from 9 to 28 million tons; of cast iron, from 4 to 18 millions; of steel, from 4 to 17.5 millions; of coal from 25 to 130 millions; of oil, from 9 to 27 millions; of electric power, from nearly two thousand million kwh. to thirty-nine and a half thousand millions. Between 1929 and 1935, the amount of gold extracted increased from 30 to 160 tons. All told, industrial production leapt from 11 thousand million roubles in 1913 to 137 thousand millions in 1940. Henceforward Russia held first place in wheat production, and second in oil, gold and iron. In this respect, she has become what the Germany of William II was half a century ago, a sort of 'America of the Old World'.

One element in the thoroughly American rhythm of production is the rise, reminiscent of the Far West of the United States, of the mushroom-towns, the industrial cities which have suddenly sprung up in the middle of the steppes or the taïga, sometimes even in the darkness of the Arctic Circle. Such is Magnitogorsk, to the south of the Urals, which has increased from 6,000 to 600,000 inhabitants, and is situated on a field of iron ore equal to those of Sweden and Lorraine combined; or Stalinsk, in the heart of the Siberian basin of Kouznetsk, as rich in coal measures as the Ruhr, Belgium, and Northern France put together. This rapid summary, to which must be added the large-scale gold-production of Siberia, explains why new books on the Soviet Union sometimes contain a new 'discovery of Russia' similar to that which took place at the beginning of the eighteenth century.

One of the factors in this transformation was the policy adopted by the Soviet Union towards native populations. The Tsarist régime had applied to them a programme of russification which, in the case of the more highly cultured nations (the Armenians, for example) had aroused a dogged opposition. The Soviets proclaimed the liberation of subject nationalities. They grouped them in autonomous republics, which were to enjoy the widest linguistic, educational, and cultural independence —within the Communist creed, of course. Despite all differences of temperament and social ideas, the Soviet Union became apparently a federation of Communist peoples.

This flexible policy was meant to attach to the Slav Empire its former subject races, and to weld to it its Asiatic dependencies. At all times Russia has been a machine for making Europeans out of Asiatics. Give your Hindu or Egyptian barrister a first-class English education: you will get an Oxford graduate, but never an Englishman. On the contrary, under the Tsarist régime, the descendant of an emir of Ferghâna, educated at the Cadet School and received at the Winter Palace, really became, even while retaining his Mohammedanism, a Russian prince. The process is even more complete to-day when, if decentralization has liberated the subject races, industrialization has standardized the way of life. 'The Turkomans devote themselves to manufacturing chemical products. The Kirghizes pass from the nomad's saddle to the electrical machine, from the shaman's drum to polytechnic education. The god of applied science fires the brains of the young descendants of the soldiers of Genghis Khan, and they prove themselves as skilful in piloting an aeroplane as their fathers were in taming the wild horse.'

Russia—statistics remind us—includes as many Turks as the Republic the capital of which is Ankara. Moreover, by acquiring the Republic of Outer Mongolia, she has gained control of the ancient patrimony of Genghis Khan himself! Even more than in the time of the Tsars, the Empire of the steppes, Genghis Khan's as well as Tamurlane's, belongs to her. But by modernizing all these Turco-Mongols, by shaking them abruptly out of the sleep of the Middle Ages into the most active industrialization, by supplying them with tools, by admitting them on a footing of equality into the secret of all our Western techniques, Soviet Russia sought to revive their hereditary virtues in the service of Communism and to restore their former vitality. She resurrected the Empire of the steppes and, assisted by the United

Nations, hurled it forward, armoured and motorized, to beat back Germany.

The power at the command of the Soviets seems enormous. To their industrial strength must be added that other great power, men. Here again, figures are eloquent: 10 or 12 million inhabitants in the two Russias in 1700, 27 in 1789, 45 in 1816, 119 in 1890, 129 in 1905, 175 (notwithstanding the amputations made by the Treaties of Brest-Litovsk and Riga) in 1937.

To move such mountains, there was needed a burning faith. 'Do you know,' wrote Dostoïevsky, 'which is at present the only people with a divine mission, the only people called to renew the world, to save it in the name of a new God? It is the Russian people.' Dostoïevksy was mistaken in one point only. A religion is not necessarily theistic. Buddhism, which was one of the great universal religions, was originally atheistic. A religion can quite well be materialistic and purely human. Russian Communism has all the collective *mystique*, the ardent proselytism, the spirit of sacrifice, of the great religions.[1] From Marxist dogma it has drawn a discipline for action. It has created a *mystique* of work, a dedication to collective labour, an eager competition among the workers which has given birth to the Stakhanovist movement without which the battle for industrialization would not have been won. In the hour of Hitler's invasion this same quasi-religious patriotism transformed
'the soldiers of Rossbach into soldiers of Valmy'
and produced Stalingrad out of Tannenberg, or rather, transformed the 1914 Battle of the Masurian Lakes into that of 1944.

Nor can we forget that the Communist faith secures Soviet Russia a considerable following among the proletariat of various non-Russian countries. Whatever Russian patriotism may be in the country itself—and four years of war have revealed its mettle—the Soviet State (Lenin insisted on this point) does not aim at being a State like others. It really constitutes a *societas perfecta* with its own values, ethics and martyrs. Like the former Moslem Khalifat or the Roman Papacy, it is a spiritual State after its own fashion, having at its command beyond its own frontiers an international *mystique* which, on all great problems, operates to its advantage. The ruler of Soviet Russia, that is, of the most powerful military empire of the Old World, the heir of

[1] Does not everything in the Slav soul become religious, even irreligion?

the Tsars who beat back Hitler, has also been the head of the
Third International, that is, of a force capable of stirring
millions of hearts from the suburbs of Paris to Milan and Barcelona, and from the Piræus to Yen-ngan and Canton.

In peace as well as war Stalin has shown the most remarkable
gifts of decision, energy and diplomatic finesse. Nor must we
overlook the sense of sequence in him and his fellow-workers,
for, by keeping the same pilots at the helm for decades in the
middle of an ever-changing universe, the Soviet government,
despite its apparent multiplicity of councils, has assured itself
a stability and continuity of action which have allowed it, both
in economic and foreign policy, to pursue long-term objectives
and develop large-scale conceptions—have given it, in fact,
just those very advantages which were formerly claimed for
the monarchical régime. If we ponder these points we shall
understand not only the secret of the Russian success, but the
pressure the rulers of the Kremlin can bring to bear on the
destinies of the West.

The Capture of Berlin

The capture of Berlin by Zhukov's armies has opened a new
phase in European history. First of all, it consummated the
triumph of the Pan-Russian idea. By the transfer of East Galicia,
the whole of the Ukraine has for the first time been brought
under the control of Moscow. Stalin has completed the thou-
sand-year-long task of the ancient *kniaz*, the unification of all
Russian lands, At the same time, this is the triumph of Pan-
Slavism, preached since Kollar's day by legions of scholars and
poets. Prague, Belgrade, Sofia, even Warsaw, all entered by the
Red Army, revolve round Moscow. Things have come to pass
as foretold by Renan, by Louis Léger, by Ernest Denis, and
Jacques Ancel. Soldiers from the fastness of the Urals pitch their
tents in Mecklenburg—once the land of the Obotrites—in
Lusatia and Meissen—once the land of the Sorbs—and in the
province of Brandenburg, which in former days was called
Brannibor. Everywhere the past history of the Slavs breaks
from the tomb in which it had been sealed by eight centuries of
German settlement. Suvarov's descendants are in Vienna. They
are on the Adriatic. Through Yugoslavia they may resume the

policies of Stephen Numanya and Stephen Dushan. By way of Bulgaria they are at the gates of Constantinople. All this they achieved as the allies of the West.

At the same time, by the reoccupation of Manchuria, they have avenged Kuropatkin and wiped out the disaster of 1905. Intervening in this theatre at the decisive hour, again in collaboration with the Western holders of the intra-atomic secret, they have set back forty years the Rising Sun of Japan. Whether at the end of half a century or of a thousand years, the Slav always comes back.

Civilization is Mortal

Astronomers tell us that the various parts of the heavens, although we can survey them with one glance in a single second, are not 'synchronistic', but exist at different times. Stars which seem to send us rays simultaneously are actually abysms apart, not only in space but in time. Some which still seem to be shining overhead may really have been extinct for millions of years. And others have been born whose rays have not yet had time to reach us. So it is with peoples! Apparently contemporary, they are actually separated by tremendous chronological gaps. The Islamic calendar has to-day reached the fourteenth century after the Hegira, and in fact a good many of its faithful are still living in the equivalent of our own Trecento. The least we can say of Hitler's invasions is that they belonged to the age of Alaric and Genseric. Whole regions of the German soul seem still to receive their light from a pre-medieval sun. And there is no doubt that under their modern uniforms the Japanese military clans were living in the sixteenth century. On the other hand, the most advanced of the Western peoples, the Scandinavians, give the impression of having already reached the year 2000.

For humanity, this chronological 'staggering' constitutes the direst of perils. Most of our misfortunes spring from the fact that, not living in the same era culturally, peoples do obeisance neither to the same logic nor the same ethics. How many wars have been caused by this difference in the development of civilizations! Indeed, in this connection, the German concentration camps have laid bare a most fearful secret: in many zones humanity is still at the level of primitive man. Now, a voice from the tomb, the voice of an American statesman[1] has reminded us that we are—more than ever—'One World'. It is indeed true that scientific progress, accelerated by the last war, has so shortened distances that henceforth all nations are contiguous. The theory of the continental drift is this time operating in reverse: the continents are being thrown together. Peoples whom we have just seen separated by psychological and cultural chasms have to exist in close proximity, to live together in a single communal house which has suddenly contracted and whose partition-walls have collapsed. In a future war the most inoffensive and resolutely neutral nation would be automatically involved. The example of Norway—to quote no other case—speaks for others.

But the West seems to have forgotten the master-word which was the key of its civilization. That magic word around which European thought had ranged itself; that driving-force which was the *primum mobile* of recent centuries, was the idea of Liberty. Liberty of thought, civic liberties, the independence of peoples—since the Renaissance man had set his course towards this ideal. For the cause of liberty he had toiled and suffered for decades. At the beginning of the twentieth century he had almost attained it. At any rate all peoples,—the most cultivated elements, that is, in all peoples, even those least advanced—boasted of modelling themselves on the liberalism of which the Anglo-Saxon nations provided the example and which was regarded as the very expression of civilization. The Treaties of 1919 strove to rebuild the world on these foundations.

Yet, when our own generation had almost reached the goal for which their fathers had died, we seemed to flag. Between 1919 and 1939 we witnessed an amazing spectacle: a society which had ceased to believe in its own *raison d'être* and become weary of everlastingly hearing the praises of Liberty and Justice, like the Athenian in the *Life of Aristides*, consigned the names of those two goddesses to oblivion. Outside the Anglo-Saxon world, one might have thought that the meaning of Liberty and Justice had been forgotten overnight. To combat the official doctrine, there sprang up denigrators who, working like the eighteenth-century Encyclopaedists but with exactly contrary

---

[1] The late Wendell Wilkie. T.P.

aim, sapped the foundations of liberal thought. Nietzsche, with his doctrine of the Superman, had dealt a blow to German liberalism, a sensitive plant ill-fitted to withstand such shocks. Now the praise of violence, loudly proclaimed by Georges Sorel, tended for its part to transform into class imperialism the socialism which Jaurès wanted to see reconciled with liberty. Finally, on the Right, liberal Catholicism which had been so influential in the days of Albert de Mun, seemed now to lose the allegiance of a part of the young men. If, during the fatal period 1933–43, liberalism almost perished on the European continent, it was from want of faith in its own power. To what martyrdom that scepticism led, we know. When the Frenchmen of our generation had lost their liberty, they understood at last what it meant: that it was, indeed, the very breath of their existence.

Now that the spiritual values on which Western civilization rests have been restored, the essential thing is to re-root them in our ways of life as well as in our laws, in the relations between free peoples as well as on a national basis. On the other hand, Emile Faguet (one of the soundest minds of his time) was aware of a certain antinomy between the idea of liberty and that of equality, if the latter was interpreted as the right of all to share alike in wealth. The fact is that states wear a rather different aspect according to whether they are based, like the Anglo-Saxon communities, on liberalism, or like the Soviets, on economic equality. As for the land which gave birth to Montaigne, it is too keen on the independence of the critical mind to concede anything on that score. There is nobody in France—least of all the Christians—who does not aim at securing for the producers the fruits of their labour. If France, as all her literary culture indicates, is in truth the country of *finesse* and moderation, it will be her task to find a satisfactory mean between these two needs.

It is not long since Paul Valéry wrote prophetic words which should be pondered now more than ever: 'We know,' he said, 'that our civilizations are mortal. We had heard of worlds that had vanished entirely, of empires that had foundered with all their men and equipment and sunk into the fathomless deep of time with their gods and their laws. . . . We know well enough that all the earth we could see was made of ashes, and that the ashes meant something. We could make out through the thick haze of history the wraiths of mighty vessels loaded with wealth and intellect. Their number was beyond telling, but their ship-wreck after all seemed no affair of ours. Elam, Nineveh and Babylon were but vague, high-sounding names, and the total destruction of these worlds had as little meaning as their exis-tence itself. But France, England, Russia . . . are not these great names likewise? . . .'

Death robbed us of Paul Valéry a few weeks before the libera-tion of intra-atomic energy multiplied by twenty thousand the destructive power at man's command. What would he have added to these reflections? Perhaps simply the service-report of Colonel Paul Tidde, explaining how in a few seconds, by simply pulling a lever or two, he had practically wiped out a city of 343,000 souls. A mere trial trip, moreover, since the war ended almost there and then. But—a new war in which the infernal weapon would be employed daily by vast squadrons of air-craft? And suppose—a hypothesis which scientists do not by any means reject—the splitting of atoms spread gradually throughout the whole of the globe until it ended in the total destruction of the planet? 'We may say,' writes Professor Jean Thibaud, 'that mankind has found the instrument of its own extermination.'

Apocalyptic visions! And to this end science has brought us. As in a nightmare, it has escaped men's grasp, rebelled and turned against them. Or rather, not science, but man alone must be blamed. 'Knowledge without conscience,' said Rabelais in his wisdom long ago, 'is nothing short of the ruin of man-kind.' Is man then unworthy of his own knowledge? The Nazi atrocities have shown us how he can be dragged back before our very eyes to the Dark Ages, nay indeed, to the age of the cave-men. And yet, at this very time, the human mind, with a single leap forward comparable to the discovery of fire or the invention of electricity, has landed in the year 3000. Whereupon it entrusts this science of the fourth millenium of the Christian era to the recking hands of the ape-man, *Pithecanthropus*. All genius—the whole genius of man—to supply fuel to man's ancient murderous instinct. How far reality transcends the most sombre mythologies of the Hindus or the Aztecs!

The speedy progress of human knowledge and the failure of human morality to keep pace has long been sorrowfully pointed out by Christians; but who has listened? After these wars involving whole continents; after the wiping out, over vast areas, of all the gains of civilization, and under the threat of destruction still more planetary in its scope, we dare no longer close our eyes. The writing is on the wall. Read while there is time. It is a matter of life or death—for the whole human race.

II

ASIA'S CONTRIBUTION

THE Asiatic East has been discovered by Europe at different times—with Alexander the Great, with Marco Polo, and in the sixteenth century; and each time it has been a fresh surprise, as if Asia were a separate planet. Each time, indeed, our classic Mediterranean traditions have seemed to be confronted by traditions very similar, though forged out of elements incomprehensible at first glance. In India and China, the original centres of culture, 'perfect societies' had taken shape with philosophies, literatures and arts all forming a co-ordinated whole. But in the three periods just mentioned, the interest caused by this encounter was little more than curiosity. The world of Alexander, so open to all Semitic or Iranian influences, was scarcely affected (save perhaps to a very slight extent, in the case of Plotinus) by Indian speculation. Again, though Marco Polo wrote a few distinctly sympathetic lines about the Cingalese Buddha, his interest seems to have been limited almost entirely to the economic aspects of Far Eastern civilizations. And lastly it was commercial, or perhaps we should say imperial, interest which was still the motive force of the Spanish explorers, notwithstanding all their professions of missionary zeal. Thus in none of these three encounters did the humanism of the Far East end in fusing with that of the West.

To-day the situation seems different. The conquest or penetration of Asia by Europe has produced, as a kind of counterstroke, the invasion of Europe by Asiatic art, and indeed to some extent by the ideas which inspired this art. Just as the West at the end of the eighteenth century, and throughout the whole of the nineteenth, had no appreciation of Chinese or Indian art save in the form of curios which were on occasion utterly grotesque, so popularized Indian or Chinese philosophical ideas to-day represent only too often isolated elements artificially reblended, or even deliberately adulterated, the better to suit the western intellectual tastes of the moment. We have, for example, been supplied with a Buddhism marked 'for export only' and diluted for literary consumption, which stands in the same relation to Asiatic thought as the Chinese screens of the Trianons or the modern curios of Shanghai to Chinese art of the great periods.

It is highly desirable to put an end to all these counterfeits by drawing up an objective estimate of those eternal values which shall represent the contribution of eastern Asia to the humanism of to-morrow. But how can one possibly summarize the eastern half of human thought? Mankind's spiritual peaks (on which have been raised the torches that, one by one, have brought light to the valleys) are few; and if half of them are grouped around our Mediterranean world, the rest are to be sought in the Far East and in India. Let us suppose that, of everything we hold dear, we have hastily to choose, in the midst of an almost total catastrophe, what is to be salvaged for our descendants of the year 3000. Along with the legacy of ancient Greece, and of course Christianity, would we not wish to preserve both the immense effort of Indian speculation and the great cosmic vision which fired the old Chinese painters of the tenth to fourteenth centuries? These are indeed among the chief treasures of our human patrimony, the most precious legacies of our ancient heritage, not only on account of all the memories which they stir in us, but because they are expressions of great and eternal spiritual forces: these forces can, if we understand them, help us to emerge from the impasse in which contemporary man is destroying himself.

India

The astonishing philosophical gifts of the Indian race (and the 'philosopher races' are not numerous) manifested themselves even before the dawn of Indian history proper. In the *Rig-Véda*, the oldest of the Vedic anthologies, dating probably from about or a little before the year 1000 B.C., there suddenly flashes forth from the middle of a wealth of animist mythology a passage in which the whole problem of Being is already stated: 'There was neither being nor non-being; there was neither the air nor the sky above. What is it that moves? In what direction? Under whose guidance? Who knows, who can tell us where creation occurred, whence it cometh, and whether the gods

were only born thereafter? Who knows whence it hath come?
Whence creation did come—whether it is created or not created
—He alone knoweth Whose eye watcheth over it from the
height of heaven; and yet, doth He know?' The metaphysical
agony which alone makes man great, nay, which alone makes
him man, bursts forth with the first words. And a little further
on, in the same collection of hymns: 'He who giveth life, who
giveth strength, whose commandments all the gods revere,
whose shadow is immortality, whose shadow is death, who is
this god, whom we honour with sacrifices? He through whom
these snowy mountains have their being and the sea with the
distant river, He who hath the regions of the sky for his arms,
who is this god, whom we honour by sacrifices?' Is not this, in
those dark ages of the end of the second millenium b.c., a kind
of pathetic appeal to which the answer was given at the other
end of Hither Asia, amid the thunder and lightning of Sinai and
Mount Carmel?

But the answer did not carry as far as the banks of the Indus,
and the drama of Indian thought began. By penetrating right
into the Indo-Gangetic and Deccan 'continent', the Aryans
came into contact with a flourishing animal totemism of which
the prehistoric seals of Harappa and Mohenjo-Daro afford us a
glimpse. No doubt it was this old indigenous totemism which
gave the Indo-European conquerors the belief in the transmigration of souls, a belief unknown to them at the period of the
Rig-Vêda but universally accepted by their descendants. Subsequently, transmigration formed the guiding thread of all Indian
philosophy. It was to escape the consequences of this dogma
(which no one ever thought of doubting, but which was none
the less felt to be secretly revolting) that Indian thought undertook its enquiry. This unconscious revolt was entirely to its
credit; in contrast to events elsewhere, man was here greater
than his beliefs. Yet the unease they caused him never drove
him to reconsider his postulates. The cycle of transmigrations
—birth, suffering, death, and rebirth to eternal suffering—was
like a Nessus's shirt which the Indian dared not cast off, but
whose burning heat drove him forward in an effort at once
pitiable and sublime. It was to free himself from the penal ser-
vitude of 'eternal' rebirths, that with Buddhism he drowned his

ego in the Nirvana, and with Hinduism in the Absolute. The disappearance of the human personality into total Nothingness or into total Being—these were really the only alternatives which the postulates it had borrowed from primitive mankind henceforward allowed to Indian thought.

From this Aeschylean drama there were to spring magnificent impulses—noble outbursts whose pathos stirs us across the ages. Imagine the final meditation of the last thinking being on the last remaining planet, awaiting the cosmic catastrophe which will plunge this universe back into night again! The protest, the profession of faith in the supreme value of the spirit, which he would fling in the icy face of infinity, were formulated in the period of the ancient *Upanishads* about the seventh century B.C. This protest against the apparent victory of dark forces over mankind—why was it raised thus early? Doubtless because Indian nature, that subtropical *milieu* into which the Aryan race was sinking ever deeper, tended to overwhelm that race, to stifle it no less beneath the swift-springing, luxuriant growths of earth than beneath the mighty meteoric manifestations of the Indian heavens.

Confronted by this seeming triumph of blind forces, the Indian withdrew into his secret thoughts and, by a heroic recovery, found there the only ultimate reality:—the Spirit, final master of the world. 'The Absolute is to be found within the heart. There, and in no other place. The wise who gaze upon it within their soul, alone possess eternal rest.' And further on: 'Thou askest, what is the Absolute? It is the very essence of thine own soul which is the inmost of all things!' Finally comes the assertion that this cosmic essence is wholly spiritual. 'Smaller than that which is smallest, greater than that which is greatest, the essence of being lies hidden in the heart of the creature. The sage whose passions are at rest sees within himself the majesty of the inward soul. Unmoving, it ranges afar; without stirring, it journeys through space. Human suffering ceases at the sight of this mighty soul, all-pervading, bodiless in the midst of bodies, stable at the core of transitory things.' A total Presence divined behind every blade of grass as behind the face of the cosmos: 'We see it not, and it seeth. We hear it not, and it heareth. We think it not, and it thinketh. We know it not, and it knoweth.'

From her earliest development India has given the world the deep meaning of her message. Doubtless, for want of an adequate vocabulary, she was already in danger of confusing the essence of the universe—which is the breath and the thought of God—with God Himself; to avoid such a tendency Biblical Revelation would have been needed. But overlooking this inadequacy (admittedly a grave defect), how many eternal truths are here! Beyond the seeming victories of matter; in spite of the immeasurable vastness of stellar space; notwithstanding the periodical phases of destruction which grind heavenly bodies to powder and plunge the universe back into chaos as complete as if it had never been or had been in vain, the Spirit survives, soars, and abides. Beyond the photons and the Milky Ways, there remains the ultimate reality, the reason of things, the link between successive universes, and through it alone the world has meaning. 'Space', the *Upanishad* teaches, 'is spun and woven within the Spirit.' That is what India, from the dawn of her recorded history, has cried out to our planet, and if she had uttered nothing else, her message would still have had supreme value. Obviously, it needs to be completed by Christian theology; but not to accept what it can give us would be less than just.

Outside Christian philosophy, there are few statements in which the supremacy of spiritual things has been more triumphantly proclaimed than in the following—made, moreover, twenty-five centuries ago: 'The earth, the air, the ether, all that moves, all that lives and all that is lifeless, has Intelligence as its guide and is founded on Intelligence. Intelligence is the foundation of the universe. The Absolute is Intelligence.' Or this: 'The Spirit is imperishable. Encompassing the earth on every side, it is greater by ten fingers' breadth. It is the past and the future, the arbiter of the universe' . . .'It is the dyke between the worlds, keeping them from collision.' Certainly, Neoplatonist philosophy was to attribute no less a rôle to the intellectual principle (the *noûs*) as the motive power of the world. But to this intellectualism India—and this was her special contribution—added the notion of the holiness of things. Behind the cosmic Spirit, India sensed the God of the Bible and was hushed before Him. 'We cannot reach Him, neither by speech nor by understanding nor by sight. We can see Him only by saying: He is.'

The certainty of finding the divine Presence in the secret places of his heart transfigured Man. Behind the pantheistic interpretation of this doctrine subsequently given by the Vêdânta, there is a kind of spiritual communion here which must not be overlooked. 'The ancient Being, imperceptible to the senses, the Being deep in the unknown, wrapped in shadow, dwelling in the abyss, lives in thy heart.' By the reflection of this divine Presence, as in the Catholic communion, the human individual becomes sacred. And the universe also receives the stamp of holiness through the same reflection, the same presence. The universe, too, is a temple, the temple of 'the one Who, being in the earth, is different from the earth, Whom the earth knows not, the inner light, the Immortal One, He Who, being in space, is different from space, He Who, being in the sun and the stars, the lightning and the thunder, is different from them all, He Who, being in the worlds, is different from them, of Whom the worlds are merely the body, but Whom the worlds know not, the inward guide, the Immortal One!' This is a commentary on the mighty line: 'Within myself I feel eternal being.'

What better introduction to Christianity is there than the conception of the sanctity of the human individual and of the universe as temples of God? In India this conception was afterwards debased into pantheism; but the important thing is that the eternal values were in fact bequeathed to mankind, before any such systematization took place, by the truest representatives of Indian thought in its pristine vigour. As in Christianity, the idea of the divine Presence gives the world not only meaning but also affective value, and sets this universe free from blind forces and from strife, so that it may live in the light of love. 'It is not really,' says the *Upanishad*, 'for love of beings and worlds that beings and worlds are dear to me; it is not for love of all that all is dear to me; but for the love of the divine Spirit. The divine Spirit is He Who must be seen, Who must be heard, Who must be thought, Who must be meditated upon.'

The end of this meditation, this spiritual communion with pure divine love, is Salvation through joy ineffable. 'Alone the sages who gaze upon this Soul within their soul; the Being that endures for ever amid transitory things; the Intelligence which hearkens to the desires of creatures without intelligence; these sages, they and no others, possess eternal rest. Therein lies happiness beyond description, therein lies the supreme peace.' This total surrender of the soul to God, this ineffable absorption of the soul in God, are translated by images in which all the wealth of Indian poetry is poured out to tell us that the soul comes from Him and returns to Him. 'Even as the sparks,' says the *Upanishad*, 'spring from the blaze and return to the blaze; even as the rivers come from the mists of the ocean and return to the ocean; so does the wise man come from the Brahma and return to the Brahma.'

The regular systems which India erected on these foundations towards the end of the ancient world and at the beginning of the Middle Ages contain no such flashes of inspiration, but are nevertheless sufficiently important to be compared with the Greek systems. Since the objects of speculation are limited in number—as are their possible combinations—Indians discovered or foreshadowed the chief intellectual positions of our classic philosophies. The *Vaiceshika* is a combination of complete atomism in the realm of matter with pure monadology in the realm of mind, a combination of the physics of Lucretius with the metaphysics of Leibnitz. The *Samkhya* system, which is more elaborate, is a kind of magnificent metaphysical poem, but a pessimistic one, like those of Lucretius, Schopenhauer or Nietzsche. Contrary to the monistic tendencies of Indian thought, it postulates two principles: Nature, and the world of souls. Nature is a blind force, perpetually in a state of becoming, of transition between the homogeneous and the heterogeneous, rather as in Herbert Spencer. The union of Nature and souls engenders simultaneously the phenomenon of representation and the affective world, that is—in last analysis—universal suffering. Salvation lies in the freeing of the soul from the attraction of Nature. To that end, the sage must free himself successively from his social or hereditary self, his individual understanding and finally all contingent thought, in order to 'become his primal self'. The human soul, thus dehumanized, becomes then a pure monad separated from the universe, insensible, inaccessible, infinitely apart, like the remotest star in the icy void,

> 'And the deathless one, alone,
> Burns silent in the night.'

This system, devoid of hope, but great with a greatness that our classical stoicism has certainly never reached, harmonized with the tendency to asceticism which is the general mark of all Indian religious feeling. Indian asceticism bears the revealing name of *yoga*, a term signifying a 'union' of the being with the supreme principle, whether it is a question, as here, of the individual monad, or, as in other systems, of the union of the individual soul with the cosmic soul, or even the union of the soul with a transcendent or personal God.

India has not always found the way to this last solution, which would bring her closer to the West. Only in some of the higher forms of Vishnuism has she verged upon it. And even in these she has suffered from an excessive mysticism, as in the *Gita govinda*. Popularized yogism has brought a host of social abuses in its train. For a people to set up as its ideal the depersonalization of the self, with all the strange practices that such an objective implies, is potentially dangerous. The very loftiest speculation may revert unwittingly to the ritual practices of primitive magic. Nevertheless, this mighty aspiration towards asceticism has a certain grandeur. Obviously it missed its way, too often turning aside into a blind alley; yet it commands respect. Where else (save in the Christian world, of course) would we find great numbers of people forsaking all to tread 'in the footsteps of God'?

India had also had her Spinozas, Fichtes and Hegels. About the time of Charlemagne, the Indian Çankara, a metaphysician of remarkable calibre, built up in Mysore the structure of the spiritualistic monism known by the name of Vêdânta. In comparison with him the three Western philosophers seem rather cramped and arid; yet our histories of philosophy devote many pages to the study of Spinoza while ignoring Çankara's very existence. To be sure, monism has always seemed to be a rather precarious intellectual position. But at least Çankara defended it with a kind of metaphysical lyricism of great beauty. In his opening words he proclaims that the pure Being, the Absolute, is unique, spiritual and inward. There is no being save this Being. The relative, the multiple, do not exist. Therefore the individual self is mere illusion, just as the 'perceptible' universe is mere illusion—a mirage, a kind of magical invocation. But what remains when external world and individual self have been swept away? What, save total God, who is none other than the essence of spirit which exists in every individual soul, and is the soul of souls and the ultimate reality? The recession of the spirit into the divine subconsciousness is here presented as the entry into pure blessedness, which is the goal of all Indian speculation. Or again, the light which illuminates man's spirit, is compared to that which lightens the universe, and both are related to the Light of lights, which is God.

The *Vêdânta* thus fluctuates, constantly at the mercy of the most glittering images, between monism and the cult of a transcendent deity, already very close to the Christian God. This wavering is reproduced by the *Bhagavad gîta* in the famous passage: 'It is I,' says the divinity to the faithful soul, 'who, stripped of all material form, have unfolded this universe. All beings are in me, yet am I not in them. And, to speak truly, the beings are not in me. Behold and wonder at my sovereign power: my being upholds all created things; it is not in these created things, and yet through it alone have they existence. As a great wind, ever moving through space, penetrates everywhere, so must it be understood that in me are all created things.' A curious passage, in which the Indian Homer tries confusedly to bring Vedantic monism to positions not far removed from the Christian.

The same power of synthesis appears in the ancient Indian cosmogonies, which transcend in sheer breadth all that the Ionian philosophers or Lucretius have left us. In them the world alternates between periods of creation (which correspond to the activity of the demiurge) and of dissolution (which correspond to the slumber of the god). During this second phase, the cosmos exists only latently, as matter infinitely rarified, a whirling dust of nebulæ which is as the dim dream of the Eternal One. Then, at the breath of the awakening Lord, matter takes shape, the universes are formed again and resume their course, to await the hour when they will be absorbed once more,—for the cycle is as eternal as the god whose supreme act it constitutes. Such conceptions come straight from primitive cosmogonies, as a glance at the folklore of the South Seas would reveal to us; but that from these ancient legends they have been able to draw poems of such amplitude serves but to add to the stature of the old Indian bards.

India and her vast literature have also given the world the example of two unequally representative states of the soul. One, developed particularly in the Krishnaïte churches, is compounded of trusting devotion (*bhakti*), the love of God, of tenderness and surrender to Him. This is not peculiar to India and may also be found in Christianity and in Shi'ite Islam. It finds expression here, especially in Bengali poetry, in charming images (little cows and shepherd-girls, alike symbolizing pious souls, raised to ecstasy by the flute-notes of the divine cowherd); but also in that excess of erotic symbolism which has always been the inevitable characteristic of certain religious faiths.

The other state of the soul, surely more dangerous, but equal in æsthetic value, is that elaborated by Shivaism. The god Shiva sprang apparently from a fusion of the storm-god of the Vedic invaders with some savage native deity, whose totem was a bull. Representing the untamed forces of nature, he symbolized in philosophic Hinduism the powers of death and destruction, associated here with the periodical renewal of the world and therefore with the renewal of life. This superior wisdom, beyond good and evil, beyond kindness and cruelty, beyond being and non-being, this Nietzschean wisdom, is the essence of Shivaism. Iconography was to make curious changes in this conception. Sometimes it made Shiva a naked *fakir*, haunting charnel-houses, a god of terror, crowned with a chaplet of skulls and dancing upon corpses, or even the crude symbol of reproduction. Underlying philosophical edification, we catch sight of the primitive beliefs of a savage tribe. At other times metaphysical thought resumes its rights, and Shiva, like the Satyr of Victor Hugo,[1] swells to the full stature of the cosmos.

[1] *Le Satyre* in *La Légende des Siècles*, II. T.R.

He becomes then (as shown by the finest Dravidian bronzes, from the eleventh to the sixteenth century) the dancer of the cosmic dance, the symbol of a superhuman—and inhuman—lyricism, by which India expressed her heroic allegiance to universal Joy, Grief, and Strength. 'Our Lord,' says a Shivaïte text, is the Dancer who, like the heat latent in kindling wood, diffuses his power through spirit and matter and makes them each dance in their turn.' A poem by Kabir, translated e.g. by Rabindranath Tagore, conveys the same idea. 'Dance, my heart, dance with joy to-day. Mad with joy, Life and Death dance together. The mountains and the ocean and the earth dance. Amid laughter and tears mankind dances!' A heroic pessimism, in which the *danse macabre* of the old Dravidian fetish-worshippers among the tombs takes up in a tone of savage violence the Stoic theme of Marcus Aurelius: 'O world, whatsoever thou bringest me is good in my sight.'

What amazing power the metaphysical genius of India has! The tomb-haunting demon, the death-god of some obscure aboriginal tribe, is now lauded as the demiurge who from time to time hurls back into nothingness what he has created: *solvet sæclum!* 'The ages during which several million gods of heaven shall succeed unto one another, after each has lived out his allotted span; the time during which several Brahmâ shall die; the time after which Vishnu shall cease to be; all this is less than an instant to Shiva. Then the time shall come that the sea, the earth, the air, the fire and the wind shall be destroyed, several millions of Vishnu shall perish, and several millions of Brahmâ shall die likewise. Then Shiva shall gather up the heads of all these gods; of these heads shall he make his necklace, and he will dance on one foot a matchless dance, wherein this necklace will rattle on his eight shoulders, and he will sing strange airs which none else can sing, and taste of pleasures which none else hath ever known.'

This is not unlike Nietzsche; and this 'totalitarian philosophy', powerful, but inhuman and even antihuman, terrifying in its last analysis, the quintessence of paganism shrinking no whit from its own ultimate consequences, is what we have seen acclaimed in Hitler's Germany. But no German has sung this barbaric theme with as much abandon as did the old Shivaïte hymns: 'When thou dost dance, the earth, at the thud of thy feet, trembles on the brink of annihilation, the heavens swoon, the host of the planets is brought down by the movement of thy arms, the firmament, at the touch of thy head-dress, is ready to collapse, so contradictory thy power doth seem, yet ever in harmony with itself. Thy gardens are the graveyards, the vampires form thy court, the ashes of the funeral pyres are thy incense of sandalwood, and lo! thy garland of flowers is a chaplet of human skulls. Grim is thy humour, and thy name is even likewise. Nevertheless thou art the supreme felicity of those who call upon thee, O dispenser of favours! Thou art the sun, the moon, the wind, the wave, the heaven and the earth, thou art the universal soul, thou art at once the Whole and each of its parts. We offer worship to Thee who art the atom and the cosmos, O beloved god! We offer worship to Thee who art the Whole, to Thee who art more than the Whole and dost contain the Whole!' A strange hymn, wherein Marcus Aurelius and Nietzsche come unexpectedly face to face, a hymn which contains all the ultimate despair implied in either, and yet all the luxuriance and lyric fire proper to the Hindu climate.

*   *   *   *

India bequeathed to the world not only heroic pessimism, but also that gentle resigned pessimism which is Buddhism. Buddhism is one of the outstanding facts of human history. Its shortcomings are obvious. It is a negative wisdom, based on the premise of universal suffering; its sole aim is the elimination of that suffering by the extinction not only of the passions but also of all desire and finally of life itself. What remains positive in it, despite its doctrinal inadequacy, is meekness, active charity, goodness, human tenderness. Buddhism, indeed, has been called a half-way house, a foretaste of Christian charity. Not that we should dream in any case of underrating this Indian *misereor super turbam*. The words attributed to Buddha Çâkyamouni anticipate the Gospels: 'To do a little good is better than to perform difficult tasks. To understand the value of almsgiving, one should share even one's last mouthful. The perfect man is as nothing unless he pours out his charity on all, and consoles the forsaken. My doctrine is a doctrine of pity; that is why the happy of this world find it difficult. . . . There is a sacrifice easier than milk, oil, and honey—it is the giving of alms. Instead of sacrificing animals, let them go. Let them find grass, water, cool breezes!"

The pity of Buddha inclines an ear to all sorrows: 'More tears have been shed, O my disciples, than there is water in the great ocean.' Unlike Brahmanism with its caste divisions and its doctrine of transmigration according to social rank, protracting into eternity the social divisions of this world, Buddhism proclaims in principle the equality of all men. It welcomes with equal affection the prince and the pariah: 'The Brahman, O disciples, is born of woman, no less than the untouchable on whom he shuts the gates of salvation.' The Buddhist monks are enjoined to practise long-suffering and be of good cheer under the worst afflictions. If wicked men abuse a monk, he must say to himself: 'They are good, they are very good, because they do not wound me.' If they wound him: 'They are good because they do not kill me.' If they kill him: 'They are still good, because they are merely delivering me from this mortal life, without jeopardizing my salvation.' Chastity, poverty, and renunciation here take the place of the inhuman practices of Brahman yogism. These pure hearts beat with a quiet goodness, a childlike joy. 'In perfect joy we live, we who possess nothing. For us, as for the radiant gods, joy is our sustenance.'

Such selfless gladness is already almost Franciscan, just as the Buddhist tenderness towards our brethren, the animals, suggests to Christian minds the *Little Flowers* of St. Francis. The *djâkata*, or previous lives of the Buddha, are contributory to this state of mind. In the course of these previous existences (for we are dealing with the country of transmigration) the Buddha has been in turn the white six-tusked elephant bestowing his tusks upon the hunter, his murderer,—the king of the stags who has just delivered himself up to the King of Benares to save a captured hind,—the heroic hare leaping into the fire to feed a famished Brahman, the good monkey making a bridge of his tortured body to enable his brethren to escape pursuit, the King of the Çibi giving the falcon a pound of his flesh to save the pigeon who has sought refuge in his bosom. This fervent humanity, extended to animals and plants, remains the glory of Buddhism.

On the other hand, Buddhist philosophy seems rather vulnerable in its starting-points. True, it attempted to counter the pantheism which was rife around it, just as it reacted morally against the ferocity and immorality of Shivaïsm. But in this reaction against mistaken ontologies, Buddha goes to the length of rejecting all ontology and refuses to pronounce on the metaphysical problem: 'Let that which is unrevealed remain unrevealed.' (Here, *mutatis mutandis*, is an attitude somewhat akin to that of Auguste Comte's positivism.) But once the divine element has been removed from the sight and life of the Indian, what remains of the world of phenomena, of transmigration or *samsâra*, becomes sadly incomprehensible. And it is not surprising that Buddhists have seen in it only an ocean of change and suffering.

The infernal cycle of rebirths knows its frightful hazards, for, after several lives of upward progress through accumulated merit, the most exalted creature may at any moment sin, fall, and be flung back into horrible reincarnations! This is the only prospect which it offers for all eternity. To escape the torrent which sweeps him along, man looks in vain for a fixed point to which he can cling. He cannot find anchorage in the universe (made of impermanence and soon to be declared unreal) nor in God (the notion of the Absolute is denied us), nor even in the human soul (no substantial self, the self being merely an epiphenomenon). The only refuge left to him is in the extinction of the soul or *nirvâna*, on the understanding, moreover, that this extinction cannot be attained by material suicide (which would only plunge him back into the most terrible reincarnations); it can only be reached—after Heaven knows how many more rebirths—by the utter extinction of desire through the practice of all the virtues. And even then we are not told whether *nirvâna* is annihilation pure and simple or an ineffable beyond, 'a way of being which is superior both to non-being and to being'.

The teachers of Buddhism, such as Nâgârdjouna, Asanga and Vasubandhu, the first in the first century A.D. and the other two in the fifth, tried to fill these gaps. Nâgârdjouna attempted to do this, if not by nihilism—as would seem on first impression—at least by a system of universal nothingness which, in the hands of so subtle a dialectician, allowed amazing verbal recoveries.

Asanga and Vasabandhu made a more serious effort by building up, some thirteen centuries before Fichte, the theory of absolute idealism, founded on the unreality of the external world and of the substantial self. 'The individual has no personality,' wrote Asanga, 'since nothing exists but idea. The self is a hypothesis. We imagine that matter is formed of atoms, that intelligent beings are persons. Now it is we who suppose those atoms and persons by the idea of them. Thanks to our perception, an exterior world is created which has no reality.' And if we ask how the idea itself is not swept away by this dissolution, Vasu-bandhu answers brightly: 'The existence of pure idea is estab-lished by the very knowledge that we have of its objective unreality.' To such verbal tinsel was Buddhism reduced (like post-Kantian German idealism later) by its refusal of any pre-liminary ontology.

Though Buddhism has had great philosophers, it has left be-hind only an imperfect philosophy. It was partly for this reason that the Indian, a born philosopher if ever there was one, aban-doned it almost entirely after the ninth century A.D. One can found a school, but scarcely a religion, still less a society, on the void. As for the subsequent versions of Buddhism in China and Japan (Amidism was a case in point) they ended in an out-and-out theism which was really poles apart from the teaching of Çâkyamouni. Hence, despite scholastic appearances, despite the enormous Buddhist literature in Sanskrit, Pāli, Chinese and Tibetan, what matters in Buddhism, what has given it its power of attraction and remains its glory, is not its philosophic doc-trine but its moral practice, its affective qualities, its spiritual climate, in a word:—its virtues.[1] 'We are confronted,' Sylvain Lévi has well said, 'with this phenomenon, as contradictory as life itself and yet in harmony with it, of a religion based on nothingness and yet carrying the practical virtues to their high-est point.' And old Marco Polo seems to have struck the true note when, after hearing in Ceylon the story of Buddha Çâkya-mouni's life, he came to the rough conclusion that the Buddha's soul had possessed too many virtues not to have been already a Christian, 'for, if he had been a Christian, he would have been a great saint, judging by the edifying life which he led.'

It would indeed give an imperfect and even unjust idea of

I am not referring, of course, to Tibetan tantrism, which is only the re-admission into Buddhism of all the devilries, cruelties and obscenities of Shivaïsm.

Buddhism to judge it from the speculative angle. Half Asia would not have taken refuge in it, had it been only a matter of verbal gymnastics of dialecticians in precarious intellectual poses. The best of Buddhism, then, is Buddhist sensibility and its profound tenderness which, despite all doctrinal negations, creates an atmosphere of fervour, religiosity and active charity. To do it justice, we must study not only its teachers but also the *Garland* of Açvaghocha, the frescoes of Adjantâ and the reliefs of Borobudur. Over all the half of Asia which is as yet untouched by Christianity, Buddhism has been the great apostle of peace, gentleness, and mercy. Its inadequacies are those of human reason left to itself. Its immense charity, however, represents the best that God has put into the heart of man and has revealed a world of unsuspected moral values to the warlike tribes of Malaya and Indo-China, Tibet, and Japan, Central Asia and Mongolia. In the brutal pre-Columbian civilizations of North America we look in vain, from beginning to end, for a smile of humanity, a sigh of tenderness: how great, then, the debt which Asia owes to the sermon of Benares! And none is better qualified to testify to this than the Christian.

*　　*　　*　　*

India has given the world a mighty art, or rather a complete æsthetic, equal in originality and power to the Greek and the Chinese. It is marked by its naturalism in depicting animals and, in Vishnuite or Shivaïte iconography, its gift of attributing to God the features of man. What distinguishes the Indian animal-painters from their Assyrian or Greek rivals, is their brotherly sympathy for the animal, the tenderness with which they reproduce living forms. This loving naturalism is manifest in the first great high-reliefs on the porticoes of Santchi, dating from the first century B.C. With their wild elephants, buffaloes, fawns, antelopes, peacocks or cobras, all reconciled around the great Buddhist peace—the vision of a St. Francis of Assisi possessed of Mowgli's knowledge—the great doors of Santchi unfold before us the marvellous poem of Indian nature, the true *Jungle Book*. Under the inspiration of the *Djâtaka*, that Golden Legend of Buddhism, the jungle has been transformed into an earthly paradise. This animal art continued to grow, its freshness

unimpaired, until it reached its zenith in the rock-reliefs of Mahabalipuram or Seven-Pagodas, near Madras, in the seventh
century A.D. What majesty in the group of elephants worshipping
the descent of the Ganges from heaven to earth! What life in
'the cat dedicating herself to austerity' by refusing to devour a
mouse! What sovereign elegance in the pair of stags watching
from a cave the mystery of the life-giving waters! Another relief from the Seven-Pagodas shows us an admirable pastoral
scene drawn from life and representing a cow caressing the
spine of her suckling calf with a sweeping movement of her
tongue. Still more astonishing is the sculptured monolithic
block which groups a family of monkeys, the male catching the
female's fleas while she suckles her young, a scene depicted with
as much humour as love. Never have our brethren the animals
been so studied for their own sakes. The finest comparable
sculptures in other countries would seem cold beside this delicate and tender realism. The little loving cows of Krishna, the
slender antelopes following the shepherdesses in the Rajput
miniatures of the seventeenth century, show us that we are here
face to face with an enduring gift of the Indian genius.

The other characteristic of Indian sculpture is an anthropomorphism, a representation of divinity in the image of man,
equal to that of Hellas. But in this land of luxuriant growth it
was translated into works of a cosmic grandeur which no Zeus
ever reached. In this respect, as shown by the Shivaïte sculpture
of the Deccan from the ninth to the sixteenth century, India
appears to us a kind of tropical Greece, fed by all the sap of an
over-fertile soil, and at the same time inspiring her artists with
unbridled visions of the genesis of the gods. The reliefs of the
rock-temples of Ellora and Elephanta, contemporary with the
era of Charlemagne in Europe, prove this. Only the Michael
Angelo of the Sistine Chapel, or Rodin, can stand comparison.
The religion which inspired these reliefs was that of Shiva, conceived as a symbol of the cosmic force, an incarnation of Nature,
the eternal creator and destroyer. Yet, a classical austerity is
everywhere present. From the very entrance, it governs the
formidable elephant-battles with which the frieze seems to support the temple-mountain. Even in the cosmic dance, or as the
god of terror, Shiva's body is simple and pure of line; the

smooth, chaste and gentle nude which declining Buddhism had handed on to Shivaism.

Like the Seven-Pagodas, the Kailâsa of Ellora offers us admirable pageants, as for example that of the titan Râvana shaking the mountain on which Shiva and the goddess Pârvatî are enthroned: the subterranean violence of the titan, the serenity of the god as he crushes him with a gesture, the wholly feminine emotion of the goddess, who clings distractedly to her spouse, show a power of breadth and vision which Greek art never knew, and for whose like we can only turn once again to the Sistine Chapel. Such is the power of that Indian classicism that it even succeeds in embracing the strangest conventions of Shivaïte iconography; for example, in the cosmic dance the god is represented with four arms. Disconcertingly repellent at first sight, this multiplicity of arms soon accords so well with the requirements of an internal law, that the divine dancer appears in perfect harmony with his dreadful joy.

This rhythmic grace which India pitted against her super-abundance did not last long. In the temples of the Tamils it succumbed to the superfluity of floral, animal or anthropo-morphic decoration that loaded the great pyramid with an in-extricable tangle of designs, so that it became fretted stone in which not an inch was wasted.

Finally, at the zenith of her Middle Ages, India gave us, in the frescoes of the Buddhist grottoes of Adjantâ, immortal painting. These were huge compositions in which the animal-painters of the fifth to seventh centuries have fixed for us all the scenes of jungle life, with the gestures and facial expressions of the elephant and its young, the buffalo and the antelope, or the various species of monkeys. The same naturalism animated the lovely human bodies playing in the subtropical light—all those feminine studies with floral and, as they have been called, Botticel-lian gestures. But the Indian idyll and the jungle flowers are there only to emphasize more strongly the representation of the divine figures—the *bodhisattva*—in which the later Buddhist ideal was incarnate. These supernatural apparitions, at Adjantâ, count among the most moving that have ever come within human vision. The mind of the Western observer turns to Leonardo da Vinci's moving 'compositions for the Last Supper'.

These great frescoes of *bodhisattvas*, these charming princes with their dreamy and melancholy grace, bending in pity over the universal suffering of mankind, are found again at the other end of eastern Asia, in the frescoes of the Hôryûji, at Nara, in Japan. For Indian art conquered all eastern Asia, and India played in that part of the world as great a rôle as Greece in the West. The bounds of Outer India may thus be considered to cover half Asia. From the beginning of the Christian era to the fifteenth century, India, Buddhist, and Brahman, has civilized Indo-China and the Indian Archipelago, organized them, and awakened them to thought and art. Its contribution to the history of civilization is therefore immense. At the time of Charlemagne, Indian artists in Java, working for Indianized dynasties, sculptured the tope-mountain of Borobudur. Far from suffering through this transplantation to a barbarian land, Indian sculpture presents at Borobudur perhaps its finest masterpieces. Gazing upon the beautiful bodies in smooth, chaste and gentle relief, the serene rhythmic gestures, the poses each of such high artistic merit, one is irresistibly reminded of certain details of the frieze of the Panathenæa, with the addition of the meditative and penetrating tenderness peculiar to Buddhist art. Actually, it conveys at times a little of the same impression as the most religious works of our Quattrocento.

About the same—our Carolingian—epoch, other Indianized dynasties established the centre of the Khmer (Cambodian) empire around Angkor. Soon there arose the great capital, which passed through many alterations and changes of design between the last years of the ninth century and the beginning of the thirteenth. Here the genius of India begat a new people, and stimulated it to produce an art which, though owing its inspiration to the Ganges and the Deccan, nevertheless remained original. The architecture and ornament of Angkor have their own—largely independent—laws. A characteristic sculpture also developed, and even succeeded towards the end of the twelfth century in giving Buddhism what the sculptors of India this side the Ganges had not yet been able to achieve: the secret smile of the Buddha or Bodhisattva savouring in his heart the peace of *Nirvâna*, a faint, elusive smile with eyes closed.

Meanwhile, on the other side of the Annamite mountains, the

Chams of southern Annam, seafaring tribes with Malay affinities, came in turn under Indian influence and produced, in the neighbourhood of Turana, an art akin to the art of Cambodia but deeply original in its force and grace; its achievements lasted from the sixth to the thirteenth century.

And finally, Buddhist missionaries had profited from the beginning of the Christian era by the opening of the great silk route across Chinese Turkestan and had devoted themselves to the moral conquest of that country: and, behind it, of China proper. In Afghanistan Buddhism had come into contact with the Greek art of Alexander's successors; it carried the Græco-Buddhist art thus created across all the oases of the Gobi Desert, to the Gates of Jade at the entrance to China. Between the third and the eighth centuries A.D., Chinese Turkestan proper, which is to-day so barren, was from a spiritual standpoint a province of Outer India where Sanskrit literature and philosophy were as much honoured as on the banks of the Ganges. It was at the same time, from an artistic standpoint, one of Alexander's posthumous conquests, where masterpieces of Indo-Greek painting and sculpture survive. Here collapsed ('Remember, civilizations are mortal') a whole section of the human edifice; but without this event the passage from the Indo-European world to the Chinese world would scarcely have been possible. As regards the Græco-Buddhist art discovered in Chinese Turkestan and dating from the sixth to eighth centuries, a strange phenomenon is to be noted. Greece, in Greece itself, had been dead for centuries, and replaced by Byzantium; but her posthumous influence continued to make itself felt beyond the Gobi Desert! In just such a way does the light of a star which has been dead for æons continue to reach us across space and time.

China

From the Aryan invasion till our own day, India has never ceased to be intimately connected with Hither Asia. Chinese originality, on the other hand, is complete by itself. Born in the central and lower basin of the Yellow River, Chinese civilization steadily extended to the continent which became its field of activity, enclosed as it was between the sea to the east, the Gobi Desert to the north-west, the Celestial Mountains and the Pamirs

to the west, and the Kuen-lun to the south-west. Thence it radiat-
ed over the countries to the north-east and south-east, to Mongolia, Korea, Japan and Annam. For good and all it established
its spiritual influence over all these. It became for the Far East
what Græco-Roman civilization was to the western world;
Chinese culture played there the same rôle as Greek in the west,
and Chinese arms and administration the same rôle as Roman
arms and administration with us. China's place in history is thus
apparent.

*   *   *   *

We have seen Indian thought plunge at its origin full into the
beliefs of primitive man. The same is true of Chinese speculation. To seek of it real spirituality would be vain.[1] True, ances-
tor-worship figures among the most primitive cults; and indeed
the ancient Chinese not only recognized the existence of a soul,
but even reckoned two to each individual. But neither of these
was really spiritual, in the Greek or Indian sense of the word.
One, the *p'o*, is the animal breath, destined after death to become a *kuei*, which maintains a shadowy existence near the body.
The other individual soul, the *huen*, which has more resemblance
to the *psyche*, ascends into heaven after death in the form of
chên; but it can remain there only so long as its substance is fed
by funeral offerings—in default of these it reverts to the rank of
a *kuei* or wandering phantom. On the other hand, China has
given us powerful cosmogonies and very elaborate social
systems; these are invariably closely interlinked through the
primitive ideas on which both are based.

This connection appeared at the outset in the official cult by
which the prince was linked in harmony with the Sovereign on
High, the August Heaven. The Sovereign on High controlled
the order of nature, regulating the time and rhythm of the
seasons, and the prince's chief function was to ensure agreement between the celestial order of the seasons and the human
arrangement of work on the land. Probably the same seasonal
and agricultural preoccupations determined the division of
things between two alternating principles:—the *yin* which represented humidity, shadow, cold, contraction, and also the female
principle; and the *yang* which represented heat, sun, activity, ex-

---

[1] With the exception of Mo Tsu.

pansion, and also the male principle. The alternation and mutations of these two principles explained both the cycle of nature
and the human cycle, since nature and man, the physical and
moral worlds, were closely related. However, despite this division, Chinese cosmogony was by no means dualistic like, for
example, the Indian *Sâmkhya*. It was not so, firstly because *yin*
and *yang* not only alternated but also controlled and condi-
tioned each other, and might even be said to set each other in
motion, by means of the central notion of the *tao*. This conception of *tao*, keystone of all the Chinese systems, is difficult
to define, because it was variously conceived by different
systems. It means Way or Direction and seems originally to
have signified the order which presides over the alternation of
the two principles, and which is, as it were, the very law of their
interdependence, and their everlasting link.

In the midst of these ideas was shaped the thought of Confucius (551–479 B.C.). He follows them faithfully, believing as
he does in a superior order with which man must co-operate;
man must contribute to the social order by the perfection of his
own conduct. Confucian ethics are therefore above all social
ethics, wholly concerned with order and harmony in society.
They are a code of good citizenship, but citizenship in communion with the cosmic order. Hence the importance attached to
the rites which constitute a kind of collaboration of man with the
laws of nature. Commentators who have reduced Confucian-
ism to a featureless conformism and conservatism, however,
seem to have been unfaithful to the thought, and above all to
the personality, of the master. Confucius himself made a very
noble effort to achieve inward perfection, especially when it
was a question of shaping man's conduct according to the *tao*:
'Perfection is the *tao* of Heaven. To seek perfection is the *tao* of
man.' There is here undoubtedly something Christian:'Thy
Will be done, on earth as it is in Heaven.' But perhaps that is
straining the text a little. More modestly then it may be claimed
that the ethic of Confucius is ennobled by the special emphasis
which he puts on the practice of *jên*, or altruism. This consists
essentially in 'loving one's neighbour'. True, the atmosphere
is rather different from that created by Buddhist self-denial or
still more by Christian self-sacrifice. It amounts to no more than

intelligent mutual aid: 'Do not unto others what ye would not have them do unto you.' It is, however, equally true that *jên*, as preached by Confucius, implies infinitely commendable social and individual virtues:—respect for human personality, recognition of one's own and others' dignity, honesty, generosity, sincere politeness, and humane feeling. Even when this became a mere formula and, in the later classicism, a simple humanism, it nevertheless constituted the ideal of a polished, refined and gentle society. And at that time China was entirely surrounded by barbarians, the ferocious Huns to the north, the aborigines in the south! The gentleness of this ideal, so far in advance of its Asiatic background, is all the more striking. The land of Confucius never lost this advance on others. Through it and by it— as much as by its administrative qualities—China proved the principal agent of civilization and progress in the whole of eastern Asia. In half of Asia, China has stood for humanism in the broadest sense of the word, and for civilization in its most precious meaning.

A special place must be assigned to the philosopher Mo Tsu. who lived at the end of the fifth century B.C. Almost alone in his country and his age, this illustrious thinker practically arrived at theism. Instead of the impersonal heaven of his predecessors, he invoked the Lord On High, a personal god, omnipotent and omniscient, essentially moral. 'The great motive for good conduct ought to be fear of the Lord On High, Who sees all that happens in the woods, the valleys, and the dark places where no human eye can penetrate. It is Him we must try to please. He desires good and hates evil. He loves justice and hates iniquity. All power on earth is subject to Him and must be exercised according to His views. He wishes the prince to be benevolent towards the people and all men to love one another, because He loves all men. . . . He hates conquerors who make women widows and children orphans.' From his theism Mo Tsu gained, indeed, a remarkably high morality. With him *jên*, Confucian altruism, became *liên-ngai*, universal love, which he carried even to sacrifice of self: 'To kill a man for the sake of the world, is not to act for the good of the world. To sacrifice oneself for the good of the world, that is to act well.' In this iron age —the period of the Fighting Kingdoms, as it has been called,

—the Chinese sage condemned war: 'The Prince should regard his subjects as himself.' And all his thought is summed up in this maxim: 'Wisdom consists in adoring Heaven and loving men.'

The teachings of this great mind were rather neglected after his own day, but have been restored to an honoured place, since the advent of the Chinese Republic, by a young school which sees in them not only a justification of democratic principles, but also 'a bridge to Christianity'.

*   *   *   *

China, apart from Mo Tsu, is considered the country of conformism and positivism. But this same country has given us Taoism. This, as the name indicates, is the philosophy of the *tao*. We met this idea in the earliest Chinese cosmogonies. Here, it is enriched and deepened. The *tao* is the superior principle of the *yin* and the *yang* which find in it their unity at the same time as their impulsion—the One who, by provoking their endless alternation, is the motive force of the cosmos—'the responsible centre which radiates the regulating forces of the universe.' It is also the cosmic continuum in which are reconciled the opposites 'life and death, subject and object, thou and I'; in which the Taoist, liberated from time and space, and from himself, identifies himself with the rest of the universe and thereby dominates the universe.

Chinese history shows only too clearly that this led in practice to spiritualism and even sorcery, and that its adoption had indeed to a considerable extent no other object. It contained the same dangers for morality and took on the same anti-social character as did Hindu *yoga*. Nevertheless, it is true that this mystical monism inspired a lyricism of extraordinary power, whose æsthetic value—whatever our fundamental reservations may be—was of the greatest importance for the later history of Chinese poetry and art.

The commentary on the first chapter of the *Tao-tö-king* is a magnificent poem, even if the idea of the divine was soon warped by a monist vocabulary: 'Before time, and at all times, was a Being existing of itself, eternal, infinite, complete, omnipresent. To name it is impossible, for human terms apply only to creatures perceptible to the senses. Now the primordial Being is essentially not perceptible. Outside that Being, before the origin, there was nothing. It is called nothingness, or mystery, or *tao*.'

The *tao* can then only be defined negatively. It is what is expressed in the four verses, so often quoted, of the Book of *Lao-Tsu*:

> 'O great square that has no angle,
> Great vase that ne'er was finished,
> Great voice that speaks no words,
> Great presence that has no form.'

But we should be fundamentally mistaken if we took it for a static monism. It is dynamism itself. The *tao* is conceived less as a being than as a force. It is all upsurge and freedom. It is 'the spontaneity which moves the worlds'; or, better still, 'the permanent principle of universal spontaneity,' the cosmic urge, identical with Bergson's *élan vital*. Wisdom consists in renouncing all desire to guide oneself, and allowing oneself to be guided by it: 'Away with the wind I went,' says the *Book of Lao-Tsu*, 'now east, now west, like a driven leaf or a dry stalk, until I no longer knew whether it was the wind that bore me or I who bore the wind.'

But it is above all to the philosopher Chuang-Tsu, the most illustrious author of the Taoist rule of life, that we owe immortal pages. His book begins with the Platonic myth of the great celestial bird soaring up to search for the *tao*. 'The great bird rises on the wind to a height of 90,000 stadia. What does it see up there in the blue? Troops of wild horses at full gallop? Primeval matter hovering in a dust of atoms? The breaths that give birth to living creatures? Is it the blue of the sky itself, or only the colour of infinite distance?' In this planetary flight on the wings of the great mythical bird, overtaking and surpassing the profound meditations of the Buddhist hermitages, in this wild aspiration to reach at a stroke the nameless force that moves the worlds, Chuang Tsu feels himself master of the universe. 'The sage in his transcendence is beyond all contingencies. Though the thunderbolt fall from the mountains, though the hurricane overwhelm the ocean; he is untroubled. Borne aloft upon air and cloud, he rides to the sun and the moon, and frolics beyond space itself.' At these heights, the individual self has long been left behind: 'How do we know if the self is what we call the self? I, Chuang-Tsu, once dreamt that I was a butterfly, and I was happy. I did not know that I was Chuang-Tsu. Suddenly I awoke and was myself again, the 'real' Chuang-Tsu. And I no longer knew whether I was Chuang-Tsu dreaming that he was a butterfly, or a butterfly dreaming that it was Chuang-Tsu.' Or there is the Shakespearean scene in which another Taoist philosopher, Li-Tsu, showing a skull which he had picked up on the edge of the road, murmurs, like a Chinese Hamlet: 'We know, this skull and I, that there is no real life, and no real death. . . .'

Taoist ascetic practice absorbs the whole being. 'May thine eyes,' teaches Chuang-Tsu, 'have nothing more to see, thine ears nothing more to hear, thy heart nothing more to know.' The danger, here as in certain Indian systems, lies in the impossible effort to think outside of categories; to reach the absolute not by adhesion of heart and faith, but by thought which is no longer part of man, by robbing the intellect of its spiritual nature. 'Spew out thy intelligence,' enjoined the Taoist canon. On the other hand, this philosophy which is intoxicated with divinity refuses to recognize God. 'The *tao* which can be named is no longer the *tao*.' Finally, there is the relativist atmosphere. Long before Renan's picture 'from the viewpoint of Sirius', Chuang-Tsu invited us to envisage things from a similar observatory: 'If you ride in the chariot of the sun. . . .' From these heights, as we have seen, 'self and others are the same, a centenarian is not old, a new-born infant is not young, a mite is as big as a mountain, a blade of grass is equal to the universe.' This relativism, or rather this universal reversibility, leads to a detached, quiet, and serene acquiescence in face of all human vicissitudes. 'O world,' Marcus Aurelius was to say, 'all that you bring me is good in my sight.' 'When we have grasped,' Chuang-Tsu likewise said, 'that heaven and earth are one vast crucible, and the creator a great smelter, where could we go that would not be for our good?'—'O master, master,' cried Chuang-Tsu in another passage addressed to the *tao*, 'thou destroyest all things without being cruel, and dispensest bounty to ten thousand generations without being good.' A moment ago we were very close to Christian resignation. Now we are thrown back towards the bleak stoicism of a De Vigny.

Primitive Taoism, like the teaching of the *Upanishads* in India, wavers incessantly between two tendencies, no doubt because it is more like a metaphysical reverie than a philosophical system in the Western sense. But however lacking in coherent deductions, it has vouchsafed us 'poetic heights' of unsuspected range, and its influence, like that of Buddhism, has been considerable in art, notably in the growth of Chinese medieval landscape-painting.

From these somewhat nebulous heights we come back to earth with the medieval philosopher Chu Hi (1130–1200), who tried to imprison the old cosmogonies in a rigorous scientific system. At the origin of things, Chu Hi puts the *wu-ki*, which is non-being, conceived as universal virtuality. From the *wu-ki* arises the *t'ai-ki*, or 'supreme summit', which is substance in its fullness, 'most lofty, most excellent, most subtle, most spiritual.' This *t'ai-ki*, rather like *tao*, sends forth the world under the action of the principle of *li* which represents the laws of nature, the 'norm', as it has been translated. It is the 'norm' which sets in motion the cosmic energy (*ki*) which, by the combination of the opposites *yin* and *yang*, produces out of primordial chaos all the beings of the universe. 'The latent force, inherent in all matter,' writes Chu Hi, 'produced gyratory movement: heaven and earth were then a mass of evolving matter, turning like a millstone. As this rotary movement quickened, the heavy parts were condensed in the centre, forming the earth, whilst the light parts, drawn towards the periphery, formed the heavens.' The cosmos thus organized is only, like the individual, a momentary aspect, 'an anticipation', of the universal energy. After some millions of years, there will begin a phase of disintegration of matter, followed by a new phase of gyratory condensation and creation, and so *ad infinitum*. But throughout this eternal cycle, it is always the *t'ai-ki* which animates the worlds and living creatures. 'It is like the moon which lightens the night,' explained Chu Hi. 'She is in the heavens and yet, when she sheds her sweet light over rivers and lakes, the reflection of her disk can be seen everywhere, without it being possible to say that the moon is divided or has lost her unity.'

The analogies of this system with Spencer's *First Principles* are striking: both speak of the passage from the homogeneous to the heterogeneous, and the return to the homogeneous, the phases of integration and disintegration throughout eternity. What is particularly interesting is the importance attached to the principle of *li*, that is, to the laws of nature, valid for all reigns and in all worlds, a permanent mould in which all ephemeral forms are moulded. Chu Hi expresses this in these terms: '*Li* is like the master of the house, who dwells within and receives his guests. He is eternal, though his guests pass on.' The laws of nature, therefore, existed before evolution: 'Certainly *li* existed before heaven and earth, and it is *li* which set energy in movement and thus produced the world.' The moral sense also has its share in the principle of *li*: in other words, the moral law is the human application of the laws of nature; it is as necessary as they, and is binding on us for the same reason.

Chuism, it may be seen, is a coherent system which lacks neither strength nor even poetry. Unhappily its results were not invariably as acceptable. By imprisoning Chinese thought in the closed circle of a mechanistic evolution, this Spencer of the Far East lessened for a time the creative urge of the Chinese genius. His doctrine, when it had become the accepted doctrine of the State, risked (especially through the faults of mediocre disciples in the Ming period) plunging Chinese society into materialism and routine. Thanks to Wang Yang Ming (1472–1528) there were re-introduced into neo-Confucian philosophy more human feeling and also more idealism.

*   *   *   *

Finding no outlet in official philosophy, the Chinese genius took refuge in art. North China, in the fifth and sixth centuries A.D., at the time of the Tartar dynasty of the Wei, created a school of Buddhist sculpture which was in some degree an equivalent of the Romanesque and Gothic sculpture of the West, which it anticipated by five centuries. It was the school, well known to-day in Europe, of the rock-sanctuaries of Yun-Kang and Long-mên. It was an essentially mystical art because it reduced form to its simplest expression and addressed itself directly to the soul—a very great religious art in which severity, even gaucherie, became by their profound sincerity like a call to meditation. All this was true of its beginnings at Yun-Kang. Later these stylizations softened. While still preserving their mystical character, contours grew more human, expressions calmer. The folds of the garments, instead of ending in great jagged angles, faded gradually away into little rounded waves. Finally, in the last years of the sixth century, at Long-mên, relief came back into favour; but, as in similar circumstances at Rheims and Notre-Dame de Paris, it remained exclusively at the service of religious feeling, steeped in sober meditation.

It has been claimed that these schools influenced the growth of our own Romanesque and Gothic art. That is geographically and historically impossible. But the achievement is none the less remarkable. We have seen how the religious thought of India with the theistic systems of Vishnuism, and Chinese thought with Mo-Tsu, anticipated Christian ideas. It is no less interesting to see that Chinese religious feeling foreshadowed the art of our cathedrals.

From the eighth century onward this great religious art grew dull and insipid in China. But Japan, traditionally the repository of the Chinese æsthetic, gathered it up and gave it a new life. In the sanctuaries of Nara or in the Kyôto of the Heian era, plastic art, emptied of its content, had become no more than an urge towards the Beyond, a prayer and a burning mysticism. Under the immense nimbus with flame-wreathed point which often crowns them, the earliest *bodhisattva* of the Hôryûji, at Nara, tall tapering statues almost bodiless in their stylization, ethereal apparitions seeming to rise up to heaven, sometimes suggest Moissac or the Romanesque portal of Chartres. This was in the seventh century and accorded with the chronological staggering usually to be found when a school of philosophy or art passed from China to the Archipelago. It was Japan, moreover, which left us what is certainly the purest masterpiece of that style, the wooden Nyoirin Kannon preserved in the Chûgûji of Nara, one of the noblest images of meditation ever created by the hand of man. As for the *bodhisattva* of the Hôryûji frescoes, their expression of fervour relates them to the 'heroes of Buddhism' whom we have just seen on the walls of Adjantâ, in India. Or rather, at such heights, Adjantâ and the Hôryûji no longer really belong to Japan or India, nor even to Buddhism, but to the religious inheritance of all mankind.

*   *   *   *

We could perhaps say as much of one whole side of Chinese poetry and painting in the Middle Ages. If we analyse Chinese lyricism under the T'ang, we find there both the great cosmic dream of the old Taoism, born of a wild urge towards the divine, and the Buddhist melancholy in face of universal dissolution. 'All pass away together,' sings Li T'ai-po, 'things and creatures, like the ceaseless waves of the Yang-tse, rolling down until they are lost in the sea.' And from the other great poet of the eighth century, Tu Fu, comes this autumn meditation whose poetic feeling leads us almost to the threshold of what might be called metaphysical feeling: 'The wind is keen, the clouds are high, the monkey voices his plaint. On the silver shores of the limpid water, birds skim the sand as they wheel. On all sides, the rustling of fallen leaves, and before one the swollen waves of the great river, rolling, rolling endlessly, never weary. To see in the distance only the desolate spectacle of autumn and to feel oneself a stranger wherever one goes. . . .'

Metaphysical anguish grows sharper in a poignant poem by Chen Tsu-ngan (about 685): 'Each lovely day that passes, comes never to return. Spring follows its swift course, and is half gone. Lost in a dream, I know not where my thoughts have wandered. Lying beneath the tall trees, I gaze upon the eternal handiwork. . . . How many creatures have lived and died since the ancient days of the great flights of wild geese! Who would recognize the most famous man of past ages, if he returned to earth to-day? The autumn wind is rising amid the quivering leaves. The flowers of the year faint and fall and are swept away, but what becomes of their perfume?'

And there is this winged meditation from another T'ang poet, Song Che-Wen: 'The rain from Mount Ki-chan had been driven away by the wind. The sun appeared, pure and radiant above the western peak, and the trees in the valley of the South seemed more verdant. I approached the holy dwelling where a venerable monk gave me friendly greeting. The monk and I were united in the same thought. We had exhausted all that words could say, and we remained silent. I looked at the flowers, likewise motionless; I listened to the birds hanging in space, and I understood the great truth.' Another visit to the monastery, by T'ao Han: 'The pines and the cypresses hide the mountain pass, but to the west I have discovered a narrow path. The sky opens, a peak appears and, as if out of nothingness, a monastery rises before my eyes. The building seems to be perched on a terrace of cloud; its parts spring up upon precipitous rocks. The night comes; monkeys and birds fall silent. The sound of bells and the chant of priests penetrate beyond the cold clouds. I gaze on the blue peaks and see the moon mirrored in the waters of the lake; I listen to the water-springs and the wind that whips the leaves along the edge of the brook. My soul, at once free and captive, has soared beyond things visible. . . .'

These great romantic themes, treated in the impressionist manner, recur with the landscape-painters of the Sung period, such as Ma Yuan, Ma Lin, Hia Kuei and Mu K'i (in the twelfth to thirteenth centuries), as well as with their Japanese imitators of the fifteenth and sixteenth centuries; such as Sesshû, Sôami, Sesson. Despite the discipline of the most accurate drawing that ever was, the world of form has become with this school, according to the Buddhist formula, 'merely a dew-world', a belt of haze through which the most precipitous peaks seem but unsubstantial phantoms. Drowned in mists and lost in distances, its landscapes are as heart-gripping as a human face. And indeed, it is the face of the world which the painters have sought to capture here in its most general aspect; or rather they have tried to convey its deep significance, the material forms being indicated only in so far as they suggest what is hidden behind them. The more that face of land and water, of valleys and mountains, is blurred by mist and simplified by distance, the better the Spirit may be grasped through it. This explains the customary composition of the Sung wash-drawings. In the foreground, lightly sketched in, there are a few trees with twisted trunks, a cottage, a boat on the bank of a river which fades into the mist that fills the valley. On the horizon, at distances impossible to gauge—the intervening mist has made us lose contact with reality—rise mountain-chains whose faint outline seems to hang in mid-air. These are landscapes in which the enveloping mist, by obliterating plane surfaces and half-veiling the concrete forms of things near at hand, ends by leaving only 'pure space' and the enchantment of distance.

It has been said that a landscape is a state of mind, and that was never as true as of the Sung wash-drawings. These landscapes are indeed a 'poetic elevation' and meditation after the manner of our own Romantics. They are the unformulated prayer of a soul seeking itself, and seeking also, behind the veil of appearances, the true Being, the ultimate Reality.

*   *   *   *

Japan

If we speak of the Chinese Buddhist sculpture of the Wei, we must also speak of the Japanese statues of Nara or Heian; if we conjure up the Chinese drawings of the Sung, we must mention the Japanese landscape-painters of the fifteenth century. Japan has at each period, although after an appropriate time-lag, become the pupil of China,—the pupil often improving upon the master! But what can Japan show us that is actually her own?

In the first place, a new conception of Buddhist tenderness, a thought born in China, it is true, but one that has really gained a special emphasis in Japan: Amidism. Amitâbha, 'infinite light' —Amida in Japanese—is a metaphysical and transcendant Buddha, full of pity, who reigns over a wondrous paradise where pure souls are reborn at his feet in the mystical lotus. This Buddhism was originally agnostic, but acquired an idealistic monism in the course of its evolution. Owing to the demands of the human heart, it ended as a state of mind that was almost entirely theistic. The distance thus covered may be measured by the changing conception of the soul and its salvation. Buddha Çâkyamouni had denied the existence of the soul, at least as a substantial entity; salvation was for him the extinction of the individual in *Nirvâna*. Amidism practically replaced *Nirvâna* by a paradise in which souls enjoyed a kind of beatific vision without losing their personality. Amida thus became a rough equivalent of a personal god and saviour. The worship paid him was the religion of the heart in an atmosphere of true quietism. For a sinner to pronounce but once the name of Amida was to be saved.

Amidism was preached in Japan by the Shônin monk Hônen, founder of the Jodo sect, or sect of the Pure Earth (1133–1212).

The sermons in which Hônen preached self-abnegation and all-confidence in Amida still have the power to move us by their genuine piety: 'There is no hamlet so forlorn that the rays of the silver moon fail to reach it. Nor is there any man who, by opening wide the windows of his thought, cannot perceive divine truth and take it unto his heart.' Persecuted for his faith, Hônen died, murmuring the famous lines:

> 'What though our bodies, fragile as the dew,
> Melt and dissolve themselves in nothingness?
> Our souls shall meet again in happier days
> Among the lotus-flowers of Paradise.'

The spiritual heir of Hônen, the Shônin monk Shinran (1173–1262), founder of the Shinshû sect, finally gave Japanese Amidism the appeal of a quietism based on the divine love and goodness. Amidism, the old Buddhist agnosticism, thus ended as its opposite, an affective theism.

Zen represented a paradox still greater, although one less happy in its applications: it was the ancient Buddhist non-violence ending in a religion of individual combativeness suited to a people of Samuraï. Zen (from the Sanskrit word *dhyâna* or meditation) means to give man, by a sort of intuitive conquest, the mastery of the cosmic force which resides in his heart. Cloaked in Buddhist vocabulary, this doctrine returned to the old Chinese Taoism, as preached by Chuang-Tsu. But the Chinese superman formed by that self-dicipline had been a supreme philosopher, detached from the world, aspiring only to lose himself in communion with nature. The Japanese Zenist stood for the opposite. The intellectual and moral discipline he imposed on himself was only an anvil on which his self was hammered into shape for action, struggle, victory. Zen, thus interpreted, became a school of military stoicism, a seminary for warriors. The ideal was no longer the tender paradise of Amidism, but a paradise in the shadow of the sword. Undoubtedly we have here in the Samuraï the concentrated violence of the island temperament which ended by remodelling Buddhism in its own image. The Indian Buddha, the apostle of extreme gentleness and renunciation, had thus strange heirs in the masters of the Bushidô, the Japanese code of chivalrous honour.

Zen has left a strong imprint on Japanese life. It ended by giving the Japanese soul its unequalled temper, its nobility, its sense of duty, its contempt for death, its total abnegation. But at the same time it helped to give it the taste for violence, the worship not only of heroism but also of war for war's sake, a worship utterly opposed to the Buddhism with which Zen claimed kinship, and completely opposed to the true nobility of man.

*   *   *   *

What conclusions are we to draw? If the great civilizations of eastern Asia have not succeeded for long in attaining what we ourselves know and feel to be the truth, they have yet, in the course of the ages, manifested by their passionate seeking after truth that they stand in poignant need of it. They are seekers—as we are. Despite the letter of their schools of thought and religions—which is often of small account in comparison with the profound tendencies they reveal—we can only bow admiringly before the sincerity of their effort. Their search for truth often strayed into blind alleys, perhaps for want of adequate metaphysical vocabularies or conceptions. This was only to be expected in view of the fallibility of all human reason if left to itself. But the spirit of Asia and the merit of the Eastern philosophic enquiry remain immense in size and depth. I would add that their Christian potentialities are infinite.

III

RELIGIOUS IMAGES OF EAST AND WEST
EUROPE AND ASIA

THE main interest of oriental studies undoubtedly lies in the comparison of values which they make possible. The revelation of Indian and Chinese thought has meant for us Westerners the discovery of different races, inhabiting other planets. But there emerges this clear conclusion:—despite the geographical and cultural barriers which for so long have separated the various cultural centres, and although they have developed independently, in almost complete isolation, the human spirit has remained one. The position which in every latitude it has been led to take up in face of the great problems has proved appreciably similar everywhere. Whether it is a question of the problem of knowledge, the origin of the world, the nature of the self or the nature of God, we find to our surprise that the answers given in eastern Asia and in the West are very similar. Hence contemporary interest in the comparative study of philosophy. But this method is not thus exhausted. Alongside the zone of discursive reason, there exists an immense field, that of religious feeling, which merits equal attention.

We know that it is not with reason alone but with his whole being that man goes to God. On this search for God; on the gropings, stumblings, and approximations to which it gives rise; on the exultant or humble joys which it affords in proportion as the sole Presence allows itself to be felt; on all these spiritual states the mystics have provided us with evidence. Their testimony is not confined to what they have written down. No less eloquent are the frescoes of cloisters and the stones of cathedrals. Often, indeed, the esoteric vocabulary of their texts proves difficult to understand, and needs even more delicate handling when one compares religions with one another. For in that case there is the gulf, the chasm which exists between dogmas. What common measure can there be between the Christian transcendent God, the Hindu Immanence and the

Buddhist Evanescence? And yet a work of art can translate these conceptions, however diametrically opposed, into representations that are often similar! How are these confluences to be explained? Does the artist—who acts like a mystic using brush or chisel—see beyond the letter of the texts into the true spirit of religions?

It would be a grave mistake to attempt to subordinate dogma to the expression of religious feeling. In fact, we are doing nothing of the sort, but are showing on the contrary, by direct reference to works of art, that often religious feeling seems to rebel when dogma (as in Buddhist or Brahman India) proves deficient. It makes good these deficiencies and heads straight for a more fully developed theology. Despite Hindu monism, Vishnuite or even Shivaïte mysticism manages at moments to suggest positive transcendency. And it is this possibility which the art of Ellora or Elephanta conjures up so often before our eyes. Likewise, while universal nothingness underlies Buddhism, and the most authentic Sutras explicitly deny the existence of the soul and of the Absolute, the mysticism of Çântidêva, for example, affords us a kind of echo of Christianity. It is 'this Christianity without Christ', as Marco Polo more or less called it, that seems to be reflected for us in more than one of the figures of Adjantâ. In this sense—and only in this sense—can we without blasphemy compare the finest religious images of eastern Asia to the portrayal of the face of God in Christian art.

There are countless varieties of mystical experience. Within the human heart the sound of the voice of God reverberates upon an infinite keyboard. But the organ notes are grouped around certain eternal themes, ranging from God's wrath to His tenderness. It is these themes which we must examine, across the ages and the civilizations.

*   *   *   *

Figures of gods

Primitive man, lacking revealed religion, experiences in the face of destiny a diffused menace which surrounds him on every side. His very terror causes him to see it suddenly take shape in the clouds. This conception prevails in the arts of negro Africa and of the Pacific Islands, and even in more developed civilizations, as witness the Chang *t'ao t'ie* or the pre-Columbian masks. The Unknowable appears as a god of terror; the supreme power takes on the semblance of the bestial and divine mask. These visions are often of striking æsthetic value and of a philosophic scope which is no less considerable, since they symbolize what, in a cosmos without God, would truly be god.

After these gods of terror, the god of majesty. Coming from the cradle of the Aryan race, the Shiva *mahêçamourti* or three-headed Shiva of Elephanta is already God, if not quite the Biblical Jahveh. Of all the divine figures which medieval India has bequeathed us, he is undoubtedly the finest and most impressive. Compared with this metaphysical apparition, dominating the worlds in the fullness of its strength and its thought, the figures of Olympian Zeus, in their serene majesty, seem very human. To define such a god, recourse has been had to the greatest verses of the *Içvaragîtâ*: 'I alone am the creator of the whole universe, alone the destroyer of the whole universe; I am the universal and eternal Soul; I am the Supreme Lord who governs all beings; and yet it is the universe which is in me, and not I who am in the universe.'

Can the term pantheist properly be applied here? Is not the absorption of the universe within the Lord, as has been suggested, an awkward and clumsy figure of speech used by the Hindus to increase divine transcendence? It is certain, on the other hand, that the Elephanta Shiva represents, as far as humble mortals are concerned, an attitude of total indifference. The giant pride of an omnipresent will, written upon the Jovian forehead, the fullness, the excess even, of vital force attested by the sensuality of the lower lip, are so many warning signs:— in spite of the impassibility of his expression, and without even altering it for a moment, the Lord can in a second pulverize this universe—or, more precisely, reabsorb it; in fact, he emits and reabsorbs it ceaselessly throughout eternity. All Hindu theology, Vishnuite as well as Shivaïte, proclaims the same teaching, which, unwittingly, Vigny rediscovered:

'Unseeing, unhearing, unheeding,
Alongside the human ant-hills I pursue my haughty course.'

This is cosmic greatness, but superhuman to the point of becoming inhuman. It is spirituality of the highest order, the spirituality of the mountain-tops, but exudes an air so rarified that our lungs can hardly breathe in it.

The same cosmic majesty, transcending centuries and worlds, emanates from the great *bodhisattva* of Long-mên, in North China, which was sculptured straight out of the rock-wall in about A.D. 676. With its back to the cliff from which it gradually stands out, this giant figure fifteen metres high, aureoled and surrounded by flames, meditates with an abstracted gaze which it lifts towards the heights. Is it Vairotchana, the esoteric Buddha whom certain sects have wished to cast for the rôle of an Absolute? Or Baichadjyaguru, the merciful *bodhisattva*, who cures bodies as well as souls? In either case, compared with the unfeeling Shiva it represents a considerable advance. This figure no longer breathes the formidable omnipotence of life, but the omnipotence of metaphysical abstraction and detachment. It is the force of spirituality. But it is part of the full current of medieval Buddhism. The spirituality to which the sculptor calls us may well seem very cold to us: the wisdom it has to offer ends in Nirvâna. And in the long run it is this impression of a cosmic Nirvâna that is left on us by the tall pensive figure on the cliff of Long-mên.

With the Christian God of majesty, we reach a positive theology. One of the most characteristic representations of Him is undoubtedly the tympanum of the façade of the Gothic Cathedral at Moissac. Christ in all His glory is there surrounded by the Four Beasts and the Four-and-Twenty Elders, preparing to judge the quick and the dead. As He appears at first sight, this Christ-king reminds us of some twelfth-century monarch sitting enthroned among his great vassals. But if the Christian presentation of the God of majesty adapts itself so well to pomp and royal attributes, it is because that symbolism has been found to express better than any other the Church's teachings on the divine transcendence. The same is true of many Byzantine Christs (for example in the apse of Monreale)[1] who represent the Second Person of the Trinity in the likeness of the *Pantocrator*, the Sovereign of the World and heavenly *basileus*. To the superficial onlooker such a notion would seem similar to the Indian idea of the *Chakravartin*, that is, the idea of the Buddha as

[1] In Syria. T.P.

universal monarch. But the Christian expression of this symbol, common to both religions, is by far the more powerful, because it corresponds exactly, not to a late development, but to the letter of the Christian doctrine. Perhaps this majestic, forceful, yet melancholy *Pantocrator* may seem to us to wear a severe— already a Spanish—expression; God who has passed through Golgotha and who, on the right hand of the Father, cannot forget the nails of the Passion. If his right hand redeems us, his left condemns sinners to eternal fire. But we must choose. Either with Shivaïsm we deify the whole of creation, vice and virtue, good and evil, spirit and flesh, or we accept the fact that, in the words of St. Luke, everything at last will be 'sifted like wheat'.

Of this god of justice and of vengeance, western art and Indian art have left us two incomparable representations. On the one hand, at the Vatican, in Michael Angelo's Last Judgment, we have Christ lashing out against the damned—an angry Olympian whose single gesture, before the terrified gaze of the Blessed, casts down to Hell a cataract of naked, writhing bodies. On the other hand, in India, at the Kailâsa of Ellora (of the eighth century), is the rock-relief which represents the demon-monster Ravâna trying to shake the Himalayan mountain on which the god Shiva sits enthroned with his wife Pârvatî. Contrasted with the subterranean violence of the Titan is the serenity of the god who, with the touch of his toe, steadies the mountain and crushes the disturber. In both scenes, so different in so many ways, there are unforgettable visions of the cosmic power of the Eternal One.

There is another aspect of the Hindu god that could have no equivalent in Europe. It is that of Shiva as the universal motive force, dancing the cosmic dance. The rhythm of his dance, stressed by the beat of his tambourine, is the very rhythm of the universe throughout the endless cycle of creation and destruction. The flame he brandishes in one hand is the original fire which alternatively animates and consumes the worlds. The frenzy of his gyration is the unleashing of the cosmic or vital Urge. His superhuman joy, as exultant in destruction as in creation, alike whether he is the source of individual suffering or the bestower of blessings, is the amorality of the pantheist god which amongst us Westerners no Spinoza has perceived, but which the metaphysical genius of India—with a freedom for which we owe it thanks—has unmasked without hesitation.

Far removed from this riot of cosmogony is the serene but somewhat chill vision of the God of Wisdom, common to Christianity and Mahâyân Buddhism. We need only think of the Buddha-statues of Borobudur, seated as they are in the lotus-pose (*padmâsana*) and making with two hands that most elegant gesture, 'the shaking of the wheel of the Law' (*dharmatt-chakra-moudrâ*), that is, the gesture with which the preaching of the Buddhist doctrine begins (eighth century): or again, in the same pose, with the same gesture and also at Java, but later (Singhasâri, thirteenth century, to-day in the Leyden museum), we find the famous statue of the Buddhist 'Holy Wisdom' (*Pradjnâparamitâ*). May we compare such works to the 'Fair God of Amiens', with His right hand giving the benediction, His left holding the Gospel, and His feet stamping upon the asp and the basilisk? Not if we consider the nature of the teaching given; for what common measure is there between positive charity, the entirely active doctrine of our Bible, and charity for *Nirvâna*, the completely negative doctrine of the purest Sutras? The analogy is only in the spirituality, the doctrinal power and security, which is common to both. But the historian recalls that for comparative philosophy, as far as speculative method is concerned—though certainly not as regards the fundamentals —there is also on occasion a certain superficial analogy between the school of mystical idealism (*yogatchara*) which inspired the sculpture of Borobudur, and the great Christian scholasticism of the thirteenth century, upon which the sculptors of Amiens and Rheims were brought up.

Independent of these edifying figures, but still very like them, are the meditative figures. One of these looms up in the semi-darkness of Cave I, among the frescoes of Adjantâ, a *bodhisattva* whose eyes are lost in reverie under his rich golden tiara and the immense arch of his eyebrows. That metaphysical gaze desires not the world of appearances which is our universe, but reaches far beyond to the universal vanity and universal suffering which are, we know, the ultimate Buddhist reality. Gentler and more peaceful are the Khmer (Cambodian) heads of the Bayon school of sculpture, at Angkhor; they belong to the end of the twelfth century. If Buddhist doctrine has for its starting-point the starkest pessimism, its morality ends, through the practice of constant charity, total renunciation and universal meekness, in ineffable blessedness.

The 'Bayon smile' with eyes closed gives expression to this state of mind: a fixed, subtle smile, mysteriously reflecting the inner light of *Nirvâna*. Moreover, it must not be imagined that this theme of the smiling Buddha degenerates into monotony by dint of repetition. Sometimes, when it lights up the face of some slender Indian, the smile is so purely immaterial and ethereal that it transfigures his entire face; sometimes it takes on a still deeper meaning, and a great peace descends on some Cambodian mask with its broad face and thick lips, earthy and wholly human.

Khmer art has no monopoly of these meditative figures. In Japanese Buddhism, at Nara, the Miroku Bosatsu of the Chûgûji (seventh century) and the Bonten of the Sangatsudô which are attributed to Ryôben (mid-eighth century), give an even more striking impression. The second of these statues, with hands resting, palm against palm, in the gesture of prayer (*andjak moudra*), eyes half-closed, face fervent yet at peace, is pure meditation. As for the long statue of Miroku Bosatsu, seated cross-legged with the right elbow supported on the knee and the right hand stroking the face, it is not a meditating figure; it is Meditation itself. While both are Buddhist divinities, they seem, curiously enough, more remote from previous Buddhist art than from our own Roman and Gothic statues. Pure coincidence? No. A metaphysical conjunction. It would certainly have seemed paradoxical to talk of metaphysics, let alone theology, in connection with primitive Buddhism, which was strictly speaking the negation of both. But medieval Buddhism had arrived at precisely that degree of evolution where, without ever formally breaking with the teaching of Çâkyamouni, it had become almost its opposite. The somewhat arid and dull wisdom of the original doctrine had changed into a mystical idealism formulated by such eminent metaphysicians as Asanga and Vasabandu in India (fourth to fifth centuries) and Huian-Tsang in China (seventh century). With them, the agnosticism of the first Sutras ended in the equivalent of an Absolute, namely in the 'Ideal Plane', which the faithful did not reach by pure thought alone, but to which they clung with the whole of their sensibility. Indeed, could it not be said that despite the negative postulates of ancient Buddhism, the secret demands of thought and heart had led medieval Buddhism half-way to the Christian position? The best proof of that lies in these tall meditative figures of *bodhisattvas*, mystical apparitions which the first Buddhist canons had certainly not foreseen and which, albeit unconsciously, brought to the peoples of Further Asia something of our own hope.

Medieval Buddhism was, all unaware, so near Christianity that it seemed to feel the need of it. It is not by pure chance that the 'beautiful *bodhisattva*' or 'lotus *bodhisattva*', a fresco in Cave I, at Adjantâ, in the Deccan of the seventh century, recalls by his bowed and slightly weary pose, by his inexpressibly melancholy tenderness, by that look of pity for human sorrow, Leonardo's Christ of the Last Supper (to-day at the Brera). And we certainly have not in mind any comparison which might seem sacrilege. No figure of any time or place could be set in a diptych with Him who so loved men that he died for them on the Cross. Now, if ever a picture of Christ approximated to the idea we have of Him, it is Leonardo's. 'A picture of infinite love, of infinite grief, of infinite compassion'; it is permeated by the *misereor super turbam*, expressed by that look of pity for universal suffering, over the treason of Judas resolved upon at that same Supper, at that same instant; over the Passion foreseen and accepted in advance, the Passion drunk and savoured, all of it, in the same chalice now circulating around the table. The tenderness of that face permeates, in the Gospel of St. John, all the Discourse after the Supper: 'When He knew that His hour was come that He should depart out of this world unto the Father, having loved His own which were in the world, He loved them unto the end.' 'Little children, yet a little while I am with you.' Death, indeed, has already touched with his wing the Christ of the Brera, has marked Him with the seal of the victim who is to be sacrificed, and has prematurely given His sad face its almost unearthly look, as if it were already no more than a divine apparition above the tomb.

Never has the dogma of God-made-Man been so closely approached; for no face more pathetically human has ever reflected so much of the Eternal.

How can we then dare to think of the fresco of Adjantâ? Just precisely because the feelings which inspired it, seem like a presentiment of Christianity. Asanga, the Indian metaphysician of the fourth century, speaks to us of Buddhist pity: 'The *bodhisattva* has in the very marrow of his being a love for all creatures which is like the love one has for an only son. As a dove cherishes her young and patiently broods over them, so does the Compassionate One with the creatures who are his children.' And further on: 'The world is not capable of bearing its own sorrow. How much less the sorrow of others! But the *bodhisattva* can bear the sorrow of all creatures, all that there are in the world. His tenderness for all created things is the supreme marvel of the worlds; or rather not so, since self and other are identical for him, and therefore the creatures are to him as himself.' With Asanga, Buddhist commiseration reaches the climax, of pity beyond even what justice requires. 'Pity for the wretched, pity for the hot-tempered, pity for the angry, pity for the slave of matter, pity for him who is obstinate in error!'

Three centuries after Asanga, another master of Indian Buddhism, Çântidêva, in his *March towards the Light*, sang of the passion for sacrifice in future Buddhas: 'Let me be for the sick both medicine and doctor. Let me, in time of famine, become myself the food and drink of the hungry. I deliver my body into the hands of all beings. Let them beat it incessantly and abuse it; let them cover it with dust; let them make of my body a plaything, an object of derision. Let me be the protector of the bereft, the guide of those who journey and, for those who desire the Other Shore, the ferry-boat, the causeway, the harbour; the lamp for those who need a lamp, the slave of those who need a slave.' From the same treatise comes this other definition of total charity: 'For the sake of the creatures the Buddhas lacerate their bodies and penetrate into hell. What they do for any living creature, we must also do for them. Like them, we must do good even to our worst enemies. From to-day, to please the Buddhas, with all my soul I make myself the servant of all created things. Let the multitude trample upon my head and kill me, that the Protector of the world be satisfied!' And, to finish with Çântidêva, there is this truly Christian thought: 'If the suffering of the greater number can cease through the sacrifice of one, that one should bring it about by pitying others as himself.'

How are such utterances of later Buddhism to be explained? Must we imagine contacts between the Christian communities ('Christians of St. Thomas') of the Malabar and Coromandel coasts and the Buddhist metaphysicians of the fourth to seventh centuries? Or did there exist mysterious correspondence between mystics of totally different worlds? In reality, these conceptions fulfil such a need of the human heart, and our souls are so naturally awaiting Christ, that perhaps where they have not received His message they may have a presentiment of His approach. But Christian art alone has been able to reach the goal, because it alone—to repeat the image so curiously glimpsed by the Buddhist mystics—followed Him who proclaimed Himself the Way, the Truth and the Life. Moreover, we would seek in vain in Buddhist art for a figure comparable (to quote only these few examples from among thousands) to the Christ of the Crowning with Thorns (*Gesu deriso*) or to the Christ of the Laying Down of the Cross by Giotto, both of which are at Santa Maria dell'Arena, Padua. Only the Man of Sorrows has accomplished the total sacrifice foreshadowed by Asanga and Çântidêva.

Madonnas

Nor is there any parallel to the Virgin. Where would we find in Buddhism a figure like the Golden Virgin of Amiens? Some students have, indeed, quoted in this connection the 'Kuan-yin, Giver of Children' of late Chinese Buddhism. Among the ivories of the Lucien Lion Collection, there are certain figurines of Kuan-yin which do present a resemblance to our Madonnas; although superficial, it has been enough to mislead some. It has been asked whether the influence of the Jesuits of Macao may not have made itself felt here. But if it is a question of Ming or T'sing ivories, these Chinese divinities derive from much earlier times than the first arrival of the Portuguese. The ivory Kuan-yins of Ming, especially those affecting the pose of 'regal relaxation', do but reproduce the image of similar divinities painted on mountain-sides, in a misty landscape of rocks and springs, by the old Sung or even T'ang masters. Indeed, at that period which corresponds to our Middle Ages, there was only *one* *bodhisattva* in question, Avalokiteçvala ('He who looks down from on high'), a kind of Buddhist Providence who, still masculine at Tuen-huang in the tenth century, only assumed a definitely feminine form in the Ming period: appealing to women in the shape of the 'white-robed Kuan-yin'. Thence have arisen these mistaken analogies between various Ming ivories and Western Virgins. The Buddhist 'Giver of Children' and our Virgin Mother represent, however, two entirely different subjects. Their interest, properly speaking, lies elsewhere, namely in that transformation of the old *bodhisattva* into a woman. Why should there be such a transformation, were it not that the exigencies of the human heart demand that the tender pitying figure, depicted by Mahâyâna Buddhism as bending over human distress, should become a female figure, a Madonna 'by allusion'?

On the other hand, in all Far Eastern art there is no representation which even remotely resembles our *Pietà*. For instance the Virgin of Giotto's 'Laying Down of the Cross' or the Avignon *Pietà* with the inscription taken from the *Tenebrae* of Good Friday: 'O, all ye that pass by, bethink ye if there be any sorrow like unto mine!' Nowhere else can we find this. Not in any other religion than ours. Not in any art other than Christian.

But does this mean that outside of such restricted fields Buddhism has known no feminine images worthy of our admiration? Of course not. There are notable representations of holy women. Some of them would surprise the profane a little, because female figures in ancient Indian sculpture are nearly always in the nude. It is, however, an essentially chaste nude and one which evoked no worldly thoughts in the pious Buddhist, as may be demonstrated from the famous relief of Amarâvatî, in which the four female worshippers, prostrate with religious zeal, bow their lithe bodies before the throne where may be seen, sole sign of the invisible presence of the Buddha, the imprint of his feet. Nearer, however, to Western conceptions is the admirable eighth-century relief of Borobudur, in Java, representing the pious young girl Sudjâtâ coming to offer a bowl of rice to the meditating Buddha. The modest reserve of the young peasant-girl, her contemplation, her freshness and fervour, handled in the chaste and gentle manner which distinguishes the art of Borobudur, create an atmosphere that is already almost Christian.

*   *   *   *

Saints and Ascetics

The psychology of saints has been studied at close range by the Buddhist sculptors and painters as well as by our Western art. The concordances here are striking. As far as the representation of divinity is concerned, the analogy naturally remained very superficial, because an abyss separates the theology of the *Pater* from the Buddhist evanescence or the Hindu immanence. On the other hand, the rules of monastic life, the practice of poverty, chastity and obedience are in general the same with both. In the Buddhist *vihâra* and in our monasteries the faithful surrendered entirely to spirituality, even if, to the metaphysician, the object of their meditations differs entirely; they lived in similar worlds. Re-read, e.g., the *Fioretti*, the *Legend of the Three Companions*, the *Canticle of the Sun*. And then turn to the famous stanzas in which the Buddhist monk describes his ideal: 'In perfect joy we live, without enmity in a world of strife. In perfect joy we live, we who possess nothing. Gaiety is our food, as it is to the shining gods.' Born of total self-surrender, the cheerfulness of these monks has the same ring on the banks of the Ganges as in the Franciscan sanctuaries.

There, as here, asceticism has re-created man. According to the striking formula of the *Upanishad*, he has 'become what he was'. With what fervour does the soul thus lightened plunge into contemplation.[1] With what sureness does it steer its way to salvation! Here (in the National Gallery) are two apostles after the school of Giotto, bowing their venerable heads in a gesture of overwhelming sorrow at the news of Christ's Passion; and there, on an eighth-century high relief from Mahabalipuram, in Southern India, is a Brahman ascetic prostrate before the miracle of the Ganges which the gods, to save man, are

[1] In an album of comparative art shortly to be published, jointly with Madame Jacques Lemaitre, the author has brought together certain figures borrowed from the most diverse schools. As a matter of fact, they have, so to speak, grouped themselves.

pouring down from heaven upon the earth. No doubt, a whole
world separates the two conceptions; but in both cases there
are the same monastic faces with long hair (coiled in the Brahman fashion at Mahabalipuram) and long beards, the same
intense fervour, the same bodies bowed in burning adoration.
. . . At Mahabalipuram, furthermore, another Brahman ascetic,
thin as a skeleton, stands erect with arms raised above his head,
in an attitude of jubilation before the mystery of the life-giving
waters; he strikes a more typically Hindu note. But here again,
allowing of course for all the difference between that running
stream of images in Hindu lyricism and the more measured tone of
Western poetry, we might recall the Franciscan *Canticle of the Sun.*

Buddhism too has given us great works on this subject. The
famous statue of the standing monk who holds the alms-bowl
(*patra*) in the eighth-century Long-mên style is, by its solidity,
by the doctrinal affirmation of its attitude, and by the austere
self-communion of its face, one of the most powerful monastic
figures of all time. Still more moving is the Çâkyamouni of the
Chinese painter Leang K'ai (roughly between 1200 and 1270).
The founder of Buddhism is here represented in the guise of an
ascetic who meditates while leaning on his stick near a torrent
in a strange landscape of steep mountains. The intensity of
thought and the power of meditation are expressed with harsh
spirituality in his hairy and almost savage face; an inner violence
as strong as the wind which howls through the mountain
gorge, stirs the strange folds of his scanty garment, and finds
its counterpart in the gnarled branches which creep and writhe
like monstrous beasts at the ascetic's feet. No less prodigious is
the painting of another Sung artist of the same period, Hu K'i,
representing an ascetic lost in ecstasy. The hermit is seated on a
mountain ledge. An enormous serpent surrounds him with its
coils and lays a menacing head upon his knees, but the ascetic
remains unmoved; the power of his mental concentration dominates the reptile. Below them, in the mountain-side, opens a
chasm from which are rising clouds that seem to bear aloft the
strange group.

With such work, Buddhist mystical theology touches Taoist
mysticism. The famous portrait of the sage Lu Tong-pin (755–
805) illustrates this. What strikes us here is no longer the flame

of asceticism in the Indian monks, but on the contrary, as befits this naturalism, a powerful vitality, spiritualized, it is true, by the profound intellectuality in the gaze, by the serenity of the expression, the majesty of the attitude, the sweep of line, and also by the figure's kindness. For was it not Lu Tong-pin who would jot down at evening in his bedside note-book: 'Saved the life of a butterfly: one merit. Bought and liberated some little captive animals: one merit by cash expended'?

In Japan, Buddhism has made all the mystical theologies of the continent of Asia grow together and intertwine. Japanese sculpture of the Kamakura period has left us moving proofs of spiritual revival. The statue of the hermit Bashisen (by Unkei, *c*. 1150–1220), with parchment-like face furrowed by fasting and vigils, and body desiccated by austerities, illustrates this. Buddhist asceticism here rejoins Hindu yogism, despite the fact that it was originally condemned by Buddha in person. Indeed, for a long time even in India itself, Mahâyânist Buddhism had been developing this tendency, which triumphed fully with Tibetan tantrism. There is the astonishing passage from Çânti-dêva's *March to the Light*, which dates from the seventh century: 'I will go to the charnel-house, the dwelling befitting the body, to put my body in the presence of the cadavers, my body vowed like them to corruption. Lo, the corruption that my body shall become: its odour shall spread to the jackals.' This is clearly the same theme as in the *Triumph of Death* of the Campo Santo at Pisa, the stark horror of the whole cavalcade, men and animals alike, a sight which Bossuet refused even to name, while Verhaeren called it up savagely with the cry: 'And you too, my fingers, will become worms.'

Seemingly at the opposite pole of spirituality, we place the statue by the same Unkei of the Indian philosopher Asanga, at the Kôfukuji of Nara, about 1208. Not an ascetic type, this time, but one properly ecclesiastical which bears the stamp of doctrinal force and goodness, its face solidly built. In Asanga's vast forehead may be read the intellectual power and grasp that make for metaphysical genius; his calm features reveal experience of the human heart and of life, leading to infinite indulgence for all creatures, as is proved by the gesture of his raised right hand —it reassures and soothes (*abhaya mudrâ*). Evoking the same atmosphere, but with a rather different expression, the portrait of the *daishi* Jichin, a Japanese painting of the thirteenth century, is equally accurate in its sacerdotal psychology: a bald old man, with strongly marked features, seated in a high-backed armchair before a table covered by a magnificent lotus-patterned cloth. Eyes full of shrewdness and acumen, intelligence and kindness, the fatherly eyes of a Churchman. Plump hands of a prelate, accustomed to handle firmly and prudently the great interests committed to their care. Indeed, a Holbein character, with the goodness of Ghirlandaio's 'Old Man with the Child'. As for the Nara Asanga, there are innumerable magisterial figures in our Gothic sculpture as well as in Quattrocento painting which could be compared to it. An example may be found in Amiens cathedral: the episcopal statue of St. Firmin, with face radiating nobility and spiritual light, his left hand holding the cross, and the right raised in a gesture in which 'there is something of eternity'. All the doctrinal security of our scholasticism is there.

A religious figure appropriate to the Far East is that of Bodhidharma, in Chinese *Ta-mo*. He was the legendary founder of the school of the *dhyâna*, that is, of meditation or more properly intuition, a term rendered in Chinese by *ch'an* and in Japanese by *zen*. To this Indian mystic, who is said to have gone to China in the sixth century A.D., is attributed a curious doctrine according to which the ultimate truth of Buddhism cannot be taught by word of mouth, but has to be communicated directly from master to pupil in the flash of a single glance. Hence those sages with flashing eyes, 'tiger eyes,' multiplied by *ch'an* painting in China or zenist painting in Japan.

Rather similar in conception are the Taoist genii, popularized in the China of the Ming by painting and ivory statuettes. Strange figures these, very human in appearance, all smiling with good-nature, but at the same time transcending our world by the metaphysical irony with which the sight of universal disquiet seems to imbue them. Here again, what insight into character lies behind such simple statuettes! These good old men with thick skulls are sometimes deliberately comical but never lose anything of their majesty; from our European shop-windows they smile at us with a slightly quizzical benevolence.

Though they appear to engage us in conversation, we are quite aware of the superior powers within them. They can at any moment, like Chuang-Tsu in his famous dream, transform themselves before our very eyes into a butterfly or a cloud, and fly off forthwith to the paradise of the Immortals! Are not these Taoist gods of happiness so many stars hanging in the depths of the heavens? Their smiles, fraternal but never identical, carry us through the whole gamut of spiritual detachment from simple Socratic irony to the 'metaphysical evolutions' of a Chuang-Tsu. One, who seems clouded by dreams and distance, almost recalls the Verlaine of Eugène Carrière; another is a Silenus having the disillusioned wisdom and the goodness of Marcus Aurelius, together with the purity of heart of Ghirlandaio's 'Old Man'. Their expressions, as befits the tone of Taoist teaching, are at once mischievous and mystical, steeped in kindly irony so as to convey to us the double response of the sons of Lao-Tsu in the face of universal grief and vanity.

Something of a surprise to us (especially in such a setting) are the young Shivaïte saints whose images have been popularized in the Indies by the Dravidian bronzes from the eleventh to the fifteenth century. In a religion scarcely given to such ingenuity, these adolescents with their hands joined in prayer or with gestures of religious jubilation surprise us by the sincerity of their fervour. It is true that the Shivaïte hymns show them intoxicated with God. With mysticism so intense, it seems that the inadmissable postulates of Shivaïsm are forgotten. And there remains only the sincerity of the soul in quest of the divine.

But at the risk of seeming unfaithful to orientalism, I must admit that of so many monastic or priestly figures not one can move me like the portraits of the saints grouped by Fra Angelico around the Christ of the Crucifixion (at the Museum of St. Mark), a fresco painted kneeling, for one feels that the artist, no less than his characters, lived every moment of that scene, that he inflicted the punishment on himself, since he was recreating it so that he might suffer himself the agony and death of his Lord. And among these figures, particualrly those of St. Francis and St. Dominic. St. Francis is on the right, a little withdrawn in his humility. 'Frail as a bending reed' (to quote Alfred Pichon) 'the saint, burning with love, puts his hand to his head no longer able to hold it up; the stigmata of the Passion pierce his hands, his feet, his side; his eyes are fixed on Jesus with an expression of supreme suffering; and a deep furrow, more agonizing than tears, ploughs its way horribly down his emaciated cheek.' Nearer to Christ, kneeling alone in front of all the other saints, at the very foot of the Cross, is St. Dominic. 'On his fine and luminous head, which he throws back meditatively and which is haggard and grief-stricken with burning piety, he unites the two opposites, infinite suffering and unshakable faith.' In these two figures, we may truly find the whole greatness of Christianity in its double aspect of doctrinal certainty and of love.

*   *   *   *

Angels

After this seraphic vision, there remain only the angels themselves. We need not speak of the Byzantine angels on Balkan mosaics or as at Monreale, where they are shown encircling Christ to the rustle of their three pairs of wings as described by the Seers, from the prophets of Israel to the Apocalypse. But the angels of Rheims have a double appeal to my mind and heart: they are at once the smile of the Christian religion and the smile of the land of France. Then there are the angels of Fra Angelico, his angel-choir dancing airily around the *Coronation of the Virgin* (in the Uffizi) to the sound of organs, viols and trumpets. If Fra Giovanni da Fiesole made them so gladsome, it was because, as his surname proclaimed (which he owed to his connection with them), he had really lived among them. These purely spiritual beings have been described admirably by that other son of St. Dominic, that other angelic friar, Thomas Aquinas, whose teachings (in the *Summa*) Giovanni had certainly pondered. Denizens of the air, dressed in the freshest colours of miniature, Fra Angelico's heavenly messengers are nevertheless not mere themes and creatures of the imagination as with so many other painters. In the first place, he made of them immaterial creatures according to the metaphysical reinstatement of St. Thomas, whose *Summa* dealt with them so astonishingly logically and precisely; he then gave them his own tenderness and joy: his tenderness at sharing with them in the service of the divine master, his joy at having become one of their number. But we must not, for all that, fail to do justice to the angelic musicians of Van Eyck or Memlinc, glorious choristers of some Flemish cathedral, worthy to ascend some day into Heaven! To reproach them for not having come down from it would be churlish.

Are the Persian angels akin to ours? The Koran after all, borrowed its spirits from the Bible. Or are they derived from Mazdaism? Suhrawardî of Aleppo, author of the 'Illuminative Doctrine' (+1191), whose treatise *On the Rustling of the Wing of the Archangel Gabriel* carries weight in the Islamic lands, clearly linked the Platonic doctrine of the *dæmons*, the Knowing Ones, with the Seven Immortals (Amahraspand) and the Seven Archangels who—in Sassanid Zorastrianism—are the immediate ministers of Ahura Mazda. Be that as it may, a Mazdaian infiltration seems quite likely when one sees in a famous miniature in the Sarre Collection (Samarkand, about 1500) a princess of the genii enthroned in a tree and guarded by a swarm of winged *houris*, i.e. pleasing female 'angels'. *Houris* too, in a no less famous miniature in the Vever Collection, dance around the Queen of Sheba. On the other hand, legions of angels, in the Biblical and Christian sense of the word, come, in Aghâ Mîrek's *Apocalypse of Mahomet* (in the British Museum; Persian, sixteenth century) swarming from the heights before the Prophet at the moment when he, riding Al-Borâq and guided by the Archangel Gabriel, has just crossed the ocean of the clouds and passed beyond the sun itself, to mount into the blue of the firmament towards the paradise of Allah.

Shall we go further eastward and compare these Moslem angels with the flying genii of Buddhism and Brahmanism, the *apsaras* who in both of these religions play the part of messengers? It would be straying from our subject of comparative mysticism, were we to take up the comparative mythology of the ancient Indo-Europeans. Let us rather return to our angels with the theme of the mystic round, a charming theme found in both Persian and Rajput miniatures. In Rajput art, we have the *motif* of the *râsa mandala*, the cosmic dance directed by the god Krishna and his wife Râdhâ. The divine pair are surrounded by three concentric circles of female worshippers carried away by the ecstatic rhythm of the dance, which in mystic manner unites them to the deities. We recognize in this the cults of *bhakti* (devotion of the heart) which, since the eleventh century, have so greatly influenced Hinduism, both Shivaïte and Vishnuite.

Is there any impiety in returning hence to Fra Angelico and recalling his rings of angels in the two Last Judgments (those of the Florentine Academy and Berlin)? In the Florentine Academy the circle of angels, or rather of Celestial Powers—Seraphim, Cherubim, Thrones, Dominions, Virtues, Powers, Principalities, Archangels—which surrounds the Second Person of the Trinity is bound up with all the theological cosmography of the Middle Ages. 'The idea of circular and mobile heavens, formed of garlands of singing souls, seems to correspond to most of the paradisiacal conceptions entertained by the artists of East and West alike.' The Procession of the Spheres occurs in Arab science, notably with Avicenna, as it does in Christianity with Dante. However, with Fra Angelico these apocalyptic visions have become humanized. The Heavenly Powers which surround Christ are still angels, the eminent dignity of some of whom is proclaimed only by the richness of their armour. In reality, it was in depicting the guardian angels that the angelic friar showed the full extent of his powers and expressed all his tenderness. They run to greet the elect, each of them taking by the hand the blessed one of whom he has had charge in this life and leading him on to the flower-spangled turf. 'Among the deep grass and the flowers, in the shade of tiny trees, about a rustic lily-pool, the innocent round join hands. The sweet memories of Foligno and Todi must have been echoing in Fra Angelico's thoughts with the song of Fra Jacopone:

> In Heaven a ring is formed
> Of all the saints in this garden,

while he depicted the tender hand-clasps, the child-like purity of his elect. But as the dance moves towards the bottom of the garden and the top of the picture, it becomes more luminous, more airy, and the two leaders of the divine train, as it approaches the Heavenly City, are already bathed in light. Now they are only to be seen in a distant radiance; their ethereal bodies and diaphanous robes are already lost in the great golden joy of the light.'[1] In the 'Judgment' (Berlin), there is a similar

---

[1] Alfred Pichon, *Fra Angelico*.

round, or rather a farandole of angels which trips merrily away on the left of the picture; the difference is that the procession does not mount towards the Heavenly City, but directly towards the sky.

Visions of Paradise

The visions of paradise to which we thus have access are found in Buddhist as well as in Christian art. The history of comparative art offers similarities, for example, in Orcagna's *Glory of Paradise* (in the church of Santa Maria Novella at Florence) and the *Paradise of Avalokitêçvara*, a Chinese painting dated 983. There is the same grouping of the members of the heavenly court, ranged in serried ranks to right and left of the divine throne. There is the same finish, worthy of miniature-painting, in these portraits of patriarchs, apostles, prophets and saints mingled with the angels at Santa Maria Novella; and at Tuen-huang of *bodhisattvas, arkats, devas* and genii, treated in the Indian or Chinese manner. Each countenance which has been vouchsafed the beatific vision, whether in Tuscany or at Kan-su, is surrounded by a nimbus or halo which will after-wards accompany it everywhere; to these glorious bodies, each of which bears the ritual attributes or makes the proper canoni-cal gesture, the costliest fabrics add fresh magic, and the heavenly interplay of colours executed with the delight in detail that is found in illuminated manuscripts, make such pictures pure enchantment. Nor must we overlook, in either, the con-temporary figures at the very bottom of the pictures—this tenth-century Chinese donor in his ceremonial costume who offers, along with the scroll of Tuen-huang, a pan of incense to the *bodhisattva;* these Florentines of the Trecento, neighbours and friends of Orcagna, whom he makes the angels lead to the threshold of the Heavenly Jerusalem.

The Buddhist paradises are as numerous as the *bodhisattvas* who preside over them. In seventh-century China, the faithful most frequently addressed their prayers to Maitreya, the future Buddha. Into his paradise they hoped to be reborn. A little later, in the ninth and tenth centuries, the banners of Tuen-huang showed the preponderance of another *bodhisattva*, the Indian Avalokitêçvara, who was just being transformed into the

Chinese Kuan-yin. A material alteration in primitive Buddhist doctrine was implied in this. If there was one principle to which ancient Buddhism had clung, it was the non-existence of the soul (*nairâtmya*), the soul being thought of only as a series of psychic phenomena destined to disappear in *Nirvâna*. But despite this negative dogma of original Buddhism, the invincible hope innate in man's heart could not be stilled—is not hope a theological virtue? For the void of *Nirvâna* it substituted ineffable paradises in which souls saved by the *bodhisattvas*' clemency enjoyed the beatific vision and infinite spiritual bliss. Under cover of Buddhism there was thus restored all that it had denied, the personal soul and the survival of the personality.

The new theology in China and Japan eventually triumphed in the shape of *Amidism*, or the worship of Amitâbha. This metaphysical Buddha (*dhyâni-buddha*) plays in Japanese Buddhism the rôle of a god of salvation. He is a personal god to whom no prayer is made in vain.

> 'His light pierceth the worlds in every part,
> His mercy never faileth those who call upon Him.'

So sang on his death-bed the great preacher of Japanese Amidism, Hônen-shônin (+1212), who has been compared to St. Francis of Assisi. Such comparisons can, of course, be made only on the ground of religious sensibility; a vast gulf separates doctrines. But Amidism, as preached by Hônen, certainly produced a spiritual climate of remarkable purity. Soul-communion with Amitâbha gave to all its doctrines the stamp of peaceful trust and inward gladness. Was it not enough for believers to utter the divine name once, in order to have their prayers answered? One act of repentance, one sincere wish to improve oneself, and the bad *karmen* could be destroyed, sins wiped out, and souls saved and reborn in lotus-flowers of a wondrous paradise at the feet of Amitâbha—the Paradise of Purity, or Paradise of the West (Sukhâvatî). Japanese painting has tirelessly reproduced the splendours of this luminous Beyond, its airy buildings, lotus lakes and celestial hierarchies. The evolution towards Christian ideals, which had begun unconsciously with Tuen-huang at the peak of the Middle Ages, continued despite all philosophical reasoning, urged on by the reason of the heart alone.

Animals

Indian and Western art have, in varying degrees, associated the animal kingdom with manifestations of religious feeling. A part of Buddhist literature which deals with the *djâtaka* or earlier lives of Buddha is founded on this theme. The dogma of transmigration (*samsâra*), universally accepted in India, obviously made the acceptance of such parables easy. But in so far as we can catch a true echo of the words of the historical Buddha in the oldest Sutras, it seems that in addition he personally showed a real tenderness which we would call Franciscan for our brethren the animals. This was one of the reasons why he opposed sacrifices: 'Instead of offering up these animals, let them go. May they find grass, water, and cooling winds!' And the Master took special pleasure in borrowing an animal theme for the text of many of the lessons which he gave to his disciples. The *djâtaka* form an immense anthology of such tales, quite unequalled in their freshness. One of the chief attractions of primitive Buddhism is its manifestation as a religion 'expressed in terms of the fables of La Fontaine'. To preach to us the forgiveness of those who have trespassed against us and to inculcate renunciation and self-surrender, Buddha teaches us that, in a former existence, he was the king of the elephants who himself made a gift of his tusks to his murderer, the king of the stags who gave himself up to redeem a pregnant hart,[1] the self-sacrificing hare who threw himself into the fire to feed a hungry Brahman, the king of the monkeys who saved his people by letting them trample him underfoot, the wild goose who cast himself down from the sky to provide additional food for a monastery. The echo this found in works of art is easily imagined. From the porticoes of Sântchî to the frescoes of Adjantâ, Buddhist art concerned itself to a considerable extent with animals; indeed the animal *motifs* became no mere subsidiary theme, but formed the chief and really religious part of high reliefs or frescoes. Between man and animal there is here a community of religious fervour based on a common nature: thanks to transmigration, they are interchangeable. Art gains thereby, albeit at the expense of reason. Look at the animals

---

[1] The *djâtaka* ends with the truly Buddhist edict, placed in the mouth of the King of Benares: 'All these forests and woods, springs and pools, I give to the stags, forbidding any to do them harm.'

adoring the tree of the Bodhi, on the east door of the great tope of Sântchî: these buffaloes, antelopes, even these savage beasts have become, by force of the compassion of the Merciful One, pious Buddhists.

Hinduism, whose Vishnuite and Shivaïte divinities have also frequently assumed animal form, favours the same artistic manifestations. The Hindu equivalent of the scene at Sântchî is (at Mahâbalipuram) the descent of the Ganges, worshipped equally by all the animals, from elephants sunk in grave meditation to the austerity-practising cat. Again, Krishnaïte pietism drew pleasing effects from these same themes, as when it shows us the heavenly herdsman making all the beasts of the stable or the forest dance to the sound of his flute. 'The peacocks dance, drunk with joy; the gazelles run to gaze affectionately upon him; the cows prick their ears as if to drink a cup of ambrosia; all the cattle come up in droves, with the grass they were munching still in their mouths; others, with tears in their eyes, stand and stare at the cowherd-god.' A symbol, the commentators tell us, of the delight of the faithful soul drinking in the divine word.

If we put aside the somewhat disturbing element sometimes found in Hinduism, Buddhist tenderness towards animals finds its equivalent in Franciscan tenderness. Consider the conversion of Gubbio's wolf: 'Brother wolf, thou art an object of terror to the inhabitants of the town, but I want to reconcile thee with them. . . .' Or the episode of the freeing of the turtle-doves: 'Little sisters, doves, innocent and chaste, why have you let yourselves be taken like this? I will snatch you from death and make you nests where you can multiply in obedience to your Creator.' Or the sermon to the birds: 'Dear birds, my little brothers, you owe your Creator deep gratitude. . . .' It is a theme which has inspired innumerable artists, beginning, at Assisi itself, with Giotto.

*   *   *   *

Feeling for Nature

All the texts show us how closely Buddhism from the first has associated love of nature with religious feeling: 'With calm intent,' declares a monk, 'I will enter the lovely forest, the abode of fiery elephants. In the forest full of flowers, in a cool mountain cave, I will bathe my body; my desire is to walk quite alone, in the vast and lovely forest. . . . When the storm-drums thunder in the sky, when torrents of rain fill all the pathways of the air, and the monk, in a mountain-hollow, gives himself up to meditation, there can be no deeper joy. On river-banks strewn with flowers and crowned with the gay garland of the forests, he sits in ecstatic meditation. Truly, there can be no deeper joy.' And further on in the Thêraghâtâ comes this other appeal to solitude: 'When shall I live in a cave, contemplating the instability of all existence? When shall I be wise despite my ragged garments, calling nothing mine, void of desire, casting out love and hate; when shall I live in such joy high upon the mountain? The places which the karéri bushes crown, the places loud with the patter of rain, with the trumpeting of elephants and the peacock's cry—these delightful retreats give rest to my spirit.'

This feeling for nature is inherent in Buddhist monasticism and appears again in the exquisite little landscapes, part-Indian, part-Chinese, which illuminate Tibetan banners: and especially so when they depict hermitages where the hermits consort with wild beasts.[1] Developed in medieval China by the Ch'an or Contemplative school, it eventually fused with the Taoist feeling for nature; this, as we have seen, was born of ecstatic communion with the essence of the universe. In the Sung period (960–1276) the two sources of inspiration practically merged. And it was precisely then that those prodigious Chinese monochrome landscapes appeared, which are composed solely of space and distances, expressing sheer meditation in face of the infinite. Sometimes, in the foreground, there is a human figure lost in the contemplation of immensity. A Taoist dream of union with the cosmic power? Or Buddhist melancholy aroused by the impermanence of things? At this level the two themes are no longer mutually exclusive. Here, transcending even Buddhism and Taoism, we attain the universal. In fact we often find more true religious feeling in a Sung landscape than in many Buddhist sculptures of the same period, at least if religious

---

[1] On the same subject, a charming painting by Lorenzetti may be seen at Florence. It represents the anchorites of the Thebaïd; in a landscape which is really rather Tibetan in appearance, the Desert Fathers are milking does, riding leopards, receiving food from the paws of bears and being buried by lions.

feeling may be taken to consist of metaphysical unease and the aspiration towards the infinite.

Does feeling for nature require a monist philosophy, as has been believed in Europe by so many German and other students of æsthetics? A pilgrimage to the sites so lovingly chosen by St. Francis for his monasteries or his hermitages answers this. And so does the *Canticle of the Sun* or, to use the Franciscan title, the *Canticle of the Creatures*. These blessings upon our brother the sun, our sisters the stars, our brothers wind, water, and cloud, our sister water and our brother fire, our mother the earth—have we not already heard them at the far end of the Indo-European world, some thousand years B.C., in the hymns of the Vêda? True, as far as the flow of imagery goes, the finest Franciscan poetry cannot be compared with Indian lyricism— Umbria is no Punjab!; but it did prove itself no less able to hold communion with the beauty around us. The whole difference between the two really lies in the fact that Franciscan poetry shared in the union with nature without letting itself be overwhelmed by nature. This reservation is of infinite importance, since that makes it both the guardian of Christian ideas on divine Transcendance, and the defender of what, from a moral standpoint, constitutes in our opinion the essence of the West.

*　　　*　　　*　　　*

In all these works of art, however separated by distance in space or time and by differences in outlook or dogma, there stands revealed one common trait:—aspiration towards the divine. Metaphysical anguish or religious faith, the whole gamut of meditation, prayer and union with God is here translated into universal language. Viewed from these heights, religious art thus represents one of the purest ways of expressing spirituality. It is one of the means given to man whereby he may rise above himself and commune with the Absolute. This holds good even if the notion of the Absolute is apparently banished from the vocabulary of a particular religion. The pathetic votive offering, noticed by Chavannes on one of the T'ang steles, is but one illustration. 'Behold me, a servant of Buddha, abandoned, alone, bereft of all who were dear to me. Before a tree shaken by the wind, I think long of them and question heaven without being granted an answer. Would that I could place myself in the hands of the spirits, so that they could lift me out of my solitude! I give, then, my wealth to carve respectful images of Buddha, hoping that through them peace will be brought to the living and the dead.' Are we not here at the very sources of religious art? And is there anything which can touch us more nearly than these humble voices which, across the ages and from beyond the grave, tell us of their anguish and their unconquerable hope? These are voices from the depths of the past, raised in prayer—voices of our brethren, voices of poor humanity.

IV

EUROPE AND ASIA

Greek and Barbarian

EUROPE and Asia—the meaning of the two geographical terms has widened with the growth of our knowledge. For the Greeks of the fifth century B.C., Europe was in fact the Hellenic world, and Asia the Persian Empire. Herodotus conveys the impression that the idea of a Europe appeared for the first time in the course of the Medic Wars. For it is only by opposition to other ideas that a concept takes definite shape. It was by taking her stand against the world-empire of the Persians that Greece finally reached self-awareness. When her writers compare her with other peoples, the ' Barbarians ', as they call them, we feel that they see in her, and in her alone, the home of the human spirit. Their attitude was certainly exclusive, for these so-called barbarians included after all the oldest civilized nations—Egypt, Babylon, and Israel, to say nothing of India and China which the Greeks did not know as yet. But the Hellenic attitude of viewing Greece as the centre of the world was justified on at least one count: if Hellenism was not the whole world, it was certainly for its time the whole of our world; it was Europe.

For three hundred years, it summed up Europe. Between the fifth and the third centuries B.C. European frontiers were not marked, as geographers later claimed, by the Urals and the Bosphorus. The Scythian steppes and forests, the woods and sandy heaths of Germany, the Celtic forests and the plateaux of Spain were still integral parts of the barbarian world. On the other hand, because an Aeolis, an Ionia and the Dorian Pentapolis had taken root on the eastern shore of the Aegean Sea, all that part of Asia Minor had become European land: so much so, that it was the home of the Homeric poems! Likewise, Italy 'entered Europe' when Greater Greece was established there and when the Etruscans, who had made primitive Rome, were themselves Hellenized.

Peoples obtained access to European civilization in so far as Hellenism introduced them to it. Of this remote spiritual ascendancy we are all more or less aware. Which of us, as soon as he was old enough to tackle Æschylus or Herodotus, has not listened with beating heart, as to some contemporary report, to the story of the Battle of Salamis? Dimly we feel that on the day of Salamis the whole inheritance of our civilization was at stake; that 'these men who are slaves to no man', as the chorus of ancients says in *The Persians*, were our true ancestors; that the liberation of the soil of Hellas, on the evening of Plataea, was to prove the pledge of all our liberations down the ages. Memories or anticipations such as these make Greek history for ever a living and topical part of our own.

The whole of that history is contained in the duel between Hellene and Barbarian, between Europe and Asia. We scarcely need sum up the facts. In 480 the whole barbarian world was in attack on two fronts; the invasion of Attica by Xerxes' armies through Macedonia was paralleled by the landing in Sicily of the Carthaginian army which marched on Syracuse. And on both fronts victory was complete. Herodotus, who had fully realized its Panhellenic character, regrets only that Hamilcar's disaster at Himera did not coincide to the day with the Battle of Salamis. At a stroke all the Greek colonies of the Propontis and Asia Minor were liberated, from Byzantium to Cnidus. In 449 the Peace of Callias consummated this triumph of Hellenism on the two shores of the Aegean Sea.

The subsequent events are equally familiar. They showed up the incredible sins of the Greeks against Hellenism. The results of their common victory were thrown away by the Peloponnesian War—that criminal civil war of Greeks against Greeks from which Pericles can scarcely be absolved—and then by the 'triangular' struggle between Athens, Sparta, and Thebes. Through their miserable parochialism, the cities contesting the hegemony were brought one by one to seek the arbitration of the Great King.[1] He it was who after 412 brought about the triumph of Sparta over Athens, which had remained more faithful than her rival to the memories of the Median Wars. Lysander's destruction of the Long Walls was, from that point of view, the indirect vengeance of the vanquished of Marathon.

[1] i.e., the King of Persia. T.P.

It is true that victorious Sparta tried to take upon herself the mission of Athens, and to regroup the Greeks against the Barbarians. The expedition of Agesilaus to Asia Minor in 396 anticipated that of Alexander. Through it, as well as through the amazing adventure of the Ten Thousand, the Greeks learnt to travel the road to Asia. But Panhellenic sentiment spoke less loudly than the ancient feuds: while the Spartan armies were far away in Lydia, their Greek rivals barred their line of retreat against them. Sparta, infuriated by such treason, became guilty of still worse. In order to preserve her hegemony over European Greece she handed over Asiatic Greece to the Persians by the Treaty of Antalcidas (386). The preponderance of Thebes, which since the Median Wars had always 'played the Persian', consummated that humiliation. A century after Salamis, entirely through the discords among the Greeks, the Great King found himself the arbiter of Hellas without ever having needed to draw the sword.

The humiliation was nowhere more keenly felt than at Athens. The most eloquent protest, as we know, came from Isocrates, who during the internecine struggles of the Greeks wished to stand apart from the conflict, the better to defend the cause of all Greece against the Barbarians. He it was who gave Hellenism the magnificent definition: 'the mark of the Hellene was rather his culture than his blood'. In the sweep of his Panhellenic patriotism and his wish to save Greece from Asia, did he not want to see the Athenian democracy enter into a voluntary alliance with Philip of Macedon?

Where, about 350, did the true interest of Hellenism lie? With Demosthenes, who, to save the independence of Greece from the Macedonian hegemony, was counselling alliance with the Persians? Or with Isocrates who, to deliver Ionia from the Persian yoke, was willing to accept the primacy of Philip? It is tragic that the Greeks, by their incurable discords, should have thus been driven to an impossible choice between the territorial expansion of Hellenism and liberty.

From Greece to the Indies

Similar uncertainty surrounds the personality of Alexander. Should we see in him the agent of the Hellenic League about to

Hellenize Asia? Or the Macedonian whom the Orient had won over and divested of Greek civilization to the point of making him a Son of Ammon and Great King? Both personalities were present in him. And the whole drama of his brief life lay in the contrast between them. When he forced the passage of the Granicus, he came to Asia, like Agesilaus before him, to take vengeance for the invasion of Xerxes. His first act was to deliver Ionia. He went on to give Hellenism the coasts of the eastern Mediterranean, Syria, and Egypt; that is, the European façade of Asia. And this part of all his conquests was the only one to prove really lasting. Egypt and Syria remained part of Hellas for nine hundred and seventy years after his day, and western Anatolia for sixteen and a half centuries. On the other hand, east of the Euphrates, on the Persian plateau afterwards conquered by Alexander, Hellenism maintained its hold for barely two centuries. And it was there that the Macedonian, for the eight years of life left to him, began to strip himself of his Greek inheritance.

But what strikes the imagination most are the two reconnaissances which he made, one across the Russian Turkestan of to-day, the other towards India. Alexander, however, halted on the threshold of the promised land. Though he conquered the rajahs of the Punjab, he failed to reach the Ganges basin which is the real India. In another direction, beyond Samarkhand and Khodjand (which he turned into a second Alexandria), he could do no more than suspect the existence of that Far East which would indeed have seemed to his Macedonians a new planet. But here—unwittingly—he made it possible for future ages, for the Roman caravaneers of the Silk Route, to link the two halves of the world. In this borderland between two worlds, all subsequent history derives from him. His Macedonian adventure remains therefore one of the most stupendous sallies on record.

With Alexander the frontiers of Europe expanded beyond the Indus. For nearly three centuries his successors, amazing adventurers, kept alive there an extraordinary, bold, and paradoxical copy of Greece at the cross-roads of the Afghan valleys and even around Lahore. Little is known of the history of these far-off Græco-Bactrian or Indo-Greek *basileis*. On the other hand, their features are familiar to us; we know them as old friends, thanks to their remarkable coinage, specimens of which have been found to the north of Kabul and around Peshawar.[1] Here is Euthydemos of Magnesia—who reigned over fabulous Bactria between 225 and 190 B.C.—portrayed as a bold and astute young man; and again as an old man with the countenance of a realist, rich in experience, strength and authority. And here is Demetrios, his son, proud and vigorous of profile, wearing as head-dress the skin of an Indian elephant, his gaze lordly and triumphant, as becomes the conqueror of the Punjab. Then, about 168, we find Eucratides, another king of Bactria who, also in helmet, looks at us, magnificently virile, a man in the prime of life, with a strong aquiline nose, powerful jaw, jutting forehead and a torso like Jupiter, and who handles his lance with as much vigour as the Dioscuri on the reverse. Here, too, is Antimachus in whom, under the Macedonian *causia*, we recognize the clear-minded, energetic and witty Greek. And finally comes Menander, the greatest of all, who (between 175 and 150, about a hundred and sixty years after the passage of Alexander) accomplished what Alexander had planned in vain: a victorious expedition right through the Ganges valley into the heart of Bihar. His profile shows the stark outline, the sheer acuity, of the portraits of Julius Caesar: the conqueror of the Rhine and the conqueror of the Ganges. . . . To few men of action has it been given to discover and understand so many new things in new lands. Caesar took care to tell us all about himself. But about Menander we know only the barest of facts. Each of these, however, sets one dreaming. On his bi-lingual coinage he styles himself in Greek the 'king of kings', *basileus basileôn*, and in Prakrit he is *maharâdja*. The Pāli sacred writings reveal him interested in Indian wisdom to the point of engaging in subtle dialogues with Buddhist philosophers—a tendency confirmed by the recent discovery near Peshawar of a Buddhist shrine erected to his memory. A strange figure, this gifted and eloquent Greek who was already so well adapted to his colonial atmosphere that he left behind him in the Church of the Buddha the reputation of a neophyte full of deference, almost that of a saint.

[1] You can see them to-day, rubbing shoulders in the show-cases of the *Cabinet des Médailles*.

Moreover, the association of Buddhism and Hellenism out-lived Greek domination in these regions. Menander's last successors disappeared about 30 B.C. Now, at that very time, on the very fringe of our own era, some Greek statuette-maker, working for some monastery in the Kabul valley, dared to take the Apollo-type as his model when representing for the first time the figure of Buddha. Since then, the whole of Buddhist statuary, multiplied throughout the ages and many lands, has merely adapted to native taste that 'first Buddha' who was in fact an Apollo and whose prototype may be lying to-day in the show-cases of our museums. . . .

The consequences of Alexander's expedition were infinite. If the Conqueror had not marched through the Punjab, Græco-Buddhist iconography would not have been born three hundred years later; and three more centuries after that surprising association, the divine image thus created would not have reached China. And the whole of the Far East would not worship—all unwittingly—at one and the same time an Indian sage and a young Greek god.

The Last Macedonians

But the Indo-Greek kings were like so many lost children, forgotten by Hellenism at the end of the world. From its very beginnings—250 B.C.—the Parthian revolt against the Seleucid empire had cut them off from the other Hellenistic kingdoms. The burden of defending the bulk of the Macedonian conquests devolved on Alexander's principal heirs, the Seleucids. Here we must guard ourselves against a common misconception: against taking these 'créole' dynasties for families of half-breeds. There was no Græco-Egyptian cross-breeding among the Ptolemies. True, in order to make the religion of the Pharaohs work in their favour, they did not fail to represent themselves to their native subjects as the legitimate successors of the old national dynasties. But this was mere political fiction, just like the one created on rupees which used to show the King of England dressed as an Emperor of India. The Macedonians on the Nile no more became Egyptian than British civil servants in Delhi became Hindus. As for the Seleucids, in spite of the Babylonian titles given them in cuneiform texts, they seem to have rapidly renounced the 'Persianizing' policy which had been Alexander's in his last years and to have concentrated on continuing his original work of spreading Greek culture. Instead of establishing themselves in Babylonia as he had done (though they founded a Seleucia on the Tigris), they placed their capital significantly enough at Antioch, near the sea which had given them birth. And they devoted the best part of their activity to Mediterranean affairs. This soon distracted them from the watch which they had undertaken in defence of Hellas in Persia. After 250 B.C. the Persian tribe of Parthians, between Khorassan and Mazandéran, shook off their yoke. It was the first revolt, the first native rising against the work of the great Macedonian.

A further historical exaggeration would be to see an immediate degeneration in Ptolemaic and Seleucid Hellenism. True, Hellenistic society did not escape, either in Asia or in Egypt, the general decadence in which the Greek element was involved throughout the entire Mediterranean world. But we have seen what Greek science owes to the Alexandrian setting. Nor must we forget that Stoicism was born in the Syrian region, in Cilicia, in Phœnicia and in Cyprus. If the Macedonian kingdoms of Greater Greece had left no other proof of their activity, they would have done enough for ancient civilization by giving it the masters of Epictetus and Marcus Aurelius. And later, in the Roman period, the winged irony of Lucian shows us that oriental Hellenism, in face of the heavy Asiatic mysticism, had almost to the end kept control of its mind and mastery of its senses.

For the moment, and for a long time yet, Hellenism maintained its intellectual hegemony. Even the Parthian princes who in Eastern Persia had revolted against Seleucid domination, even the dynasts of equally Persian stock who had similarly shaken off the yoke in Asia Minor, would 'Hellenize' themselves as a matter of either fashion or inclination. Every one, even in the very act of freeing himself from the Hellenistic kings, was proud to proclaim himself a philhellene. Their revolt, which could not have succeeded but for the domestic quarrels of the Seleucid family, and the fatal rivalry between Seleucids and Ptolemies, remained timid and hesitant. There was still time to check it.

All the Seleucids, in their effigies and in their history, present a family likeness which is not without its charm. The first Seleucos had been a brilliant cavalier, an epic adventurer. As for Antiochus the Great, a brilliant cavalier was all that he was, with his fiery spirit, his grand manner, and also his instability and incredible inconsistencies. Even so, he still showed, as Renan says, 'something of Alexander's genius.' Determined to put an end to internal disturbances in Persia as well as Asia Minor, he undertook a mighty raid from Sardis to the Indus, in the course of which he renewed the exploits of the Conqueror and repeated his achievements. In 201 all Asia, from the Aegean Sea and Palestine to Afghanistan, was reunited under his sway. The Macedonian empire had been restored.

These results were ruined by the war which the same Antiochus the Great afterwards waged against the Romans. Beaten at Magnesia by the legions, he had to accept the Peace of Apamea which reduced his Seleucid empire to the proportions of a mere Syrian kingdom. The Romans boasted of having thus conquered, in his person, both Darius and Xerxes! What they had really done was to conquer Alexander the Great and gravely compromise everywhere the work of the Macedonians —the hegemony of Hellas over Asia. In Persia they had ruined it irretrievably. The real gainers from the defeat of the Seleucids were the Parthians, who were becoming more and more the avowed champions of a native revival.

One of the sons of Antiochus the Great, Antiochus Epiphanes, tried to react (175–164 B.C.). How are we to judge him? The superior strength of the Romans made it impossible for him to secure the triumph of Hellenism by force of arms. But the expansion of Greek nationality was the whole *raison d'être* of the Seleucids. Antiochus Epiphanes was therefore obliged to undertake the conquest of the oriental soul by introducing Hellenism to the native peoples. His bid, an intellectual's programme for the Athenian education of the Aramean people, was, in sum, Alexander's thought adapted to the necessities of the Roman protectorate. Unhappily, there was in Epiphanes, as in the Emperor Hadrian later, a certain antiquarian extravagance. Like his distant imitator, the Emperor Julian, he showed an enthusiasm for Greek culture which was not altogether devoid of sectarianism. He embarked officially on the persecution of the Jews (the first religious war in classical antiquity!) and failed—a passionate Hellene who, having once dreamed upon the Acropolis, foolishly believed that he could conquer the genius of the desert.

The defeat of Epiphanes marked the triumph of Asiatic reaction against Hellenism; it was a Semitic reaction in Palestine, where the Jewish theocracy prevailed; a Persian reaction in the East, where the Parthians in 129 B.C. finally drove the Seleucids from Mesopotamia; an Aramaean reaction even in Syria where in 84 B.C. the last Seleucids were dethroned and where the first Arab infiltration began, harbinger of strange events to come.

Rome, the Soldier of Hellenism

Having no inkling of the great Asiatic problems, Rome (after the Battle of Magnesia) had left the former Macedonian empire to local rule. But as soon as she subsequently annexed the kingdom of Pergamum which became the province of Asia (133 B.C.), her point of view changed. Protector of Hellenism throughout the world, and heiress willy-nilly to the Macedonian tradition, she had to assume her responsibilities. She was all the more obliged to do so by the appearance on the scene of a new champion of Asiatic revival, Mithradates Eupator, King of Pontus.

There is no doubt that in Mithradates was incarnate the re-awakening oriental soul. Descended as he was from a family of Achæmenid satraps, and himself (as his Mithraic name shows) a Persian by cult and culture, it was of no consequence that, like all the dynasts of his time, he affected a veneer of Hellenism. This make-belief was in any case necessary to seduce the petty Greek politicians. In 88 B.C. he had driven the Romans from Asia Minor and occupied part of Greece: it seemed then that the wheel had come full circle. Two centuries after Alexander, a ' barbarian' garrison was camped on the Acropolis. Macedonia had become a satrapy of Pontus.

The Romans nipped the new Achæmenian empire in the bud. When the old king died in the Crimea where he had sought refuge, all Asia Minor was obedient to Rome (63 B.C.). The death of Mithradates and the submission of Armenia left the Romans a free hand. They could decide whether to base the relations of the Hellenistic and oriental worlds upon new foundations. Such a task was undertaken by Pompey, who must not be judged by the taunts of his erstwhile friend Cicero. Pompey's action in the East was as judicious as Caesar's afterwards in Gaul. The Roman peace-maker took over everything of Alexander's achievement that had stood the test of time. In every region where Hellenism had taken firm root, he set up the power of Rome. True to the practical genius of Rome, he abandoned all the remoter parts of the Macedonian conquest. He thus revived the Seleucid tradition, profiting from experience. Asia Minor and Syria seemed sufficiently Hellenized for Pompey to attach them to the Republic. Persia he thought irrevocably lost: in it therefore he did not intervene. Regarding Mesopotamia, outwardly Greek but fundamentally Aramæan, he hesitated; and after him Rome hesitated for another four centuries.

In all, the Romans showed themselves the conscious heirs of the Macedonians. Like them, they were the protagonists of Hellas in Asia. They Latinized only their western and barbarian provinces. Wherever they found Hellenism, they respected it as one of the two official forms of their dominion. East of the Ionian Sea and the Syrtes, the Roman Empire remained Greek. And the really Hellene period lasted long! Western Anatolia for example enjoyed Greek civilization from Alexander to Mithradates, while, in comparison, the Roman period lasted from Pompey to the Palaeologi: Hellenism owed to the *Pax Romana* the best of its conquests. Once Persia had been sacrificed as indefensible, Alexander conquered Asia in the days of the Caesars. In the East, Rome performed not her own work but that of Macedonia. Moreover, the Romans brought to the Greek world an inestimable force which Alexander and the Seleucids had vainly tried to confer on it: namely political unity. It was the Byzantine Empire which was to realize Alexander's idea— Macedonian Panhellenism—in face of an Asia in revolt, and realize it for the Greeks; but it was thanks to Rome, in the first place, that it was so realized.

Pompey had made the Euphrates the eastward limit of the Roman lands. For seven centuries—from Pompey to Heraclius —it remained the frontier of Europe. The excavations at Doura-Europos have shown us what the life of the garrison was like in one of the forts of this *limes* during the Romano-Parthian period. Despite many common features—notably as far as Hellene art is concerned—they give the impression that this frontier marked indeed the meeting of two worlds. Several times the Romans tried to overstep that borderline. In the north, the Armenians were to them a source of permanent friction with the Parthian empire. To the east, there survived in Mesopotamia a certain number of Seleucid colonies, including Seleucia itself, which naturally looked to Rome for help against their Parthian master. There was an 'unredeemed Greece' there, cut off by the Parthian conquest from the rest of the Hellenic community, which the Romans felt they ought to liberate. The proconsul Crassus made the attempt and was killed. That was the disaster of Carrhae (53 B.C.), similar in its consequences to the disaster that befell Varus later in Germany. It was written that in the east the Euphrates, and on the west the Rhine, should mark the limits of European civilization. Caesar, it is true, was planning on the eve of his assassination to go and avenge Crassus. His expedition against the Parthians—the war which never took place and about which, nevertheless, we cannot help dreaming —would doubtless have changed the face of the world. The Ides of March stopped dead this expansion of Europe.

Yet, the greatest of the Roman emperors, Trajan, took up Caesar's plans again. He routed the enemy near the historic field of Arbela, entered Ctesiphon, the Parthian capital, as a conqueror, and reached the Persian Gulf (A.D. 116). Were the legions about to climb the Persian plateau in the tracks of the phalanx? But now, when the Romans sought to restore the empire of Alexander, the soul of the East rose up to declare its hatred of Greece and Rome. Already under Nero the author of the *Apocalypse*, that passionate Semite inspired by his hatred of all that was Greek, prophesied the death of the Roman Beast; and he looked for salvation to the Parthian cavalry. During Trajan's war with the Parthians, the whole Jewish world, from Cyrene to Asia Minor, rose up against him, not without heroism. The Jewish revolts are interesting in that they allow us to catch a glimpse of the reactions of Asiatic peoples against Roman domination. They form a continuation of the risings of the Maccabees and foreshadow the Hegira. Already the flame of Islam was setting the ancient East on fire!

The Jewish revolt, and Trajan's death, put an end to his projects. His successor Hadrian, though the most Greek of the emperors, gave up the idea of conquering Persia. This renunciation must ever be regretted, since it prevented the Græco-Roman world from piercing the Parthian barrier and communicating directly with the Indian and Chinese world. In particular it prevented Alexandrian thought from making contact with Buddhist feeling.

Although the Parthian kings were the incarnation of the defence of Asia against Græco-Roman imperialism, they claimed to be philhellenes. It was precisely this attitude which (in A.D. 224) provoked their fall. The Sassanid dynasty overthrew them and took their place on the throne of Persia by directing a violently national reaction against everything which recalled the Hellenic hegemony. Representing Persian nationalism in the political field, and Mazdaian pietism in the religious sphere, Sassanid Persia—during the four centuries of its existence (224–640)—proved itself the indomitable enemy of the Roman world. It is no accident that the Persian epic of the *Châh-nâmek* neglected the Parthian interlude and linked the first Sassanids directly with the last Darius. In fact, they lost no time in trying to recover the former Persian possessions—Syria and Asia Minor—which were still in Roman hands. In the course of that struggle, the second of the Sassanid kings took prisoner the Emperor Valerian (259). Sassanid bas-reliefs immortalized that unprecedented scene: the Persian monarch trampling underfoot the captive Caesar!

By an unlooked-for chance, the Roman frontiers in Syria were saved, not by the legions, but by clients of Rome, the princes of Palmyra, who under a rather superficial Græco-Roman veneer could not disguise their Arab origin. For twelve years (260–272), until the destruction of its capital by the Emperor Aurelian, 'the Palmyrene Empire' dominated Roman Asia. What a strange episode, a Palmyrene emirate detaching

from the Romans, without apparent rupture, their Asiatic provinces! In truth, the event merely revealed the results of a
revolution which had passed unnoticed, namely the occupation
of part of the Hellenic East by the Arabs. It was a slow, imperceptible taking over, comparable, e.g., to the penetration of
the Slavs into the Balkans in the eighth century. Whilst the
official history of the Roman province of Syria mentioned only
the pomp of governors and proconsuls, a great task was silently
accomplished there. The tribes of the desert, the nomads of the
great tents, were gaining ground, little by little, as far as the
Lebanon. Just as part of Roman Gaul was Germanized before
the Great Migrations, the *Völkerwanderung*, so part of Roman
Syria was to become half Arab well before the Mohammedan
invasion.

The Eastern Question and Religious War

The struggle between Rome and the Persian world took on
a special aspect, and the Eastern Question changed its com-
plexion, when about 325 the Emperor Constantine definitely
adopted Christianity. Still more was this the case when the
Roman Empire, which had become in the East the Byzantine
Empire, assumed after 395 a strictly confessional character.
Romanism, in the Byzantine sense of the word, became synonymous with Christian orthodoxy,—just as Persia had identified
itself with the Mazdaian faith after the Sassanid 'restoration' of
224. The struggle between Hellenism and the oriental spirit
entered the field of dogma. In that respect Islam, when it came,
merely aggravated a situation which had existed since the fourth
century. The Eastern Question, hitherto merely ethnic and
cultural, had become a religious question.

Asia's reaction against Græco-Roman rule manifested itself
not only by Persian opposition to Christianity, but also in the
very bosom of Christianity itself by the schism of the Eastern
Churches. When, from the fifth century onwards, Syria and
Roman Mesopotamia had accepted baptism, they took advantage of the spread of the Nestorian and Monophysite heresies to
set up independent churches of the Syrian rite; their thought
and literature thus shed Hellenism. This loss of the Greek in-

fluence and the rising to the surface of the old Semitic sediment were yet another forecast of the great Mohammedan tide which in the seventh century finally destroyed the work of Alexander the Great together with the Romans in Syria.

In Persia, the Sassanids were not long in becoming aware of the advantages which they could draw from the theological quarrels between the Christians. Without giving up any of their intransigent Mazdaism, they tolerated and (up to a certain point) protected the Nestorian faith among their Syrian subjects, especially after this creed had been proscribed as heretical by the Byzantine Empire in 489. But Nestorianism to them was only another weapon against Byzantium.

*　　*　　*　　*

A sum of history such as this enables one to descry here and there certain outstanding facts which govern subsequent developments. At one point, Alexander conquering the Persian Empire, from the Hellespont to the Indus. Then Khosroes Parviz restoring to the Persians, for about twenty years, all that Alexander had won from them. In 613 he wrested Syria from the Byzantines, and in 614 Palestine. One of his armies penetrated to Egypt; the other, traversing the whole of Asia Minor, reached the Bosphorus and set up the siege of Constantinople in conjunction with a Mongolian horde of Avars who beleaguered on the Thracian side 'the City in God's Keeping'. But a great emperor, Heraclius, had ascended the throne of Constantinople. By an incredibly bold diversion, while Persians and Avars were surrounding his capital, he marched through the Caucasus to threaten the King of Kings in the very heart of his 'paradise' of the Zagros. Khosroes fell in the course of the struggle and Heraclius recovered all, and more than all, of the territory lost.

What matters here is the character—that of a holy war—which this gigantic duel assumed on both sides. When they captured Jerusalem, the Persians carried off the True Cross. After his victory in 630 Heraclius commanded the Cross to be returned to him and solemnly restored it to the Holy Sepulchre: a 'crusade' already. But the victory left Byzantium as exhausted as Persia at the very moment when, to the peril of both, the mighty threat of Islam was darkening to the southward.

The lightning successes of Islam can only be explained by the fact that the new faith had been conceived in the midst of the revival of the ancient East, just when the latter was engaged in a fight to the death with Hellenism. It was not even Mahomet who converted the struggle into a holy war; such had already been the character of the conflict between Heraclius and Khosroes. Nor was it Islam which first launched the tribes of the desert upon Byzantium and Persia; for a long time they had been infiltrating into the province of Damascus on the one hand, and into ancient Babylon on the other. But Mahomet gave all these Bedouin a faith and a flag. His Islam was first and foremost Pan-Arabism. More generally, in the eyes of all orientals, he came to undo the work of 'Iskander the Roumi', of that Alexander who had given the Greeks the rule over the old world for more than a thousand years, had then left it to the Romans, and afterwards to the Byzantines. The Middle Ages had begun. After the conversion of Constantine, Hellenism presented itself to Asia in the shape of a faith. With the Koran, Asia replied by the *djihâd*, the unrelenting holy war of Mohammedanism.

The ease with which the Arabs conquered Syria and Egypt between 634 and 643 is no doubt explained by the secret harmony which existed between them and the native population. Both at Antioch and Alexandria the Monophysite Christians whether of Syrian or Coptic rite, persecuted as they were by Byzantine orthodoxy, became accomplices in the invasion. Amid the applause of the native races, Hellenism was flung into the sea. The fall of Alexandria in 641 marked the end of a world. The Egypt of the Alexandrian savants, the neo-Platonists and the Fathers of the Church, was gone for ever. Alexandria, since the decline of Athens the capital of European thought to a far greater extent than Rome, ceased to be 'in Europe'.

Byzantine Epics

With the fall of Antioch and Alexandria, relations between Asia and Europe entered a new phase. Europe, which had for so long imposed its will on the East, was everywhere on the retreat. In every sphere—ethnical, religious, literary, artistic—the East was clearly gaining. It was Asia's great revolt against the ideas, the religion and the rule of Greece and Rome. In the face of this rising tide the Byzantine Empire, which represented at one and the same time Greek civilization, Roman politics and the Christian faith, found itself alone (save for Armenia). A mighty ground-swell that had arisen out of the depths of Asia, stirring first the deserts of Arabia and afterwards the steppes of central Asia, beat upon the New Rome on the Bosphorus: there, in the night of the Dark Ages, had taken refuge all the knowledge of the western world, all its treasure of ancient wisdom and beauty, all the past and all the future of our European civilization.

With a single surge, the wave of Arab invasion submerged Mesopotamia, Syria, Egypt, and the further parts of Africa. All these old Semitic or Hamitic lands, where Hellenism had been represented only by the urban element, returned to Semitic rule. The colonies founded by the Macedonian *basileis* of yesterday were lost to the Byzantine *basileus* of the seventh century. Antioch, the capital of the Seleucids, and Alexandria, the capital of the Ptolemies, now obeyed caliphs and emirs. Nor did caliphs and emirs halt there. Going beyond the former home of their race, they broke into the Greek lands, invaded the Anatolian peninsula which at that time was the chief centre of Hellenism in the world, and pitched their tents on the Asiatic shore of the Bosphorus. Twice in half a century, in 673 and 717, the 'City in God's Keeping' saw itself thus besieged. But it proved secure in Byzantine hands: on the first occasion it was rescued by Constantine IV, and on the second by Leo the Isaurian.

Europe owes a debt of gratitude to these tough Byzantine emperors of the 'Dark Ages' for having thus saved the repository of its civilization. The Battles of Constantinople in 717–718, in which Leo the Isaurian broke the Arab offensive on the Bosphorus, rank with the Battle of Poitiers of 732 in which Charles Martel broke the same attack in the West.

In Europe itself, on the Danube, the Byzantine Empire also encountered Asia. Beyond the Danube there spread across the Russian and Asian steppes the vast Turco-Mongolian world,

which at that period was getting ready for its immense migration. From East to West, from the sands of the Gobi desert to
the Hungarian *puszta*, a continual movement, like an overflow
of humanity on the march, was driving the nomad peoples,
Huns and Avars, Bulgars and Magyars, Comans and Petchenegs,
ever towards new pastures and new prey. The life of these
pastoral races, the last-comers in the share-out of the globe,
was truly wretched. Hence they never ceased to cast covetous
looks upon the old civilized empires whose dread they were—
on China which they invaded so frequently; on India which
they also ravaged; on Mazdaian or Mohammedan Persia, their
age-long enemy; and, after the end of the fourth century, on
the Byzantine Empire. Byzantium and Ch'ang-ngan (or, according to the period, Byzantium and K'ai-fong), the 'golden cities'
of the Middle Ages, became their chief objectives.

The great Byzantine cities were for months cut off from the
rest of the universe. Then, beneath their walls, there began the
musterings of hordes which sometimes appealed to each other
for help, and sometimes fought each other, sometimes banded
together for common pillage, and sometimes destroyed one
another. The Byzantines at the peak of the Middle Ages, so
refined in their manners, so complex in their culture, found
themselves confronted by a ceaseless swarm of barbarians. Sole
survivors of the world of Plato and Marcus Aurelius, contemporaries of the old dead civilizations, they remained in a universe which had sunk back into barbarism, conscious of their
vast moral superiority and proud of their glorious past. Often
greatly weakened, sometimes victims of the worst humiliations,
yet they never lost courage. Never did they renounce one jot
or tittle of their historic rights, never did they forget the sacred
character of their mission. Neither as heirs of Rome nor as
representatives of Hellenism did they ever surrender. At times
their soul seemed to fall into the torpor of the great medieval
lethargy, just as their art suffered from a conventional religiosity shown in their mosaics. But that was only outward. Under
the rigidity of the motionless figures of, for example, Athos,
there persisted passions to whose fiery intensity the Byzantine
Epic of the tenth century bears eloquent witness.

Byzantium recovered in the second half of the ninth century with the advent of the imperial dynasty to which a happy chance has given the great name of 'Macedonian' (it was really of Armenian origin, like so many military families in the Byzantium of the time). External circumstances were favourable. The Arab empire which, under Harun ar-Rashid at the end of the eighth century, had made the Byzantines tremble, had just fallen. The effective power of the Caliphs was limited to the neighbourhood of Baghdad, whilst the remainder of their empire was partitioned between Mohammedan provincial dynasties—Persian in the Middle East, and Arab in the Near East. The mission of defending the frontiers of the Islamic world against Byzantium devolved upon the emirs of Aleppo, a minor local Arab dynasty, which was unequal to such a rôle. Furthermore, a schismatic caliphate of the Fâtimids was established in Egypt after 969. This was a very serious secession, for it affected both the political and the religious field. Between the Abbasid Caliphate of the Sunnite faith, recognized throughout almost all Mohammedan Asia, and the Fâtimid Caliphate of the Shi'ite faith, recognized in Egypt, the gulf was as great as the one which in the Christian world separated Byzantium from the Pope.

To reap advantage from such a split in the ranks of the enemy, Byzantium could call upon a group of great soldiers in whom there lived again something of the Roman prowess. One of them, Nicephorus Phocas, whose exploits earned him the purple, reconquered Cilicia, to him the key to Syria (965), and then Northern Syria itself; the re-capture of Antioch by his lieutenants in 969, three hundred years after the flight of Heraclius, consummated this unlooked-for return of the legions. John Tzimisces, another general whose victories carried him to the imperial throne, led a triumphant expedition in 975 across the whole of Syria to Damascus and into Galilee. Everywhere the local emirs, whom the Caliphate showed itself powerless to defend, submitted and became vassals of the *basileus*. In 1030 the reconquest of Edessa (present-day Orfa) to the east of the Euphrates and in the north-west of Djéziré, completed the Byzantine reconquest.

A brilliant revenge, certainly. But it lacked the crowning

achievement that might logically have been expected: the deliverance of the Holy Sepulchre. Why did John Tzimisces fail to think of it at the end of his triumphal march through Syria, when he had received the submission of the Emir of Damascus, and when (as we are told by a letter attributed to him) he had made the stirring pilgrimage to Mount Tabor and Nazareth? Why did Basil II in his turn not think of it in the course of his Syrian campaigns between 995 and 999, when he captured Chaizar and sacked the suburbs of Tripoli? Was it the 'Gibraltar of Tripoli' which made them pause? At any rate, it was a unique opportunity which never again came their way. Byzantium had let slip the honour of completing a Christian crusade.

Armenia's Part in the Christian Resistance

In the great duel between Europe and Asia, Armenia had thrown in her lot with European civilization, or, as it would have been put then, with Christendom. Even before the Emperor Constantine, namely at the beginning of the fourth century, she had accepted the Gospel. This great act determined her destiny. Just as France and her fourteen centuries of history flow from the baptism at Rheims, so Armenia was born in the sanctuary where St. Gregory the Illuminator baptized King Tiridates in 305. On that day the Armenian people accepted the heaviest but also the most glorious historical mission which has ever fallen to a nation's lot. It was admitted to the heritage of ancient culture, to the society of Christian nations, to the intellectual and moral life of Europe. But at the same time, by thus becoming the advanced outpost of our civilization in the East, it found itself exposed to the hatred of all Asia, first of the Persians, then the Arabs, and finally the Turks. In 419 the Persians did away with the Armenian dynasty and annexed the country; but the Church took the place of the vanished monarchy. When the Persian governors, in order to make the Armenian people lose its specific character, tried to force it into apostasy, it rallied around the clergy under the leadership of the famous warrior Vardan Mamikonian. Vardan's heroic death on the field of Averaïr in 451 was no vain sacrifice, since, thirty years later, the Persians, discouraged by the indomitable resistance of the Armenians, granted them religious independence and political autonomy.

When the Arabs succeeded the Persians and ruled the East, they in turn sought to break Armenian resistance. After more than two centuries of persecution, however, they realized how futile this was. And in 886 they themselves restored the Armenian monarchy, choosing the princely family of the Bagratides in the person of its chief Achod the Great. It mattered little that the new Christian realm was an essentially feudal and federal monarchy, in which local princes had almost as much power as the sovereign himself. In their eagles' nest, safe and strong thanks to the precipitous rocks of these high lands, they braved the attacks of Islam and maintained their Christian faith and their liberty. A friendly and allied Armenia proved itself the best of satellites for the Byzantine Empire. It was an external bastion which protected it against assaults from the depths of Moslem Asia. But unhappily, at the moment when Byzantium reached its greatest brilliance, the Emperor Basil II was not content with this indirect service rendered by Armenia. He decided to annex it. And one by one, the three royal houses which shared the country had to resign their states into the hands of his imperial troops (1002, 1045, 1064).

The annexation of Armenia by the Byzantine Empire was a misfortune for Armenia, for Byzantium, and for Christianity. There had always been bitter hostility between Greek orthodoxy and the Gregorian Church of Armenia. After the annexation, this disagreement was aggravated by the pin-pricks inflicted by the orthodox bishops on the Armenian clergy. Moreover, the military defence of Armenia, instead of being instantly assured by her own princes who had always been on the alert among their mountains, now depended on orders from distant Constantinople. The country which had been the citadel of Christendom thus became its most vulnerable province. Furthermore, mistrusting the Armenian people, the Byzantines had replaced their sturdy militia by mercenaries devoid of local patriotism. And all this had been done just when the Turks were on the march.

Asia Minor, the New Turkestan

The Byzantine recovery, like the restoration of Armenian independence, had been made possible only through the decay and the parcelling-out of the Arab empire. Now, in the middle of the eleventh century, the Arabs were replaced in the leadership of Moslem Asia by a young military race, the Turks, who gave a new impetus to the holy war of Islam. They were Seljukids and came from the steppes of present-day Russian Turkestan; and their chief, Toghril-Beg ('Prince Sparrow-hawk'), having conquered Persia, compelled the Caliph of Baghdad in 1055 to accept him as temporal vicar. The Abbasid Caliphate was thus duplicated by a Seljukian sultanate; and the Arab empire by a Turkish empire.

In reality the Arab empire abdicated in favour of the Turkish empire. Just as the consecration of Charlemagne by the Pope in the year 800 had given the Germanic kings the heritage of Rome, so the consecration of Toghril-Beg by the Caliph made the Turks the heirs of four centuries of Saracen history. A Turkish Caliph and a Turkish *basileus* were one day to emerge from the consecration of 1057. As Knight of Allah and understudy of the Caliph, the Seljukian hero became the second person in the Moslem world; the Turkish race became the imperial race of Islam.

At once the Turks resumed the struggle, long since abandoned by the Arabs, against the Byzantine Empire. Their warlike temperament found a vast field of conquests; at the same time, they made the rule which they had assumed over the Moslem world legitimate in its eyes. Few conquests have been more rapid. In 1064 the Turks wrested Armenia from the Byzantines. In 1071 Sultan Alp Arslan ('The Strong Lion') defeated and captured the Roman Emperor Diogenes in the great battle near Manzikert. This Western defeat at Manzikert was one of the worst disasters in European history. For centuries the strength of Hellenism had lain, no longer in the Balkans which had been largely occupied by Slavs, but in Asia Minor. In proportion as Hellas suffered loss of population and became impoverished (and in Plutarch's time it was already almost empty) a new Greece, vast, rich, and densely peopled, had taken shape in Anatolia. What finally remained of the Macedonian conquest was this New Greece in Asia Minor. Contrary to what had occurred in Syria and Egypt, Hellas had taken root there because it affected not only the urban or littoral populations, but also the rural element. It was from these sturdy Anatolian peasants that the *basileus* recruited his armies. And it was the Anatolian landed gentry who supplied the Empire with its most illustrious generals.

The disaster of Manzikert involved the fall of the greater part of Asia Minor. Between 1078 and 1081 the Turks occupied not only the cities of the periphery like Nicaea and Smyrna, but also the strong places of the interior, such as Iconium, the modern Qonya. The worst feature of this development was that it did not limit itself to the political conquest of power by the Seljukian sultans or emirs, but meant the effective occupation of the soil by the Turks. The Turkish peasant replaced the Greek peasant. At one blow Hellenism was deprived of its territorial base and its rural class.

The Hour of the Crusades

At the end of the eleventh century, the Turks thus seemed poised for the conquest of Europe. Not only had the gains made by the Macedonian dynasty in Armenia, Mesopotamia and Syria been lost for ever to Byzantium, but a great part of Asia Minor was occupied by the Seljuks. The harbours of the Aegean Sea, such as Smyrna and Ephesus, belonged to emirs. Even Nicaea was in the hands of the Turks, who washed their horses in the Sea of Marmora and were only waiting for an opportunity to cross over into Thrace and get a foothold in Europe.

Against eternal Asia and in defence of their Western civilization, the leading nations of Europe had risen in turn—Alexander and the Greeks; then Pompey and the Romans; later John Tzimisces and the Byzantines. They had all gone their way, and the unchanging East had reconquered its former lands, just as the sands of the desert cover the broken columns of vanished cities. Now the soul of Asia, burning brightly in Islam, and the strength of Asia, represented by the Turkish race, resumed their age-long march on Europe. The Semitic world and the empire of the steppes moved as one, united as they were by religion. The danger was the same as in the far-off days of Xerxes, Mithradates, and the first caliphs. Or rather, it was much more threatening this time, for behind the Islamized Turks of Anatolia moved all the Turco-Mongols of Upper Asia, the enormous mass of nomads wandering from Mongolia to the Caspian, who were presently to cross the isthmus of Persia and the bridge of Asia Minor, all intent on reaching the dome of St. Sophia.

St. Sophia had replaced the Parthenon, for European civilization is one, and Christianity now appeared as the highest form and the culmination of Græco-Roman thought. The defence of Christianity in the Middle Ages, on these borderlands of Europe and Asia, was the defence of the Western spirit itself. As in the days of Themistocles at Salamis, what was at stake was the treasure of our Western world.

*   *   *   *

It was from France that salvation came. The Crusade—*gesta Dei per Francos*—was essentially the work of the French, of Frenchmen from the Kingdom and from Lotharingia, of Normans from Normandy or the Two Sicilies, who took up instinctively the work left unfinished by the Hellenes, Romans and Byzantines: namely the task of safeguarding the approaches to Europe. 'From the day,' says Madelin, 'when a great idealistic movement urged Europe to withstand the East, the Frank took the lead. It was from the centre of France, from Clermont in Auvergne, that the movement sprang; it was a French Pope, Urban II, who unloosed it. It was a French monk, Peter the Hermit, who preached it. And if the Crusading army of 1095 was composed of German, Italian, and French contingents, it remains rather remarkable that the leaders of even the German and Italian sections were French-speaking—Godfrey of Bouillon, Duke of Lower Lorraine, and his brother Baldwin, Count of Boulogne, at the head of the so-called German troops; and at the head of the Italian troops, those Sicilian Normans who were still so thoroughly French, Bohemund and Tancred, the grandsons of Tancred of Hauteville.'[1]

The rôle of the Papacy proved decisive. It acted as 'the conscience of Europe,' just as at other times. Never did it

---

[1] Louis Madelin: *L'Expansion française, De la Syrie au Rhin*, p. 9.

deserve that title more. About 1090 Turkish Islam, having almost entirely driven the Byzantines from Asia, was preparing to invade Europe. Yet ten years later, not only was Constantinople freed, not only had a third of Asia Minor been restored to Hellenism, but coastal Syria and Palestine too had become Frankish lands. The catastrophe of 1453, which almost happened in 1090, was warded off for three centuries and a half. And all this was the deliberately planned work of Urban II. The great Pope's action held back the onrushing stream. The course of destiny was halted and turned sharply back.

This is not the place to review the origins of the crusading idea. The author has shown elsewhere what were its elements.[1] First, the 'precedent' of the Spanish *reconquista* in which so many French barons had already taken part. Then the religious factor itself, the collective *mystique* created by the Pope, a religious fervour which was to rouse the world; from that aspect, the crusading idea of the Council of Clermont can be compared only to the Panhellenic idea of the Congress of Corinth in 336 B.C., which had launched Alexander the Great and the whole of Greece upon the assault of Asia. After the crusading *mystique* had led to success, there came the intervention of other factors, which may be called the fact of conquest and the fact of colonization. The preaching of 1095 gave rein to the territorial imperialism of the Capetian or Lotharingian baronage and to the economic imperialism of the Italian maritime republics; the pilgrim became a *conquistador* going to carve out kingdoms beneath the eastern sun. And finally, once the conquest had been made, the needs of the situation imposed on the barons of the Holy Land a singularly realistic colonial policy and a native policy which was often very liberal. The success of the Crusades arose from the interplay of these various elements.

Moreover, the First Crusade was to benefit from an unlooked-for combination of circumstances. The Turkish Sultan Melikshah, who reigned from Turkestan to the Mediterranean, died in 1092. His vast domains were partitioned among his sons, who ruled Persia; his nephews, who ruled Syria (one of them held Aleppo, the other Damascus, and they were at daggers drawn); and a cousin, who ruled Turkish Anatolia. Egypt, of

---

[1] See M. Grousset's *Histoire des Croisades* and *L'Epopée des Croisades*, both published by Librairie Plon.

course, still belonged to the 'heretic' Moslems, the Fâtimid caliphs who were separated from the Turks by a religious gulf. Instead of uniting against the Crusade, these various Moslem princes attacked it one by one, and one by one they were overwhelmed by it. Between them, they thus ensured its success.

A delicate problem of international law confronted the crusading leaders after they had passed through Constantinople. The regions which they were going to reconquer from the Turks, at least those of Asia Minor such as Nicaea, or of Northern 'Syria such as Antioch, had belonged in the very recent past to the Byzantines. Were the Crusaders to keep them for themselves or return them to Byzantium? The latter solution was at first adopted, at least in the case of Nicaea which was handed over to the Emperor Alexius Comnenus as soon as it was retaken. The Byzantines also profited by the alarm which the passage of the Crusaders occasioned among the Turks to recapture from them Smyrna and the rest of the eastern shores of the Aegean Sea. That was an indirect result—but not the least important—of the First Crusade. Urban II's enterprise had thus reached its first objective. Constantinople had been saved and the greater part of Asia Minor had been restored to Hellenism.

So far, the Crusaders had recognized Byzantium's first claim or 'mortgage' on the recovered lands. But when in 1098 they had driven the Turks from Antioch, they dropped this attitude. The parts of Asia Minor which the Byzantines themselves succeeded in recovering continued to be returned to Byzantium; but all territories won by the Crusaders in Syria remained henceforth in the hands of the Franks. Thus was founded a *Latin East* which maintained itself on the Asiatic continent from 1098 to 1291. The Franks showed themselves no less successful in their policy towards the Moslems. They made use of the split within the fold of Islam, where the Seljuks, the masters of Mohammedan Syria, were separated from the Fâtimids, the masters of Egypt. This schism was caused by both racial and religious hatreds. The Seljuks were Turks and Sunnite Mussulmans; the Fâtimids, Arabs and Shi'ite Mussulmans. When the Crusaders arrived in Syria, they did not hesitate to ally themselves with the Egyptians against the Turks. Whilst they were attacking the Turks at Antioch, the Egyptian army was conquering Jerusalem from these same Turks. Then, as soon as the Turks had been beaten and Antioch captured, the Crusaders turned upon the Egyptians and wrested the Holy City from them in 1099.

The Strength and Weakness of Frankish Syria

Everything gave way before the strength of the Franks. The Turkish power which had subdued the East bent before it. However, immediately after the conquest of Jerusalem, while the Franks still possessed only a small part of the coastal zone, the crusading army broke up. It was a singularly premature demobilization which brought on incalculable consequences. Most of the crusading chiefs, their vows accomplished, hastened to return to Europe with their followers, leaving behind Godfrey of Bouillon with only a skeleton force. Content with victory, they gave thought neither to the exploitation of their victory, nor to the occupation of the conquered territory, nor to the expansion of this conquest. Deeming their duty done by the liberation of Antioch and Jerusalem, they neglected to make an end of Syrian Islam while they had the force to so do. But their successors were never to enjoy the advantage of surprise which they thus omitted to exploit. True, these successors managed in the next twenty-five years to complete the conquest of western Syria and Palestine. But despite all their efforts they were never able to take Aleppo, Hama, Homs, and Damascus. The interior of Syria, supported by the whole of Turkish Asia, remained in the hands of the Moslems. Hence Frankish Syria was limited from the beginning to a coastal fringe whose depth varied from time to time, but which was always in danger of being overrun.

Notwithstanding this grave initial weakness, Frankish Syria continued to prosper for nearly half a century. Indeed, its history may be divided into two parts, whose contrast explains all its destiny. During the first part the Frankish monarchy, solidly established by that man of genius King Baldwin I of Jerusalem, was confronted merely by disunited Moslems, namely some Turco-Arabian emirates whose mutual hostility was enhanced by the sectarian hatred which separated Arab and Shi'ite

Egypt from Turkish and Sunnite Asia. Later, the situation was reversed. The Frankish monarchy was disrupted and the Frankish society sank into feudal anarchy. Meanwhile the Moslem world, first under the *Atâbegs* of the Zengi family, and then under the sultans of the House of Saladin, recovered its unity. This unity was at once political and sectarian, and therefore correspondingly formidable. One more step, and this Moslem monarchy became an absolute monarchy under the Mameluk sultans. It enforced military obedience from the Nile to the Euphrates and could deal with the leaderless Frankish colonies in which civil war was permanently raging. The issue, then, could not be in doubt.

The Frankish Achievement in the Levant

The figure of one man dominates the whole of the first period of Frankish Syria. It is the founder of the Kingdom of Jerusalem, Baldwin of Boulogne—Baldwin I (1100–1118). Few leaders in history have had a more striking personality. He did not, like others, build with existing materials. He had to create out of nothing. His kingdom and his kingship were alike the work of his genius. It was he who conceived this kingship, imposed it on recalcitrant prelates, and substituted it for the colourless 'recognition' accorded to his brother Godfrey. By the sheer weight of his personality he invested the rule thus established with a dignity, a majesty, a legitimacy which set him up on Mount Sion in the Biblical tradition of David and Solomon. His kingdom, first consisting of a few fortresses scattered around the barren plateau of Judaea, was quickly taken out of such isolation by his conquest of the sea-coast which gave him direct communication with Europe. Beyond the boundaries of the new kingdom, still too narrow for his liking, he linked up with the other Frankish states—the County of Edessa, the Principality of Antioch, the County of Tripoli. Out of the most unruly of these barons he succeeded in making lieutenants who became almost docile. While forcing them to combine under him, he helped them to complete the conquest of their own domains. Though a famous conqueror of Islam, he could appreciate Moslem society and indeed win its esteem, because from the moment of his accession he substituted for religious intransigence an intelligent, firm and yet supple policy towards it. Like his rival Tancred, he took pleasure in posing as a Christian 'great emir' in the eyes of the sons of the desert, whom he knew how to win over by some chivalrous gesture. For eighteen years, always in the saddle at the head of some foray in the Frankish fashion or some counter-*rezzou* in the Arab manner, he lived in a riot of victories. His shadow covered the land he ruled, from the gorges of Diarbékir to the shores of the Red Sea.

The colonizer in Baldwin of Boulogne was no less great than the hero of legend. His chaplain, Foucher de Chartres, who was also his confidant, has recorded the first results of this work. The passage was written about 1125, on the very morrow of the sower's death. Already the whole harvest was beginning to shoot up: 'The Italian or the Frenchman of yesterday, transplanted hither, has become a Galilean or a Palestinian. The man from Rheims or Chartres has been transformed into a Syrian or a citizen of Antioch. Already we have forgotten our places of origin. Why should we return to the West, since the East entirely fulfils our desires?' A settlement, evidently with no thought of return, and one which lacked only numbers. To supply them, and supplement the inadequacy of Frankish immigration, Baldwin I had appealed to the native Christians, whom he brought in great numbers from Transjordania and the Hauran. Then, to shelter the settlements he had thus encouraged from *rezzous* and counter-crusades, he began, and left to his successors to complete, the building of that splendid network of fortresses which, from the County of Edessa to the Land Beyond Jordan, and from Bagras to the Krak de Monreale,[1] still remind a forgetful world of the enduring quality of the Frankish achievement. The centuries pass, the stones remain. What, at first sight, strikes the traveller in Syria to-day is the mark left upon the land by the passage, first of the Romans, and afterwards of the Franks: Baalbek and Palmyra; Our Lady of Tortosa and the *Krak des Chevaliers*. It is also the secret continuity which, across an interval of ten centuries, links the knights to the legionaries as empire-builders and pioneers of

[1] *Krak de Monreale* = one of the many Crusaders' Castles in Syria which are the finest expression of the architectural genius of thirteenth-century France. The largest of these fortresses was the *Krak des Chevaliers*, several times referred to in this section. T.P.

the West. In the temporal as well as in the spiritual sphere, the knights continued the work of Rome.

The region of Yamilé will always bear their mark. Not only the stones but also the texts bear witness. They show us in particular how close the Franco-Moslem association sometimes was, under the rule of the Latin kings. There is the Emir Ousâma telling us, about 1140, of the affectionate reception which 'his friends, the Templars' gave him at Jerusalem, and of how, in their own monastery, they contrived to enable him to practise his Mohammedan religion! Or the Arab traveller Ibn-Djobair who, about 1184, concluded after an investigation on the spot that the condition of the Moslem peasants was much better in Frankish than in Islamic territory. The same unimpeachable witness describes a certain religious building in the neighbourhood of Acre which was shared amicably by the two religions, half-church, half-mosque: it would be difficult to carry toleration further! Despite the holy war, the Franco-Moslem union ended by ushering in peace. The barriers between the two societies were lowered. East and West were joined together, and Frankish Syria was their connecting link.

The kings of Jerusalem did not fail to reap advantage from their skilful native policy. The second of them, Baldwin II or Baldwin of the Bourg (1118–1131), spent his reign in playing with remarkable facility on the dissensions between Moslems. He almost succeeded in getting Aleppo handed over to him by the Bedouin, and Damascus by the famous sect of the Assassins with whom he had contrived to make an alliance. However, he failed; and soon afterwards it was too late. We have come, in fact, to the moment when, in those impregnable bastions of the hinterland, there appeared a focus for Islamic union in the person of the *Atâbeg* of Aleppo, the redoubtable Turkish chief Zengî (1128–1146), and then in his son, the famous Noûr ed-Din (1146–74). There was then reached a balance of power. On the one side was this Moslem monarchy which had reappeared at Aleppo; on the other the Frankish monarchy, still powerful at Jerusalem under King Fulk of Anjou (1131–43) and his two sons, Baldwin III (1144–62) and Amaury I (1162–74). It was still, however, a very successful period for the Frankish colonies. Wisely, prudently, like the Capetian kings in France,

Fulk made himself the protector of the weakest emirate, that of Damascus, with which he maintained very friendly relations, so as to stand up against the strongest, that of Zengî of Aleppo. The story told by Ousâma, the ambassador of Damascus, shows the cordiality of the relations established on this occasion between emirs and barons. The fact that the same ideal of chivalry was common to both societies facilitated the establishment of contacts. Does not the chronicle of the *Eracles* describe how the Atâbeg of Damascus and the Prince of Antioch rode side by side 'like good and loyal companions'?

Unhappily, these alliances were never more than truces. When King Fulk died, the Atâbeg of Aleppo, Zengî, took advantage of the minority which followed to wrest from the Franks the important county of Edessa (1144). His successor, the Atâbeg Noûr ed-Din, doubled his territories by annexing the rival Moslem kingdom of Damascus in 1154. In the interval a Second Crusade, provoked by the fall of Edessa, had landed and completely failed in 1148. The reason for this failure lay chiefly in the cleavage of temperaments between the newly-arrived Crusaders and the Frankish creoles—the 'Colts', as they said in the West, using the term in the sense of 'Levantines'. The pilgrims practically looked upon the Colts as semi-Moslems. The difference thus manifested bore witness to the extent to which the Latin colonists had adapted themselves to their new country and become acclimatized.

If only this colonization (though in any case the number of settlers was too small) had had time to take root! But the lack of harmony between the barons of the Holy Land and the Crusaders of 1148 deprived the Frankish colonies of the reinforcement of new crusades. It left them to their own resources at the very moment of mounting danger, for Noûr ed-Din, by adding Damascus to Aleppo, had just united Moslem Syria against Frankish Syria. Henceforward, whatever the circumstances, the unitary constitution of that Mohammedan kingdom prevented any possibility of Frankish expansion eastwards.

King Amaury I of Jerusalem—a strong personality and a far-sighted politician—then decided to turn Frankish expansion into a new direction: he opened the Egyptian Question. In

reality, this question opened itself. At Cairo the Fâtimid caliphate had fallen into such decay that it 'asked for invasion'.
There was obviously an opening there for a successor. Who
would profit by it, the king of Frankish Syria or the *Atâbeg* of
Moslem Syria, Amaury I or Noûr ed-Din? Amaury almost won.
Called in by the court of Cairo as an ally against Noûr ed-Din,
he was hailed by the Egyptians as a liberator. Egypt spontaneously accepted his protection in 1167. It was a brilliant success:
the kingdom of Jerusalem, if backed henceforth by the valley
of the Nile, would have been invincible. But Amaury did not
know when to stop. Not content with having won the protectorate over Egypt, he attempted to annex it. He thus drove
the Egyptians into the arms of Noûr ed-Din and was himself
driven from the Delta. Noûr ed-Din's lieutenant found himself
master of Egypt. Now this lieutenant was none other than
Saladin, one of the greatest men in Moslem history. When Noûr
ed-Din died shortly afterwards, this fortunate Saladin succeeded
him also at Damascus and Aleppo.

The political and religious unity of Moslem Syria and Egypt
had been achieved. And it had a leader—both a political and
military leader—such as the East had not known for a long
time. Frankish Syria, encircled on the north, east, south, and
south-west, was doomed. Guy de Lusignan cannot therefore
be blamed too much for that fatal Battle of Hattin in 1187 which
saw the destruction of the Frankish army. The situation created
for the Franks by the appearance of Saladin's empire was un-
tenable. Sooner or later the catastrophe would have taken place.
But in what was only a 'skeleton colony' the capture of all its
knights uprooted the settlement at one stroke.

It was an October evening in 1187. The last defenders of
Jerusalem had just capitulated. Before victors and vanquished,
ranged around the Mosque of Omar, Saladin demolished the
great golden cross with which the Franks had crowned the
dome of the building. When it fell, so the Arab chronicle tells
us, 'there arose from the ranks of the two armies an outcry that
shook the earth.' That great cry of joy and of despair is still
echoing across the centuries!

We know that the Kingdom of Jerusalem—without Jerusalem itself—was partly restored by the Third Crusade in 1191.

But the Crusaders could only recover the coastal strip with St. Jean d'Acre as their capital, while Jerusalem and all the hinterland remained in Moslem hands. The treaty concluded on this basis between Richard the Lion-Heart and Saladin in 1192 provided at least an acceptable *modus vivendi* and some mutual toleration, notably as far as pilgrims to the Holy Places were concerned.

Frankish Syria in the Thirteenth Century. New Motives and New Aspects

The Frankish colonies thus restored survived for another century (1191–1291). In reality, however, the situation was completely changed. The Kingdom of Jerusalem had hitherto been a strong monarchy with a fairly broad territorial base. Henceforth it represented only a thin band of maritime towns in which the royal power grew weaker until central government finally disappeared, leaving a feudal and anarchical republic comparable to the Poland of the *liberum veto*.

Frankish colonization had been hitherto directed by two chief motive powers: religious idealism and territorial imperialism. The thirteenth century brought a change of attitude. If the West continued to be interested in bases in Syria, it was for their economic importance, since they formed the chief entrepôt for trade with the Levant. The rich colonies of Venice, Genoa, Pisa, Marseilles or Barcelona which were established at Tyre or at St. Jean d'Acre received there spices, fine fabrics and jewels direct from Mohammedan Asia, India, and the Far East. The affairs of Syria were henceforth considered less for their own sake than as a function of Venetian or Genoese maritime interests. It could be said without too much exaggeration that in 1099 the Kingdom of Jerusalem was created by faith; but when in the thirteenth century the merchant replaced the knight, it was maintained by the spice trade.

*　　　*　　　*　　　*

A great pope, Innocent III, tried to repeat Urban II's gesture and to re-establish the Kingdom of Jerusalem in its entirety. This led to the Fourth Crusade. It was deflected from its goal by the Venetians and resulted in the unexpected creation of a 'Latin Empire' at Constantinople in 1204.

This 'crusade that took the wrong turning' was one of the most fatal accidents in the history of Europe. The earlier crusades had led to the first colonial expansion of the Christian West at the expense of Islam. The Fourth Crusade, however, diverted Latin colonization towards the Greek lands. For two and a half centuries French knights and Italian navigators devoted their best energies to exploiting the basin of the Aegean Sea. It was an ill-regulated enterprise which led only to a squandering of energies and a pulverization of power worse than in Syria. Alone, the second Latin Emperor of Constantinople, Henry of Hainaut (1206–1216), an intelligent politician and successful soldier who reminds us of the founder of the Kingdom of Jerusalem, showed himself capable of controlling this tumult. At Jerusalem, however, Baldwin I had had a series of remarkable princes as his successors. After Henry of Hainaut, the Latin Empire knew none save insignificant sovereigns. The rest of its history was forty-four years of steady decay; it was increasingly harassed by the Greek element, which eventually confined the last Latins within the walls of Constantinople. When in 1261 the soldiers of Michael Palaeologus recaptured the city, thus restoring the old Byzantine Empire after an eclipse of fifty-seven years, the empire created by the Fourth Crusade had long been the merest fragment.

The diversion of the Fourth Crusade, apart from the irreparable harm which it caused the Greek world, had consequences no less serious for Frankish Syria. Just when this stood most in need of reinforcements for its relief, it was deprived of them, and even their source was dried up for a time. By diverting the Frankish effort from Acre to Constantinople, the crusaders weakened the unfortunate colonies of the Holy Land. It may be said that the ephemeral Latin Empire cut the life-line of Frankish Syria at the crucial moment.

*   *   *   *

To save the Holy Land, or what was left of it, there remained only one possibility: to resume the programme of King Amaury I, raise the Egyptian Question and give it a Frankish solution. In historical geography—from the Pharaohs and Ptolemies to the Anglo-Egyptians—Palestine has almost always lived in close unity with the Nile Valley. What strength the Frankish state would have gained if (as King Amaury had dreamed) it could have been bolstered up by Egypt! There existed after all a Coptic element, very influential in the Egyptian towns, which could have been of great assistance to the Latins. The Fifth Crusade, led by King Jean de Brienne, was thus following a well-judged programme when it landed in the Delta in 1218 and seized Damietta in 1219. It failed, however, in consequence of a diplomatic mistake—the refusal to exchange Damietta against Jerusalem for a term of years—and also a material error: the unpardonable ignorance shown by the crusading leaders as regards the behaviour of the Nile floods.

A purely diplomatic crusade, that of the Emperor Frederick II, had more success. A strange crusade indeed, that of the sceptical sovereign who in his Sicilian lands had been enamoured of Arab culture since his youth. On the other side, the master of Islam was the Egyptian Sultan Melik-el-Kâmil, the most elegant representative of that chivalrous liberalism which had remained a tradition in the family of Saladin. Between the two men (who entered into an extensive correspondence) agreement was not very difficult. Without striking a blow, but simply by making use of his Moslem friendships, Frederick obtained in 1229 from the Sultan the restoration of part of Palestine, including Jerusalem. In reality, Jerusalem, recognized as a holy city by both faiths, was placed under a religious condominium. The Christians recovered the Holy Sepulchre, but the Moslems kept the Mosque of Omar. Were the Crusades about to end in a régime of religious toleration and cultural sympathy between Christendom and Islam? Such hopes proved too far in advance of their time. When in 1248 St. Louis embarked on his crusade to Egypt, Jerusalem had fallen again, four years previously, into the hands of the Moslems.

By choosing the Delta as the objective of his Crusade, St. Louis resumed the programme of Amaury I and John of Brienne. It was a judicious choice, since the keys of Jerusalem were indeed in Cairo. Damietta, whose capture had brought so much misfortune to Brienne, was taken at the landing in 1249. The best course would then have been, as the Count of Brittany proposed, to complete the strangulation of Egypt by seizing

Alexandria. However, the march upon Cairo which the majority of Louis's advisers preferred could also be justified. There is nothing to prove that after the Mansourah canal had been crossed success was not within sight. In spite of the wise dispositions of Louis IX, however, disaster befell the army when the Count of Artois disobeyed orders.

There are defeats, when the vanquished refuses to bow the knee, which are tantamount to victories. The moral strength of the saintly king, his calm heroism in prison in face of the Mameluks' threats of death, impressed even these wild men. Christian asceticism has always inspired in Islam a deep respect. Despite its military failure, Louis IX's crusade added to the prestige of France. So did the four years which the king spent in the Holy Land after his liberation, years so well employed for the restoration of the country; so, above all did the alert understanding of oriental problems which he then showed, beginning with the Mongolian question.

From Genghis Khan to St. Louis. The Mongolian Crusade

The Mongol empire then covered Asia. The Great Khan Mongka, grandson and third successor of Genghis Khan, was master of Upper and Central Asia, half China and the whole of Persia. A cousin of his reigned over the Russian steppes as far as the frontiers of Poland and Hungary. In the six centuries' duel between the Cross and the Crescent, might not the intervention of the Mongolian factor prove decisive?

Travellers had learnt that there were a great number of Christians in the armies of the Great Khan and even in his entourage. Indeed, several of his ministers were Nestorians, as well as several princesses of his family, including his own mother. Nestorian Christianity in fact had long been widespread among the Turkish tribes of Upper Asia whose ruling families were closely united to the House of Genghis Khan. It was to make use of these sympathies that Pope Innocent IV in 1245, and then St. Louis in 1253, had dispatched envoys into Mongolia, the former sending Plan Carpin, the latter Rubrouck. Their reception, admittedly, had not been very encouraging, because the Mongolian emperors could not imagine an understanding with Christian princes in any other form than that of a vassalage to be imposed on the Western rulers. But where the Latins had failed, the Armenians succeeded.

The history of the Armenian people is one of the most interesting known to us. As the advance-guard of Europe in its outposts towards Asia, it never ceased to warn Europe (generally in vain) of the perils that threatened it and of the methods of salvation.

When the Crusaders arrived in the south-east of Asia Minor, they had found established in Cilicia a sturdy Armenian peasantry, who had emigrated there with their Church and their feudal lords, after the conquest of Greater Armenia by the Turks. Cilicia, with its eyries and its fertile plain, was in process of becoming the new Armenia which, thanks to the diversion caused by the Crusades, could at the same time shake off the last traces of Byzantine rule and defend its independence against the Turks. The Armenian principality thus established played a considerable rôle in the history of the Latin East. Throughout the whole duration of the Crusades, the Franks had no more faithful ally. Frankish and Armenian houses were repeatedly united by marriage, so much so that the royal family of Jerusalem ended by being a Franko-Armenian dynasty. The institution of chivalry was introduced at the Armenian court, and French became the second language of the nobles. In 1198 the Papacy sanctioned this close understanding by granting the Armenian prince Leo II the Great the royal crown.

The son-in-law and successor of Leo II, King Héthum I of Armenia (Haython, as the Franks wrote it) intensified this policy. Father-in-law and faithful ally of the chief Frankish baron—Prince Bohemund VI of Antioch-Tripoli—he conceived a grandiose scheme, for the benefit of the Franks as well as for his own. This was, to win over the enormous Mongol power, canalize it for the profit of Christian civilization by directing it against Islam, and thus turn the terrible Tartars, the grandsons of the Conqueror of the World, into the saviours of the Latin East. It was a difficult task; but, thanks to Nestorianism, Héthum knew that he could count on the Christian sympathies of the Mongols. And he was well aware that the latter, after conquering almost the whole of Asia, saw before them one last obstacle, which was precisely the Caliphate of Baghdad in Irak and the last nephews of Sultan Saladin in Syria.

The Armenian monarch therefore had no hesitation in making a journey to Mongolia. On 13 September, 1254, he was received near Karakorum by the Great Khan Mongka, to whom he did homage. Not only did the grandson of Genghis Khan welcome him most cordially; not only did he declare that he would take the kingdom of Armenia and Armenian Christianity under his protection; but he also announced to Héthum the imminent despatch of a great Mongol army charged to destroy Baghdad and crush the Moslems of Syria. It was, as has been said, the launching of a vast 'yellow crusade', rising from the depths of Upper Asia and capable of squeezing Islam in a vice between Mongols and Franks.

These things came to pass. On 10 February, 1258, Mongka's brother, Hulagu Khan, took Baghdad. The fall of the great city, pride of the Arab world and capital of the Moslem Holy See, had prodigious repercussions in the East. The event seemed to the Christians a miraculous revenge. 'It was five hundred and fifteen years, wrote an Armenian chronicler,' since the foundation of that city. During the whole time that it had maintained its hold, like an insatiable bloodsucker, it had swallowed up all the world. But now it restored all that it had taken. It was punished for its toll of blood, for the evil it had done, when in the eyes of God the measure of its iniquities was full. The rule of the Arabs had lasted six hundred and forty-seven years.' The terrible Mongols thus appeared as the avengers of oppressed Christianity, the providential saviours sent from the vastness of the Gobi Desert to take Islam in the rear and shake it to its foundations. In Baghdad itself, the wife of Genghis Khan's descendant, Princess Dokuz-khatun who was a very pious Nestorian, granted favourable terms to the Christians and associated them openly with the victory.

After Baghdad, Moslem Syria. At the beginning of 1260 the Mongol army commanded by Hulagu Khan, which had been joined by King Héthum of Armenia and Prince Bohemund of Antioch, captured Aleppo. In March, the Mongol general Kitbuqa also took Damascus. Aleppo and Damascus, the virgin Moslem cities which no Frankish army had ever been able to take, fell before the 'Mongolian crusade'. Kitbuqa, who was a Nestorian and was personally assisted by the King of Armenia and the Prince of Antioch, had several mosques of Damascus transformed into churches; he authorized the ringing of bells everywhere, and, like his master at Baghdad, gave first place to the Christian element. In that crucial year 1260 Moslem Syria, still contained on the seaward side by the line of Frankish fortresses, and taken in the rear by the Mongol invasion, was on the point of collapse.

The Nestorian Mongol, master of all inland Syria, stretched out his rough hand to the Franks, who remained masters of the coast. But the barons of St. Jean d'Acre repulsed this hand. Fearing the coarseness of the descendants of Genghis Khan, they refused the proffered alliance, preferring to come to an understanding with the Mamelukes of Egypt, to whom they granted free passage for a surprise attack on the Mongol army. On 3 September, 1260, the Mamelukes, aided by this advantage, crushed the Mongols in Galilee and drove them beyond the Euphrates.

For this blindness, the Franks paid dearly. The Mamelukes, upon whose gratitude they had reckoned, immediately turned against them. This Turkish 'Great Company', a real standing army at a time when the Franks, apart from the Military Orders, had only temporary feudal levies at their command, had become one of the best instruments of war of that day. The Mameluke sultanate, even more than the empire of Saladin had lately been, was an absolute monarchy, obeyed from the Sudan to the Euphrates. What had ensured success to the Franks at the beginning of the twelfth century had been their strong military monarchy, contrasting with the Moslem anarchy. Now the situation had been reversed: Moslem military monarchy faced Frankish anarchy. Moreover, from 1260 to 1277, the Mamelukes were headed by a captain of genius, a former slave from the Russian steppe, the Turk Baïbars, the very god of action and victory. Since the Franks had repulsed the Mongol alliance which had come to save them, Baïbars had only to take advantage of their folly. In a few months, and with the greatest ease, he made a clean sweep of half their strongholds, from Jaffa and Antioch to the *Krak des Chevaliers*. As for the Armenians, he took a fearful vengeance on them by putting Cilicia to fire and sword. King Héthum, broken by these disasters, abdicated and retired into a monastery.

This failure of the great Armenian monarch was the failure of the Crusades themselves. It was the failure of Europe. As Baïbars dominated thirteenth-century Islam, Héthum had dominated the Christendom of his time; he embraced in his calculations all Asia from Pekin to St. Jean-d'Acre and had seen in the vast Mongolian upsurge the salvation of the West. But none had understood his genius. The Franks, whom he had tried to make the allies of the Mongols, had not grasped the supreme importance of such a connection; the Mongols, whom for a moment he had been able to make the protectors and saviours of eastern Christianity, turned away from that thankless rôle when they met only distrust and hostility from the Latins. But in taking leave of the Armenian prince who had not shrunk from the journey to Karakorum in order that he might enlist for the benefit of Christendom the mighty Mongol power, historians should salute one of the most lucid and powerful political geniuses of the Middle Ages. King Héthum remains the man who, if the West had but listened to him, could have turned the course of European history at the hour when the Mongol earthquake, altering the face of Asia, was opening up fresh channels for the age-old rivers.

What the great Armenian had envisaged was a Mongol empire stretching as far as Egypt, the protector of both a restored Kingdom of Jerusalem and a strengthened Kingdom of Armenia, a Mongol empire gradually becoming Christian under the influence of its Nestorian subjects and also of Armenian or Latin monks, a Mongol empire of the West which would become Syrian as the Mongol empire of China became Buddhist and the Mongol khanate of Turkestan became Moslem. It was over this vision of a lost world that King Héthum, when he had become the monk Macarios, was wont to ponder in the cloisters of Tzaragh. Whilst these possibilities of yesterday vanished like a dream, the rough hand of Baïbars steered history back into its former course.

*   *   *   *

In 1287, the Christians seemed to be given a last opportunity. Frankish Syria was reduced to St. Jean-d'Acre, Tripoli, and a few other ports, when there disembarked at Naples the strangest of ambassadors. This was a Mongolian prelate known as Rabban

Sauma. He has no secrets for us since Abbé Chabot discovered his biography in an ancient Syrian manuscript. He was born near Pekin, of a Turkish Nestorian family. With his friend Maraos—the future patriarch Mar Jabalaha—he set out from China about 1275 to make a pilgrimage to Jerusalem. In 1287 the Mongolian court of Persia, which had made Rabban Sauma's companion a Nestorian patriarch, sent Rabban himself on an embassy to the princes of the West to propose a military alliance against Islam. The offers of the Mongol khan (Arghun Khan, noted for his Christian sympathies) were very precise. He explicitly proposed to encircle the Mameluke sultanate by an attack on two fronts, to take it between a Latin landing at St. Jean-d'Acre and a Mongol invasion from the direction of Damascus. The dates are important: in 1250 St. Louis, after landing in the Delta and taking Damietta, had marched on Cairo; in 1260 the Mongol general Kitbuqa, after taking Damascus, had threatened Egypt. Both had failed, because in that interval of ten years the Mamelukes had had time to beat them separately. But what the Khan of Persia proposed in 1287 was precisely to co-ordinate and synchronize the two operations, 'to strangle the land of Egypt,' as the Mongolian diplomatic documents put it in their barbarous Latin.

To grasp the possibilities of salvation that lay in such a proposition, it would have taken an Urban II, or an Innocent III, far-sighted and swift in decision. But the pontifical monarchy, the intelligence and will of Europe, was passing through a lamentable interregnum. From Rome, Rabban Sauma went to take the Mongol offers to Philip the Fair and King Edward I of England. He received the most courteous welcome, but no definite promise: the rulers of Paris and London were keeping a close watch upon each other, and neither was willing to weaken himself for the other's profit by setting out for St. Jean-d'Acre. When taking ship to return to Persia in the spring of 1288, Rabban Sauma did not conceal his disappointment: 'What shall I say, what shall I tell the Mongols on my return? Christendom grows indifferent to its possessions. . . .'

These bitter reflections corresponded only too closely to reality. Scarcely had the Mongolian prelate returned to China than the Mamelukes took from the Franks their last capitals: Tripoli in 1289, St. Jean-d'Acre in 1291. The Armenian kingdom of Cilicia maintained a Christian bridgehead on the continent for nearly a century longer. In 1375 it too was destroyed by the Mamelukes.

The Historical Rôle of the Crusades

Frankish Syria was dead. The chronicles which tell of its history—chronicles of the *Eracles*, those of Ernoul, Novare or Joinville, the *Gestes des Chiprois*, and *Flor des Estoires de la terre d'Orient*—constitute the day-to-day story of France's first colonial expansion Without knowing it, those soldier-historians, poet-knights, and prelates who were also men of action, have written us the epic of a New France. Their literary work is immortal. Why was it that the political work in which they also colla-borated, Frankish Syria, perished after two centuries? The chronicles are there to make the reason plain. These first French political historians tell us repeatedly that last-minute heroism is of no avail, if partisan passions have obscured the sense of common weal. With what grief did a William of Tyre or an Ernoul see with their very eyes those supreme blunders which rendered useless the persistent skill of diplomats, the genius of generals and the blood of martyrs! The modern reader (I con-fess) cannot help sharing their joys, their hopes, their anger, the more so since the dismantled stones of their fortresses are there to remind us of their cause.

Call to witness these stones themselves and their indestruct-ible mass, from Cahyoûn to the *Krak des Chevaliers*, from the *Krak* to the castles of Moab: they still make their silent protest against the treason of destiny—Frankish Syria could have sur-vived! Where have greater faith and genius left a more lasting imprint? But also what history has, in its later stages, been punctuated with more ghastly and suicidal political blunders? Even at the last moment, during the supreme vigil of arms of 1287–1290, why were the France of Philip the Fair and the England of Edward I powerless to save their colony in the Levant? Because, even to the end, Capetian and Plantagenet were paralysed by jealous suspicion of one another. And the result? Frankish Syria was flung into the sea in that fatal spring of 1291. Asia was avenged on Europe, and two centuries of heroism apparently rendered vain.

*   *   *   *

What judgment shall we pass on the Crusades in this Sum of History, and what has been their part in the world? We tend to see in them only a magnificent movement of idealism corresponding to no historical necessity. If so, we neglect to set them against the history of the Eastern Question. But this must not be overlooked. When the first Crusaders arrived on the Bosphorus, the Turks were at Smyrna and Nicaea. The immediate result of the Crusade was to push them back as far as the heart of Anatolia. And the capture of Constantinople by the Moslems, which everything proclaimed to be imminent at the end of the eleventh century, was postponed until the middle of the fifteenth. The Crusades thus constituted an invaluable diversion which delayed the invasion of Europe for three hundred and fifty years. During that time Western civilization took shape and fitted itself to receive the heritage of dying Hellenism.

The very choice of objective of the Crusades had been fortunate—Jerusalem. Even had there been no religious motive, the Moslem colossus could not have been struck in a more tender spot than Palestine, if the required diversion was to rescue threatened 'Romany'. The crusaders' fortresses of Judaea and of the Moab region cut Islam in two; and whoever holds them, intercepts the caravan routes between Egypt and the Magreb on the one side, and Irak and Persia on the other. Furthermore, Palestine and the Moab control the routes to the Hedjaz, the route of the Hadjj. In the eleventh century Islam, installed in Ionia and on the Sea of Marmora, threatened Constantinople which was still the intellectual capital of Europe. By a remarkably effective counter-thrust Christendom replied by establishing itself at the weak points of the Moslem world, in Transjordania and in the Djeziré, at the *Krak de Monreale* and at Edessa, half-way between Cairo and Baghdad, between Qonya and Mecca. Constantinople was saved. The bold policy of the Comneni became possible. For the European civilization of which Byzantium was the gem, this was a magnificent achievement.

We are vaguely conscious to-day that in face of indomitable

Islam and the enormous 'yellow world', the rulers of Europe
ought to show themselves—or, alas, ought to have shown
themselves—good Europeans. The men of the Middle Ages
recognized the same duty, which they called the defence of
Christendom. From the Battle of Dorylaeum to the Battle of
Lepanto, the Crusades were neither more nor less than western
society's instinct of self-preservation in face of the most formidable danger which it had ever encountered. This became
obvious enough when the West gave up the attempt.

The weakening of the notion of Christian duty in the men of
the Middle Ages, from the fourteenth century onwards, that
'retreat of Christianity', brought down real catastrophe upon
Europe. This is shown by the results of the failure of the
Crusades. An economic disaster ensued; the abandonment of
the Syrian warehouses, handing over to the Mamelukes the
monopoly of trade with the Indies, produced a fifty per cent
rise in the price of many goods which had become indispensable to the West. But even from the territorial standpoint, it
was not in the power of the Latins to cut their losses. By resign-
ing themselves to the failure of the Crusades, the contemporaries of Philip the Fair had renounced all hope of colonization
in Moslem Asia. Now, less than half a century after the departure of the last Crusader from the Holy Land, it was Moslem
Asia which invaded Christendom, attacking it at the most
vulnerable point—the Byzantine Empire.

Consequences of the Fourth Crusade: the Dismantling of 'Romania'

Through the failure of the Crusades, the Byzantine Empire
became again in the fourteenth century what it had been in the
earlier Middle Ages: the furthest frontier and outpost of Europe.
But the West, by the Fourth Crusade, had committed the
historic crime of dismantling this bastion. Certainly, when
substituting their rash Latin Empire for the old Byzantine
monarchy, the Crusaders of 1204 had flattered themselves that
they could take the place of the Greeks in the age-long 'Watch
on the Straits'. But they had quickly had to sing small. The
State they had improvised on the Bosphorus, far from forming
a barrier against the Mohammedan world, proved a source of
weakness for the whole of Christendom. This Latin Empire,

which had owed its brief renown to the talents of Henry of Hainaut, was really doomed from the start. The handful of barons and knights suddenly superimposed on Byzantine society had neither the forces nor the cultural superiority needed to make good their hold. The diversion of the Fourth Crusade—that act of international piracy which Innocent III had denounced from the start—was, and remained, a misfortune for Europe. The victors of 1204 had broken Byzantine unity without replacing it by an effective State. The Greek restoration of 1262 certainly could not repair the damage. It by no means restored to the old empire all its territories of 1203. In this 'Romania', irretrievably broken into fragments (or 'Balkanized' as we should say to-day) by the attack of 1204, the invading Turks met with little resistance after 1350. The Fourth Crusade proved to have paved the way—far in advance, no doubt, but nevertheless surely—for the Ottoman conquest.

To do justice to the achievements of the Fourth Crusade, we ought, of course, to remember not only the miserable Latin Empire, but also the Frankish lordship over Greece proper. The principality of Morea under the Villehardouin dynasty and the Duchy of Athens under the House of La Roche were in the thirteenth century brilliant centres of French civilization. 'The noblest chivalry of France,' wrote the chronicler Muntaner, 'was the chivalry of Morea. The French spoken there was as good as that of Paris.' Similar testimony, until after the fifteenth century, was given on behalf of the Lusignan kingdom of Cyprus, that other French foundation in a Greek country: 'All the people of this land, and especially the gentlefolk, are as good Frenchmen as we are in France.'

This period of purely French hegemony in the Greek seas hardly extended beyond the beginning of the fourteenth century. After 1278 the principality of the Villehardouins, in the Morea, passed under the protection of the Angevins of Naples; it thus came under Italian influence, and it was from Italian lords that in 1430 the Byzantines managed to reconquer the country. The French Duchy of Athens likewise passed to Catalans (1311), then to Florentines (1387). As for the Greek islands, they had been divided between the maritime empires of Venice and Genoa. Even at Cyprus, the Seigneury of St. Mark eventually filched the heritage of the Lusignans in 1489. As a result of the French eclipse brought about by the Hundred Years War, Italians had finally appropriated the last conquests of the Crusades. . . .

They were in no condition to defend them. These Italian colonies, these Frankish lordships in a Greek land, soon passed their hour of brilliance and of economic prosperity. They also were skeleton colonies, not supported by immigration, and moreover were small territories, incapable of protecting themselves. Their existence therefore depended on the mastery of the sea. As long as the squadrons of Genoa and Venice held the Archipelago, Chio, Pera, and Caffa remained Genoese; and Euboea and the Cyclades, Venetian. On the day when the Ottoman admirals dominated the Aegean Sea, this precarious colonization collapsed. The Veneto-Genoese maritime empire of the Aegean in the fifteenth century resembled in this respect the Dutch empire of the Sunda Seas in the nineteenth. The temporary success of both was due to the fact that for a time they were, so to speak, overlooked in a backwater of history, in a pause of destiny. When they had to brave afresh the storms of the open sea in contact with world empires, they were swallowed up. In the Greek seas as well as in the Levant, the hour of the Turks had come.

The Ottoman Conquest

The principal outcome of nine centuries of Ottoman history was the compact establishment, around 1080, of the Ottoman race on the Anatolian plateau. But the Turkish dynasties never succeeded in making either Persia or Syria Turkish, even if they established a political control which repeatedly lasted centuries. It was a kind of exception to the rule that in Anatolia the elimination of the Greek element was almost total. The New Turkestan which sprang up immediately played a decisive part in the great duel of the Crusades, because it formed a massive barrier between Europe and the Frankish colonies of the Levant. True, the First Crusade had succeeded in momentarily piercing this barrier; but all those which followed failed to do so. It was only overland, by using the old transcontinental route from the Straits to the Taurus, that the strong immigration, needed by the Crusading States if they were to survive, could reach Syria. Once this route was closed, there remained only the sea-way, which then could convey only a trickle of colonists. The Turkish barrier therefore proved, in the long run, the decisive factor in the failure of the Crusades.

However, though the Turks were definitely established on the plateau of Asia Minor, they considered this was but a halt in their advance on Europe. The movement which for centuries had been carrying these nomad herdsmen in the direction of the West was like a force of nature. From the deep gorges of the Altaï Mountains and from the Turcoman steppes to the shores of the Sea of Marmora, came a creeping tide of black tents, broken tribes and powerful dynasties: it was the anonymous movement of mankind on the march. Sometimes an obstacle arose which, for years or centuries, halted the migration. Patiently the Turks waited until the obstacle had disappeared. And then they resumed their onward march. As soon as the Crusades and the Mongolian domination had ended, each of the emirs who in Anatolia had succeeded to the sultanate resumed for his own benefit the policy of the Turkish conqueror of the eleventh century. Each wished to have his Greek town and his outlet on the Archipelago, and the boldest made the cupola of St. Sophia the objective of his raid.

After 1261, Byzantine Hellenism was again entrusted with the defence of the Straits, the keys of Europe. But the partition of 1204 had, by 'Balkanizing' Romania, irretrievably weakened the old empire. Hellenism, restored to Constantinople by the Palæologi, but practically confined to Thrace, part of Macedonia and the western fringe of Anatolia, could not defend these last possessions for long. The Ottomans had been established on the borders of Bithynia since the beginning of the fourteenth century; they seized Broussa in 1326 and Nicaea in 1331, then, passing into Europe, went on to take Adrianople (1362).

The establishment of the Turks in Europe. . . . In other times, what an upsurge of the crusading spirit would have broken out at such news! But not in the middle of the Hundred Years War, on the morrow of the Treaty of Brétigny. Italy and the Holy Roman Empire had by now been cut into tiny fragments. The Papacy was in 'captivity' at Avignon, awaiting the Great

Schism. The Middle Ages were coming to an end. There was
no longer a single Europe. The Turks were thus able to crush
the Serbian army at Kossovo in 1389, in a victory which gave
them the Balkans.

The Ottomans reached the Danube. Directly threatened, the
Hungarians implored the aid of the West. It was no longer for
Tripoli or St. Jean-d'Acre that Crusades now set out, but for
Belgrade and Nicopolis. What a withdrawal, in a mere hundred
years! What became of the 'crusade to Nicopolis', at the head
of which rode the future Duke of Burgundy, John the Fearless?
Into this life-and-death struggle for the liberation of eastern
Europe, the irresponsible Franco-Burgundian nobility brought
the spirit of Crécy and Agincourt. But no one in the West sus-
pected that the Ottoman army, under the orders of Sultan
Bayézid, had become a precise and well-disciplined military
machine.   The day of 13 September 1396 remains one of the
worst disasters which our civilization has suffered in all its long
history. From that day the Balkan peninsula was struck out—
for more than four hundred years—from the muster-roll of
European lands.

A phantom Byzantine Empire, lost in the midst of Ottoman
territories, had hitherto maintained its precarious existence.
After the disaster at Nicopolis its days seemed numbered. Yet
thanks to an unexpected raid from the fastnesses of central
Asia, it was rescued. The victory which in 1402 the Trans-Oxian
conqueror Tamerlane won at Ankara over Sultan Bayézid broke
the Ottoman power for a quarter of a century and gave the
Byzantines a respite of fifty years. The West, however, failed
to take advantage of this last smile of destiny. Europe no more
existed than at so many other crucial hours when the historian
looks for it in vain. This first half of the fifteenth century was
the worst period of the Hundred Years War; it also saw the
Hussite Wars and the Great Schism. No one, then, took advantage of the eclipse of the Turkish power; nobody freed the
Balkans. Only the Hungarians, directly involved as they were,
made a tardy effort in that direction. In 1440 their leader, John
Hunyadi, rescued Serbia and Bulgaria for a moment. But it was
too late. The terrible Turkish infantry had had time to re-form;
moreover, the West remained inert, save for the powerless

Papacy. Beaten at Varna and Kossovo, the Hungarians were flung back to the north of the Danube. From that moment Constantinople was doomed.

No disaster was more clearly foreseen and so little guarded against as the fall of Constantinople. The crusading spirit had disappeared completely. Europe paid dearly for its scepticism and its inertia. The wretched quarrels of the Balkan peoples in Macedonia; the out-of-date rivalry of Greeks and Latins on the Bosphorus; the absorption of France and England in the Hundred Years War; and the Burgundian schism—all were preparing for part of Europe a slavery which plunged it into darkness for four centuries.

The siege of Constantinople lasted from 6 April to 29 May, 1453. During these two months, against the 160,000 war-hardened soldiers of Mahomet II, the West placed at the service of the defence no more than 3,000 Venetian, Genoese or Catalan residents, and 3,000 miscellaneous sailors, pirates and adventurers scraped together from heaven knows where. None of the powerful Italian squadrons set sail in time. The stake, nevertheless, was the whole future and, one might say, the whole past of the old Europe. Tradition has it that on the day he entered Constantinople Mahomet II, as he was crossing the Hippodrome, struck down with his mace the trophy which the Greeks had created out of the spoils of the Persians, after the Battle of Plataea. The tale is apocryphal, but no symbolic act could have been more appropriate.

Christendom, which would not save Constantinople, paid dearly for its selfishness. Once they were masters of the Straits, the Turks could devote themselves to the Danube front. The Balkans once subdued, it was Hungary's turn, whose enslavement followed on the Battle of Mohacs in 1526. The wave of invasions which had begun in the eleventh century in the remotest parts of Turkestan swept up to the gates of Vienna, where it was halted in the autum of 1529. More threatening still was the fact that the migratory hordes of nomad horsemen who had brought about these amazing results could adapt themselves to the most unforeseen conditions. The sons of the steppe became sailors! They captured Rhodes from the Hospitallers and Cyprus from the Venetians; their corsairs established themselves at Algiers, organized the Berbers of that region, besieged Malta and even raided the coasts of Provence. When in 1571 the Battle of Lepanto destroyed their fleet, it could not wrest from them any of their conquests.

That a people from the Altaïan Mountains, of Arabic religion, and Arab-Persian culture, could win such a place in the destinies of Europe is the measure of the decline of European society at the end of the Middle Ages. This statement does not belittle Moslem civilization in itself—Spain, for instance, owed to it part of its greatness; nor does it cast aspersions on the Turk—the Republic of Ankara has shown us what he can do, once he is free of his chains. But what the Osmanlis brought into Europe in the fifteenth century was the brutal rupture of Western development. In the Christian countries where they imposed their régime, all freedom of thought, all scientific and intellectual progress, were halted for many a long day. No liberty of conscience or association was possible. Political institutions could not rise above the most primitive despotism. A part of the European population was cut off from Europe. Noble races, which might have taken part in the movement of the Renaissance, were kept at the same level as the Bedouin of the Nejd, the Kurdish partisans or the Kirghiz herdsmen.

The Breakdown of the First European Colonization

The history of the Eastern Question beats to an uneven rhythm. With Alexander, the frontiers of Europe had been carried to the basin of the Indus. With the Romans, they fell back to the basin of the Euphrates. The Arab invasion made them draw back further still, to the Taurus; and the Seljukian invasion to the Aegean Sea. The West replied to these attacks by the counter-attack of the Crusades. From the eleventh to the fourteenth centuries, the Western peoples, and in particular the French and the Italians, colonized the Levant; that is, in chronological order, coastal Syria and Palestine (1098–1291), Cyprus (1191–1571), 'Romania' (1204–1261), Athens (1205–1458), the Peloponnese (1206–1430), the Greek islands (thirteenth-sixteenth centuries), even the Crimea (1266–1475). Their influence latinized to some extent the Armenian kingdom of Cilicia (1098–1375).

This was the first colonial expansion of the Christian West Its original cause, and its subsequent pretext, was the spiritual impetus of the Crusades; its lasting motives were the desire of the French barons for territorial conquests and the commercial interests of the Italian maritime republics. Powerful ideals underlay it—the liberation of the Holy Sepulchre and the suppression of the Greek schism. It unleashed the political imperialism of Capetian France and the economic imperialism of Venice and Genoa. With this backing at the outset, the enterprise succeeded. French was spoken at St. Jean-d'Acre, at Nicosia and at Athens. Italian was spoken in Crete and the Crimea. To a contemporary of St. Louis, this expansion of spiritual influence would no doubt have seemed definite. To a contemporary of Marco Polo, this economic grip might have seemed unshakable.

But of this brilliant Western expansion nothing survived. Islam recovered everything. In 1291 St. Jean-d'Acre, the last Frankish capital in the Holy Land, fell again into the power of the Moslems. In 1430 the last wreckage of Frankish Morea returned to the Greeks, before passing to the Turks in 1460. No colonization was ever to be more completely obliterated.

Now, this colonization represented the best of Europe's efforts—'the upsoaring of Europe,' as Louis Halphen called it—over a period of three centuries. What were the reasons for that failure? Above all, the shortage of Frankish man-power. The Frankish principalities of Syria and Romania remained skeleton colonies, not true settlements. The mass of the population remained Moslem or Syrian in Syria and Greek in Cyprus or the Morea. After the Moslem reconquest of Syria, and the Byzantine recovery of the Morea, nothing of the Franks survived there. Another cause of failure must be found in the defectiveness of feudal institutions, of which the *Assizes of Jerusalem* give us only the purely theoretical aspect. Such a régime paralysed the State and condemned it to impotence. These principalities were merely military colonies, encamped in enemy territory. . . .

Blame also attaches to the ruinous conflicts between Armenians and Greeks, or Greeks and Latins, and the fratricidal struggles among the Latins themselves. In Syria there was strife between the Ghibellines and the Imperialists, the Templars and the Knights Hospitallers; and everywhere, both in Syria and in Romania, the Venetians fought the Genoese. Everywhere the Latin East, divided against itself, cut its own throat. Everywhere the achievements of the Crusades were destroyed by their own builders and their own beneficiaries.

Thus Asia took revenge upon Europe, and conquered an appreciable part of it. About 1118, after the success of the First Crusade, the frontiers of Europe, as in the days of the Caesars, had been advancing between Edessa and Mosul, even into Mesopotamia; by 1529 they had receded as far as the gates of Vienna.

The Lusiads

The triumph of Ottoman arms in the sixteenth century can also be explained in terms of technical superiority. The spahi cavalry, the infantry of the janissaries, and even the Turkish artillery (cast and directed by German instructors) were for a time the best in Europe. Similarly, the Ottoman fleet, served by a host of Greeks, almost gained the upper hand of the Christian squadrons in mobility and fire-power. However, in this last field the Turkish advance was not maintained. On the whole, the Christian powers kept the mastery of the sea. While the Moslem armies thrust forward into Austria, the Christian squadrons, thanks to Portugal, were taking ruthless revenge in the Indian Ocean.

The Portuguese epic is doubly linked to the epic of the Crusades. Once their national territory was liberated, the Portuguese intended to continue the *Reconquista* on the other side of the sea by hurling the Moors back into Morocco—the first stage, as it turned out, on the road to Guinea, the Congo and the Cape. The great achievement of circumnavigating Africa, successfully concluded by Vasco da Gama in 1498, thus had for its starting-point the capture of Ceuta by King João in 1415. And again, it was the failure of the Crusades which lay behind the great voyages of discovery. The fall of the Frankish colonies in Syria, by reserving to the Sultans of Egypt the exclusive—and much abused—monopoly of the commerce of the

Indian Ocean, drove the explorers of the Far East to seek the
direct route to the Indies by rounding the Cape.

The close correspondence of dates is significant here. In 1498
the Ottoman advance-guards penetrated Venetia as far as
Vicenza; but Vasco da Gama landed at Calicut. In 1503, Venice
lost to the Turks Moron, Coran, and Lepanto; but in 1509 the
Portuguese viceroy Francisco d'Almeida secured the mastery
of the Indian Ocean by destroying off Diu the united fleets of
the Sultan of Egypt and the *zamorin* of Calicut. In 1522,
Suliman the Magnificent captured Rhodes, but in 1527 the
Portuguese scattered the fleet of the Shah of Gujerat. In
1532, the Turks ravaged Austria; but in 1537 the fleet which
they had sent to the aid of Gujerat was routed by João de
Castro.

Thus at the very hour when, with the Ottoman conquest,
Asia's most powerful assault upon the heart of Europe was
fully launched, the West, outflanking Asia by the sea-route,
took the vast continent in the rear and attacked the Moslem
world in its 'soft underbelly'. The moment chosen proved
especially propitious for such a riposte. In the first half of the
fourteenth century India had constituted one vast Moslem
sultanate which it would not have been easy to attack. But at
the end of the fifteenth century that empire had long been
splintered, and the peninsula was a prey to such anarchy as it
had never known before. The west coast of the Deccan, in
particular, upon the harbours of which the Portuguese had
designs, was shared among several rival Moslem kingdoms
—Gujerāt, Khandêch, Ahmednagar, Bijapur: and there was
also the Hindu kingdom of Vidjayanagar, their common enemy.
Once the fleets of the Shah of Gujerât and the *zamorin* of Calicut
(no other counted) had been destroyed, none of these states,
which were in any case ignorant of all things maritime, was
capable of opposing the Portuguese. Portugal also possessed a
crushing superiority in artillery; and the Portuguese viceroys
very ably gained the support, against the Indo-Moslem kings,
of the mass of the Hindu population; they also awakened the
latent Christianity of the old Nestorian communities of the
Malabar. This sagacious policy bore fruit. The occupation of
Goa, the chief port of the Sultanate of Bijapur, by Albuquerque

in 1510 proclaimed the establishment of the first European maritime empire in the Indies.

The Portuguese were perfectly aware of the historic greatness of their work. Confronted by mighty Asia, they felt that they represented Europe; they felt also the eminent dignity this conferred upon them. In the epic *Lusiads* may be read the eloquent apostrophe addressed by Camoens to the great Western nations which left his tiny country the honour and the burden of this formidable mission.

As far as both the Hindu and the Moslem worlds were concerned, the Portuguese had arrived at a moment propitious to themselves. Contrary to established opinion, the Indian people, at certain periods of their history, have not feared to take to the sea. Towards the year 1000, the people of the Carnatic possessed a fleet which commanded obedience as far as the Sunda Seas; but in the sixteenth century this had become a mere memory. Similarly, the Buddhist kingdom of Ceylon had had its hours of greatness. But this greatness had been succeeded by utter decay, which allowed the Portuguese to secure the control of the island. Again, Java and Sumatra had in the Middle Ages known powerful maritime states or 'thalasso-cracies', the extension of whose influence was due to the sea-faring aptitude of the Malayan peoples. But when the Portuguese established themselves at Malacca, the Malay Archipelago had relapsed into an anarchy of petty principalities. Despite the warlike character of the Malays, the invaders, like the Spaniards in the Philippines, were able, if not to undertake the methodical occupation of the country, at least to hold in force the points essential for the command of the sea and of the spice trade.

The Portuguese did not find the same opportunities in China. Here they encountered a great unitary empire with a dynasty, the Ming, which still commanded respect. Their situation would have been even more unfavourable had they arrived a little earlier. In the reign of the third Ming emperor (1405–1424) the Chinese fleets had for a time secured naval hegemony in the Sunda Seas and the Indian Ocean. They had established the supremacy of their flag on the coasts of Indo-China, Java, Sumatra, and Ceylon, and cruised as far as Aden and Jedda, the port of Mecca. What would Asia's destiny have been, had the

Spanish navigators, on reaching India and Malaya, found established there a Chinese maritime power? But the Sons of Heaven had neglected their fleet. Still, the Portuguese had to be content with a strictly controlled factory at Macao, and were unable to penetrate further north.

The First Japanese Expansion

In contrast to a receding China, Japan was in the course of a maritime and colonial expansion when the Portuguese arrived. This is a story too often forgotten; but it explains many features of the later drama. Throughout the sixteenth century, hordes of Japanese pirates raided the coasts of China, sacking or holding to ransom towns like Ning-po and Nankin. At the end of the century, they tried to drive the Portuguese from Macao. In the opening years of the seventeenth century, a Japanese adventurer established himself in Formosa; and when the Dutch landed on the island they had to reckon with his comrades. In the previous century, other Japanese colonies had been set up in the Philippines (where they similarly tried to oppose the Spanish conquest), Annam, Cambodia and Siam. After 1579, the kings of Siam had a bodyguard composed of Japanese *samuraï* whose chiefs often dictated the law of the land. Not for the last time, the Empire of the Rising Sun attempted at one and the same time the colonial conquest of the 'South Seas' and the military conquest of the continent. In 1592, the Japanese dictator Hideyoshi sent an expeditionary force to conquer Korea and afterwards attack China: 'I will assemble an innumerable army; I will invade the land of the great Ming; and the writhings of the great serpent that adorns my sabre shall fill the sky of the Four Hundred Provinces. Let Korea be my advance-post!'

Nobunaga and Hideyoshi, the two dictators of the years 1573–1598 who thus launched Japan upon the path of conquest, did not hesitate to welcome the navigators from the West, and especially the Portuguese, with whom they intended to establish fruitful commercial relations and on whose advice they counted for the equipment and modernization of the country. This first fever of Europeanization, which redounded to the benefit of Christian missionaries, lasted about thirty years. It ceased abruptly at the beginning of the seventeenth century with the advent of the Tokugawa shôguns. Not only were the Portuguese residents driven out and the missionaries expelled, but the Shôgun's government forbade its subjects to strive for colonies, sail the high seas, or trade with foreigners. At one stroke Japan halted her expansion dead, and shut herself up.

This dead-halt, decided upon independently of any external pressure, has caused surprise. But the Tokugawa had realized that a policy of expansion was hastening the country to its ruin. Already the expedition to Korea had ended in disaster. The Chinese masses, having recovered from the first shock, had overwhelmed the proud samuraï by dint of numbers and driven them into the tip of the Korean peninsula. And what would be the outcome of a naval war against the Spanish fleets? Would it not draw the foreigner on to their islands and bring upon the Japanese Archipelago the fate of the Philippines? In sum, the Tokugawa government, wiser than that of the *epigoni* of the Meiji era, refused to run 'the risk of 1941'. Rather than do so, it withdrew Japan from outside contact, and abandoned the Far Eastern seas to the European fleets.

The Dutch Indies

The expulsion of their residents and the sealing-up of Japan were nevertheless a defeat for the Portuguese. Moreover, the general situation in seventeenth-century Asia was less favourable for Europeans than previously. In India, the Great Moguls, from Akbar to Aurungzeb (1556–1707), had restored the territorial unity of the immense Indo-Moslem empire which, by the outset of the eighteenth century, again included almost the whole of the 'Indian continent'. From the Punjab to the Carnatic, from Bengal to Mysore, India was unified under a strong power and defied attacks from the sea. Moslem valour and Hindu wealth, at the command of the timorous Padishah in his palaces at Delhi and Agra, made him one of the supreme potentates of the age. What was the power of a Louis XIV or a Peter the Great compared to his? In face of such might, what did the Portuguese, Dutch, French, and English factories amount to? They were tolerated on a purely commercial basis in a few ports of Konkan, Malabar or the Carnatic. Their situation was hardly any better than that of the inhabitants of the

Pera district of Constantinople in relation to the seventeenth-century Osmanlis.

The Dutch Company, which was then at its zenith, was ready to meet such a situation. To Portuguese naval imperialism, it opposed a purely commercial policy. Its strict religious neutrality, contrasting with the ardent proselytism of its rivals, won it the support of the native populations which, in Ceylon and at various points of the East Indies, openly helped it to supplant the Portuguese. In Japan it accepted an almost humiliating situation, in order to maintain its Nagasaki factory, going so far as to lend its aid to the Shôgun's government against the unfortunate Christians on the islands. In the regions on which it had most definite designs, it carefully avoided showing any desire for conquest. Two hundred and eighty years were allowed to elapse between the foundation of Batavia in 1619 and the submission of the sultanate of Atchin! The Dutch were also the victims of the first Asiatic reaction of any consequence against European colonization. In 1625 they had occupied Formosa, then a no-man's-land. In 1662 they were driven out by a Sino-Japanese pirate, the famous Koxinga; the official annexation of the island by the Chinese Emperor K'ang-hi followed twenty-one years later.

The Manchu dynasty which had just established itself at Pekin in 1644 had restored the old empire's former splendour. Under K'ang-hi (1669–1722) and K'ien-long (1736–1796), China had again become one of the greatest powers of the world. Not only had she, by the annexation of Formosa, 'made a maritime gesture' for the first time for centuries, but in Manchuria too, at the Treaty of Nertchinsk in 1689, she obliged the Russians to draw back. And in 1792, by subjugating Nepal, she threatened to begin interfering in the affairs of India.

Dupleix, Founder of the European Empire in the Indies

If the China of the Manchu emperors still cut a great figure throughout the whole of the eighteenth century, India had suddenly collapsed. After the death in 1707 of Aurungzeb—the last Great Mogul worthy of the name—his empire had been torn to pieces. Separate Moslem dynasties had established themselves in the Ganges provinces, and also in Hyderabad and the

Carnatic. Hindu reaction, represented by the Mahratta dynasties, had prevailed against them in the north-west of the Deccan and in Central India, while the Sikhs took possession of the Punjab. Everywhere different races, castes, and religions were at war. Any notion of a central power, any notion of a single State, all feeling—one cannot say of patriotism, for the word would have no meaning in this context—of an Indian community had disappeared. The most complete political anarchy, spiritual torpor and national indifference prevailed. India was a prey for all to seize on.

The first to perceive this was Dupleix. A man of outstanding gifts, he understood the possibility and the necessity of transforming the purely commercial policy of the European trading companies into a policy of territorial acquisition. By subscribing to the legal fiction of the Mogul's authority, he hoped to make the French East India Company, in its sphere of influence, the due and formal mandatory of the imperial power. In 1751 he secured, through the subadhar of the Deccan, letters patent from the governor-general of the southern territories, extending from the Krishna to Cape Comorin. He thus laid the foundations for a European empire in India. At the same time as he thus acquired legal title to the possession of the soil and founded his colony by due process of Indian law, he perceived the decisive superiority of European weapons over native armies—of his handful of fusiliers over their multitudes, and of his cannon over their elephants. Strong in convictions based on these observations, he turned king-maker throughout the whole of peninsular India, to the very great profit of the Company. Clear-sighted if ever a man was, and thereby showing himself a true son of eighteenth-century France, he saw right through the Mogul's flimsy show of authority. But being much too shrewd to make his discovery public, he carefully upheld this authority, while appropriating it to his own use and deriving from it, for himself, his employers and his country, a prestige wellnigh royal.

He failed, because—amongst other things—the shareholders of the French Company wanted dividends, not conquests. His true heirs were Clive and Warren Hastings, to whom their employers gave more rein. Turning Dupleix's ideas against his compatriots, they made their Company a feudal and territorial power, embarked upon the labyrinthine sea of native intrigue, and in their turn became king-makers and protectors of emperors. And by bringing their efforts to bear on the same points as Dupleix had indicated, they made the Carnatic and Bengal the foundation of the Anglo-Indian Empire.

From the Indian Empire to the Indian Nation

The unity of India, from the fall of the Gupta Empire to the sixth century of our era, had always been imposed upon it from outside. At the opening of the thirteenth century the Turco-Afghans had created the historical empire of India; the Great Moguls of Timur's race restored it at the opening of the sixteenth. But the conquerors of India, from the first Aryans to Alexander the Great, Babur, Nadir Shah, and the Dourrâni, had always followed the land route, entering through the passes of Afghanistan. The British conquest was the first which, instead of coming down from the mountains, came up from the sea. This penetration, relatively easy when made across the inclined plane of the Carnatic or along the broad opening provided by the Ganges, was much more difficult when it involved scaling the steep escarpment of the Western Ghâts. Despite their excellent base of operations at Bombay, the British took no less than forty-four years (1775–1819) to bring the Mahratta Wars to a successful conclusion. The wars against the Sikhs for the annexation of the Punjab were shorter (1845–1849); but then Britain only decided upon them rather late, thus finishing the conquest of India in the regions where previous conquerors had begun it. For long, the British seemed to think that the Punjab belonged less to the Ganges than to the Persian world; a view which, climatically speaking, was equally tenable. In reality, they were caught in the mesh of Indian affairs and found their policy dictated by the physical structure of the Indian continent. Almost despite themselves they brought about, by virtue of the momentum they had gained, the definitive re-union of the Indian lands.

India, when they began the conquest, seemed to have no other unity than that conferred by its geographical situation. What maintained the notion of a single Indian entity was the barrier of the Himalayas with the double ditch of the Sea of Oman and the Bay of Bengal. Similarly, it had been only the Alps and the two seas which had maintained the notion of a single Italian entity in the eighteenth century. Like Italy in 1789, or the Germany of the Holy Roman Empire, India had become no more than a geographical expression. People spoke of 'the Indies', as in the time of Commines they had spoken of 'the Germanies'.

But the achievement of empire-builders outruns their intentions. The Roman aristocracy which conquered the Greek world in the second century B.C. did not suspect that they were thereby working for the unification of Hellenism and for its political expansion throughout the world; nor did they imagine that these despised *Graeculi*, when once they had become the proud Byzantines of the Middle Ages, would one day inherit Rome's achievement. Nearer our own day, when the French Revolution and Napoleon I brought order and simplification into the Teutonic chaos, little did the French dream that they were preparing for use against their own country the birth of German patriotism and unity. Likewise the British, in effecting the unification of India, intended only to make, for their own profit, a coherent empire out of a geographical expression. But the consequence of their policy outran their intentions. When they established that vast administrative unity from the Himalayas to Cape Comorin, in the framework apparently prepared by nature, it so happened that they unintentionally unified the men as well as the land—or so it seemed. By creating the Indian Empire they had, unwittingly, paved the way for the making of an Indian nation.

What had hitherto maintained the division of the country was partly its immensity and partly the mutual hostility of its component races. Between the 300 million Hindus and the 60 million Moslems (to use recent figures), the age-long duel was always latent. From the time of Mahmoud the Ghaznevid, the struggle against Hindu 'paganism' had remained for Moslems a holy war. As for the Hindus, oppressed for ten centuries by such rulers as Tughluk and Aurungzeb, they nursed undying resentment against their former masters. And even among non-Moslems, the Tamils of Madras, the Sikhs of Lahore, the

Mahrattas of Bombay and the Bengalis of Calcutta were separated by such huge geographical distances and such great differences in outlook that they did not feel themselves to be members of the same community. But the railway and the telegraph brought Bombay close to Madras and Calcutta to Lahore just when British centralization was imposing a minimum of common life on Mahratta and Tamil, Bengali and Sikh. Simultaneously, industrial development was contributing to break down caste barriers: docks and factories were compelling acquiescence in contacts hitherto forbidden. Lastly, the Western ideal, which with its fine sense of *fair play* the British administration spread by means of books and schools, worked both to modernize the most gifted members of the various races and to draw them closer together.

From these lessons in liberalism emerged the Indian Congress, a kind of unofficial parliament which met for the first time at Bombay in 1885 and subsequently continued to bring together increasingly numerous representatives of various sections of Indian opinion. Although at the outset the intellectuals who were its pioneers scarcely represented anybody but themselves, the creation of Congress was nevertheless the most important event in Indian domestic history since the coming of Akbar. For the first time since the great emperor's day, Hindus, Moslems, and Parsees, or at least the most enlightened leaders of these groups, shook hands in public. It may be claimed that the new India—Mother India—was born of these gatherings.

But the Congress leaders could conceive this Indian country only after the Anglo-Saxon pattern. Having sat at the feet of the British parliamentary system, they vied with each other in imitating the great debaters of Ottawa and Sydney, and indeed of Westminster. Their sole objective at this period was to raise their country to the dignity of a Dominion. Even the Radical leader Tilak (1855–1920) recommended the use, against British authority, of British methods of opposition. It was only with Gandhi that this opposition ceased to be modernist and, on the contrary, became regressive, modelling its ideal future on the remotest Indian past. But who can say what hidden Christian influences were inextricably mixed up with the Vedic archaism of Gandhi?

Truth compels us to admit how much India owes both to the work and the example of the British. It matters little that in the first place it was for the convenience of the British administration and the profit of British interests that the country was equipped with modern economic plant; in the end India stands to be the chief gainer from its installation. Moreover, if the poverty of India still remains all too real, the fault certainly does not lie with the 'bridge-builders', as Kipling calls them, the civilians who worked so cheerfully in famine areas, but with the system of landed property itself, with the wholly feudal organization of society—fabulously rich rajahs and a people dying of hunger—and with the caste system, from the Brahman caste 'downward' (for the intellectual ability of many Brahmans does not wipe out the abuse of Hindu clericalism). The English are sometimes reproached for having simply superimposed themselves as a superior caste at the tip of the pyramid which crushes the Indian people, instead of having laid dynamite to the base of the whole structure. But would so bold a step have been for the good of the masses, and would the masses themselves have endured it? In India social institutions are based on theology. How can they be touched without arousing that sectarian or caste feeling which in India takes the place of national sentiment?

Moreover, the Indian intellectual renaissance, even in the most nationalist university circles, owes much to the British atmosphere and example. It is the work of British Sanskrit scholars and archæologists and the admirable labour of the Archæological Survey of India which have restored to a people ignorant of its own history, a people without annals, the fabulous greatness of its own past. And finally, alongside Hindustani English constitutes for every Indian intellectual a second tongue in which the Tamil and the Punjabi are most likely to understand each other.

But it would be asking too much of peoples which have been colonized to expect them to recognize their moral debts to the colonizer. India has therefore hastened towards freedom with all the impetus which she received both from her modernization at British hands and from the lessons in liberalism and patriotism given her by the British. The last war accelerated the final steps towards complete independence. India and Pakistan, carved out of this single sub-continent, emerged in 1947, free States within the British Commonwealth of Nations. But the difficulties are immense. The intellectual races are not the military races. The brain is Bengali, but the sword is Sikh. And once the English have departed, who will protect the land? The chaos which followed the death of Aurungzeb is a warning. Finally, despite the religious resignation of the masses, what may not come in the wake of the infiltration of Soviet ideas? As always, when old problems are solved, new ones arise.

The Partition of China

China, in the nineteenth century, almost suffered the fate that befell India in the eighteenth. It is the very rhythm of Chinese history that the imperial lines, after three or four generations of men of ability, fall into decadence. Then the old empire, which the founders of dynasties periodically rebuild, dissolves again, and with it sink society, urban and rural economy, the very foundations of public morality, and even the age-old intellectual order. The decadence seems irremediable, and the chaos final. Often the foreigner seizes the opportunity to invade the territory and conquer a part; sometimes even, as in the thirteenth and seventeenth centuries, he subdues it altogether. Decades pass, sometimes a century or two, and then there reappears a new principle of internal reorganization. The foreigner is driven out or assimilated. The enormous resources of the Chinese soil, exploited by the most hard-working peasantry in the world, and by the most industrious and most commercially-minded urban population, make it possible to wipe out even the memory of previous invasion and devastation. The human anthill, having repaired its losses, hurls itself once more upon the neighbouring lands. Once more great China dominates one whole side of the planet.

This rhythm, which ought to be familiar to the historian of China, came as a surprise to nineteenth-century Westerners. At first they believed the Manchu empire to be stronger than it really was; afterwards they took the Chinese people to be weaker than was actually the case. This double misconception explains their mistakes. The Manchu family, which ascended the throne of Pekin in 1644 and kept it till 1912, was not exempt from the law which governs Chinese dynasties. After the death of the Emperor K'ien-long (1796), its degeneration was obvious and grew worse as time went on. As ill-luck would have it, this period of dynastic exhaustion, which led to the paralysis of the whole Chinese organism, corresponded to the era when the rest of the world, under the influence of the scientific spirit and of machinery, was being transformed. Hence, between China and the West, a time-lag opened up. In the seventeenth and eighteenth centuries, China had maintained herself almost on the European level, as was shown by the expulsion of the Dutch from Formosa and the retreat of the Russians at the Treaty of Kertchinsk. By about 1840, she found herself several centuries behind, seemingly medieval and indeed mummified.

The lead which Europe had thus gained over the rest of the world was truly extraordinary. Once before, but only once, in the great days of Greece, there had existed a similar inequality between Hellene and 'Barbarian'; but it had been much smaller. The future historian will write with astonishment of the fabulous period of the nineteenth century when, according to the old formula of the Pharaohs, Europe 'planted her frontiers wheresoever she pleased'. The white man landing on the shores of Asia appeared like a demi-god out of another universe. His situation was a little like that of the companions of Cortez and Pizarro whom the American Indians took for mythological characters. This phenomenon extended over the whole planet, but was nowhere more striking than in China, because of the ancient civilization of that country, which had suddenly fallen pitiably behind Western techniques.

In reality, China was most backward in relation to herself. The first Manchu emperors, such as K'ang-hi, had been open-minded, eager to be up to date, anxious for the Jesuits' instruction in contemporary science. What a contrast to their sorry nineteenth-century descendants who refused all contact with the 'Western Barbarians', persecuted Christianity and tried to force all European trade to pass through the ridiculous bottle-neck of the Hanist organization at Canton. Europe, represented by England, was bound to react in protest. It is a humiliating thought that it found no more honourable pretext

than the importation of opium. But the 'Opium War' and the
campaigns of 1858 and 1860 at least brought about the opening
up of China to international trade. Since the conflict had revealed the hopeless decadence, the bad faith and the stupidity of
the Manchu dynasty, it is strange that the Western Powers
should have consented to save it from the T'ai-p'ing, that is,
from the well-justified revolt of the Chinese people. True, these
revolts threatened the positions won by international trade,
notably around Shanghai. The Powers, therefore, helped the
Tartar dynasty to bring the Chinese nation beneath its yoke
again for nearly half a century (1864-1912). In fact, they found
it to their advantage to prolong Chinese decadence in this way,
and to maintain on the throne of Pekin, as on that of Constantinople, a 'Sick Man' incapable of resisting them. When the
first Sino-Japanese War in 1895 had finally proved the military
incapacity of the Manchus, they no longer hesitated, or rather
Imperial Germany and Tsarist Russia no longer hesitated.
Germany, in full peace time, seized Kiao-chao, the key to the
rich province of Shantung, in 1897; and Russia forced the
Chinese to surrender Port Arthur, the key to Manchuria, in
1898. England, for her part, in addition to Hong Kong which
had been hers since 1842, seemed to be reserving for herself,
like a second Egypt, the reversion of the Yang-tse valley. The
partition of China was gaining momentum. The Boxer insur-
rection, so easily suppressed, could only confirm the Westerners
in their belief that China was merely another Turkey.

What saved the independence of Asia then, was the rivalry
between the European Powers. Now that Europe, by her in
credible blunders, has fallen from her former hegemony, it
needs the historian's imagination to recall the time when she
was the mistress of the world. She destroyed with her own
hands her incomparable prestige. History will remember those
years 1890-1900 as having ostensibly marked Europe's zenith.
Ernest Lavisse then addressed his prophetic warning to the
masters of the hour: 'All strength gives out; the faculty of
leading history is not a permanent attribute. Europe, which
inherited it from Asia three thousand years ago, will perhaps
not always keep it.' But who listened to that warning? In the
Far East the Powers, which seemed to be collaborating for the

expansion of Europe, were preparing, on the contrary, to ruin it because each was really working against the others. All were feverishly striving after their own aggrandisement, in China as elsewhere, each seeking to safeguard itself against its rivals, each suspicious of the others hindering them in every way possible, and trying to raise the local population in revolt against them. A lunatic game that could end only in common disaster! History was repeating itself, on a vaster scale than ever. Just so, from the thirteenth century to the fifteenth, had the Maritime Powers then behaved—Venice, Pisa, and Genoa, responsible in their day for the defence of the West. Which of them had ever hesitated in their time to seek the temporary alliance of the Moslem, their common foe, against the other two? In the seventeenth century, did not the Dutch use every means, including stirring up the hatred of the Japanese and Chinese, to destroy the Portuguese empire? And did not England do the like against the Spanish empire? When has a united Europe ever existed against Asia?

The Ascent of the Rising Sun

The British government followed these historical precedents in 1904 by employing Japan to beat Russia. The issue was clear enough. The triumph of Russia over the only modernized Asiatic power might have been thought of as the consecration of white hegemony on this planet. A Japanese victory meant, willy-nilly, sooner or later, the revolt of Asia, the great revenge of the eastern races, the end of white domination, and the first withdrawal of Europe since the days of the *Conquistadors*. These considerations forced themselves on the attention of the least far-sighted on the morrow of the Russo-Japanese War. 'The day may come.' I wrote in 1924, 'when the action of the English in India, in urging on the Japanese armies against the Russians, will seem like that of the first emperors of Byzantium when they launched the Goths against the Western Empire.' That day—which even I myself did not believe so near—came, alas, in 1941! Not only did the Russo-Japanese War of 1904–5 destroy the legend of white invincibility, but it roused to fury a Japanese imperialism unbridled in ambition.

Japan's victory over Russia radically transformed the traditional setting of the Far Eastern Question. Since the end of the eighteenth century, it had been regarded as a problem of partitioning and colonizing Asia by the European Powers. After the Russo-Japanese War, the Eastern Question was Asia's revolt against her European masters. Whatever care Japan took—for the moment—to conceal from the European chancelleries that side of her victory, no one after Port Arthur could be blind to the significance of the deed. 'It was not Russia beaten by Japan, it was not the defeat of one power by another, it was something enormous and prodigious, the victory of one world over another, Asia's revenge for the age-long humiliations she had borne, the hope of the Eastern peoples beginning to dawn.'[1] At Tokyo, the university and the general staff resumed the programme of Japanese expansion, as it had been manifested in the sixteenth century before the 'introspection' of the Tokugawa period. Already Korea had been annexed, in accordance with the testament of Hideyoshi. In Indo-China, Siam, the only native state which had succeeded in maintaining its independence, began, as in the sixteenth century, to look towards the Rising Sun. In the Philippines the last followers of Aquinaldo were turning in the same direction, hoping one day to see the Japanese victors of Tsushima drive away those of Cavite.[2] In the East Indies the Malay aristocracy began to compare Dutch weakness with Japanese strength. In Tonkin, the Kodama report taught the French what they had henceforth to fear. And in Congress India many nationalists celebrated the victory, certainly not because the ally of the British Empire was victorious, but because European troops had recoiled before an Asiatic army.

China had remained neutral during the Russo-Japanese War; but the issue of the struggle decided her fate. On the eve of the conflict, the Powers seemed on the point of partitioning her. On the morrow of the Treaty of Portsmouth (1905) no one thought of it. Moreover, it was in China that the repercussion of the Japanese victories was greatest. They had proved that an Asiatic people, if it voluntarily Europeanized itself, could beat Europe. The Revolution of 1912 and the foundation of the Chinese Republic were the fruits of that

[1] The Author thinks of Russia as a European, not an Asiatic Power. T.P.

[2] An American victory in the Spanish-American War. T.P.

realization. The prime mover and theorist of the Revolution, Sun Yat Sen, was simply being logical when, during his last visit to Tokyo in 1924, he sought to federate China, Japan, and the Soviets into an Asiatic Holy League against the colonialism of the West.

Japan's Suicide

The Japanese military and naval clans had not the intelligence to grasp their opportunity. Two policies lay before them. They might accept the alliance of the young Chinese democracy and, having thus freed their hands on the continent, devote all their strength to the maritime struggle with the Anglo-Saxon world which their ambitions made inevitable. Or else, in order to have leave for continental aggrandisement, they might loyally maintain towards England that rôle of 'brilliant seconds' to which, on the whole, they owed their victory over Russia. They failed to choose, or rather they pursued at one and the same time towards China a continental policy of threats, territorial encroachments and brutalities which was to alienate that country irretrievably, and in the Pacific a policy of maritime and colonial imperialism which was to change into hostility the former Anglo-Saxon sympathy.

Behind the screen of her monarchy of divine origin, Japan had fallen back into complete feudal anarchy. From 1603 to 1862, the Shogunate of the Tokugawa had, by pitiless repression, checked feudalism and maintained absolutism. After the Restoration, the *tennô* of Meiji, Mutsuhito, the god come down to earth, had profited personally from a quasi-mythical prestige under cover of which the wisdom of the *genrô* had been able to pursue a moderate and skilful policy which had been crowned by the profitable English alliance (1866–1912). But when the generation of statesmen who had made the new Japan had followed him to the grave, the country found itself without stable guidance. As in the worst days of the fifteenth century, clans and coteries disputed the government. The army and the navy, rivals for influence, each had its own policy; worse still, each group of armies conducted its particular policy, seeking prestige and involving the country in enterprises which invariably led to war. It was thus that the Japanese nation found itself committed by a *fait accompli* to the occupation of Manchuria in 1931, the rupture with China in 1937, and war with the Anglo-Saxon Powers in 1941.

As in the sixteenth century, Japan had undertaken a task far beyond her strength. Like her German ally, she was committed to the madness of risking, nay provoking, war on two fronts. And what fronts! All China had to be occupied, 400 million people to be conquered, and to be kept beneath the yoke after conquest. All the Pacific, all the South Seas had to be controlled, all their archipelagos to be won and then defended, from Sumatra to the approaches to Pearl Harbour. The war in China in itself was to prove a discouraging, exhausting operation, so much so that a halt had repeatedly to be called. It resembled Napoleon's war in Spain, but on a fabulous scale as far as men and distances were concerned, with millions of guerillas. New forces are born through opposition to something. It was Napoleon's domination as much as Fichte's preaching which begat German patriotism. It was the Japanese aggression as much as the teaching of the Kuo-min-tang which finally resuscitated the patriotism of the Chinese.

To be sure, the Japanese retorted that their imperialism had always been supported and stimulated by one or other of the great European Powers. This is only too true, In 1905, they might have claimed that it was as soldiers of England that they drove the Russians from Port Arthur; in 1914, they acted as mandatories of the Allied Powers when they seized Kiao-Chao, and afterwards the German Pacific islands. In 1942 it was at the instigation of the Axis that they occupied Indo-China, the Philippines, and the East Indies, and threatened India and Australia. By stages, but always with the encouragement of part of Europe, and in order to assist one of the European *blocs*, they were expelling the Europeans from Asia.

China's Hour

The day of 2 September, 1945, which saw MacArthur come in the *Missouri* to receive the surrender of the imperial government in Tokyo Bay, put an end to this dream. But for all that, white hegemony has not been restored. The admirable Anglo-Saxon effort which, there as elsewhere, saved the world, could produce its full effect in the Pacific only because Chinese resistance on the continent was absorbing part of the Japanese forces. In the hour of victory the Anglo-Saxons loyally acknowledged their debt. The Chinese Republic ranked as one of the five main Powers of the United Nations and was even commissioned by the American friends of France to occupy half French Indo-China before France could take over.[1]

The observer cannot help noting how the march of history eludes man's forecast. The twentieth century, from its opening decade, proclaimed itself to shrewd observers as bound to witness the re-awakening of the peoples of eastern Asia. The first people likely to profit by this resurrection were obviously the Japanese. The Anglo-Saxons, it is true, who so far had had sole control of the Indian Ocean and the Pacific, might have opposed the appearance of this young rival and frustrated its effort at the outset. Instead, in the decisive years 1895–1905 they helped to arm and equip it; they supported it morally and materially. Japanese imperialism was in many respects their handiwork, until the day when, belatedly awake to the peril, they showed splendid energy in wiping the danger from the earth.

To-day the rank of great power from which Japan has just been deposed should pass legitimately to the Chinese Republic. No Asiatic state has deserved it more. By its antiquity, its wealth and the quality of its culture, the place which it has occupied in the history of civilization, its zest for work, and the profoundly humane character of its ideals, China is entitled to all respect. And what a mighty future is reserved for it! This country of over two million square miles and some 400 million inhabitants—a fifth of the population of the globe—can it be endowed by the United States in the coming decades with agricultural and industrial equipment? Knowing the resources of the Chinese sub-soil, and the amazing capabilities of the Chinese worker, as well as of the Chinese captain of industry

---

[1] It is interesting to observe that the territory in Indo-China assigned by the United States to Chinese occupation corresponds exactly to the zone held by the old Chinese Empire in that country from 111 B.C. to A.D. 939, the date at which the Annamite nation won its freedom. Similarly, as has already been said, the forbidden zone marked out by the Germans when they occupied France in 1940 corresponded to the frontiers of the Holy Roman Empire in 1610. So may maps which are apparently provisional and fortuitous be full of meaning for the historian.

and business-man, no one can doubt that this great Asiatic republic will one day become in its own sphere another United
States. Sinophils should therefore rejoice if America's plans for
equipping China as she formerly equipped Japan can be carried
out. And certainly no one would dream of drawing any analogy
between the land of the *Samuraï*, with its age-old militarism,
and the hard-working, peaceful Confucian democracy. Furthermore, the economic equipment of the 400 million Chinese could
for decades absorb the surplus production of America, prevent
the re-emergence of an unemployment problem from New York
to San Francisco, and provide a field of action for the enormous
industrial capacity of the United States.[1]

Just as the Americans, by their intervention in the affairs
of Indo-China, have seriously mortgaged the future in that
region, so have the British thought it their duty to give the
problem of the Levant a Pan-Arab solution whose form, if not
the principle applied, may one day bear them some curious
fruits. Colonel Lawrence, the Kipling of the Arab world, has
always appealed to British imagination and, no doubt, has never
been more alive than since his death. In June, 1945, his spirit
was at the back of British action in those dire 'Damascus days'
which (with the best will in the world) Frenchmen find hard to
put right out of mind. Nothing could be more legitimate than
the idea of an Arab League destined to revive in federal form
the Omayyad Caliphate of long ago. But the whole question is
whether the British were well advised to assist the Moslem
population in attacking the long-established position of another
Western power, and that power their ally France, just when she
was temporarily weakened. The procedure then adopted belongs to those liable, in these days of native nationalist movements, to be employed some day against their instigators.

To conclude this part of our Sum of History. In the eighteenth
and nineteenth centuries the West, thanks to the superiority of
its industrial and military technique, subjugated Asia. At the
same time it transformed her morally by its ideals. In the
twentieth century Asia has turned against the West firstly
the ideas taken over from Europe and then, on the battlefield,

---

[1] The author, of course, wrote this before recent (1950) developments in
China. T.P.

the armament itself which she had borrowed from Europe and America. The introduction of European techniques into Asia has resulted in the revolt of Asia against Europe. The East has shown itself a rebel against European tutelage precisely in the degree to which those subcontinents were themselves Europeanized.

The year 1900, the zenith of total 'white' hegemony, is a time long gone, already fabulously far away. In the intervening years, what centuries have passed! By its frenzy of materialism, the West, as Lavisse foresaw, has lost its ancient leadership. It has even been near to extinction and been saved on the very brink of the gulf only by Hitler's attack on Russia and the Japanese onslaught on America, which form two other different Europes, almost two new planets. And these are the two new worlds which henceforth control us. As for Asia, once more her hour has come.

V.

AT THE SOURCE OF INVASIONS

Nomad and Settler

ATTILA, Genghis Khan, Tamerlane . . . names every school-boy knows. The narratives of Western chroniclers and Chinese or Persian annalists have made them familiar figures. They emerge, these great barbarians, in the midst of civilization. And suddenly, within a few years, they turn the Roman or the Persian or the Chinese world into a heap of ruins. Their coming, their motives, their disappearance seem inexplicable, so much so that some historians almost adopt the judgment of ancient authors who saw in them the scourge of God, men sent for the chastisement of the old civilizations.

But never can it be said more truly that men are the children of their environment, immediately 'transparent' in their motives and their behaviour once their setting is known. These squat and stunted bodies, unconquerable after surviving the conditions of their homeland, were the product of the steppes. The biting winds of the high plateaux, the excessive cold and the torrid heat, modelled these faces with their slit-like eyes, prominent cheek-bones and thin hair, and toughened those gnarled trunks. Pastoral life, governed by the movements of flocks. imposed nomadic habits upon them, and the facts of nomad economy determined their relationship to sedentary peoples; it was alternately one of timid borrowing and of sanguinary raids.

Moreover, the three or four great Asiatic nomads who suddenly arose to tear up the web of Western history appear exceptional only because of our ignorance. As against three of them who have had this amazing chance of becoming the conquerors of the world, how many Attilas and Genghis Khans failed, or rather succeeded only in establishing empires limited to one quarter of Asia, from Siberia to the Yellow River, from the Altaï Mountains to Persia? This is still an adventure of some magnitude. One is tempted to conjure up a picture of the multitude of great barbarians on their march across ten centuries of history, as they move from the frontiers of China to those of our West. . .

But this is not the root of the matter. The ancient world knew many varieties of invading 'barbarians', many that is, who were so termed by neighbouring civilizations. For long, the Celts were 'barbarians' to the Romans, the Teutons to Gaul, and the Slavs to the Teutons. Similarly, the future South China long remained a 'barbarian' land in the eyes of the original China of the Yellow River. But in these cases the land of the 'barbarian' was just as suitable for agricultural life as that of their invaded neighbour; the people living there, however backward they might be, were gradually won over to the other, the 'civilized' mode of existence, so that after the peak of the Middle Ages almost the whole of our Europe, Hither Asia, Persia, India, and China had long reached roughly the same stage of material civilization.

However, a considerable zone had been by-passed. This was the broad belt stretching along the centre and north of Eurasia, from the frontier of Manchuria to Budapest, the zone of the steppes together with the Siberian forest on its northern border. There, geographical conditions allowed agricultural life to develop only in a few isolated spots, and condemned the population to the endless pursuit of a pastoral life, a nomadic life which the rest of mankind had known thousands of years earlier, at the end of the Neolithic Age. Certain of these tribes, those of the forest zone, even remained at the cultural stage of the Magdalenian hunters. The zone of steppes and forests thus remained a reservoir of barbarism, not indeed because the peoples living there were inferior to others, but because it perpetuated conditions of existence which had long since been left behind everywhere else.

The survival of these tribes who remained at the pastoral stage when the rest of Asia had long since arrived at the advanced agricultural stage, has been very largely responsible for the drama of the history here considered. It produced a kind of chronological rift or time-lag between neighbouring peoples. Men of the second millenium B.C. were living, as it were, side by side with men of the twelfth century A.D. To pass from one to the other, it was merely necessary to come down from Outer

Mongolia to Pekin, or to go from the Kirghiz steppe to Ispahan. The difference was extreme, and filled with danger. For the sedentary peoples of China, Persia or Europe, the Hun, the Turcoman and the Mongol were savages who had to be intimidated by occasional military expeditions, amused with glass beads and titles, and kept at a respectful distance from cultivated lands. As for the nomads, their feelings may be guessed. In the years when drought withered the grass of the steppe the poor Turco-Mongolian herdsmen wandered from one dried-up oasis to another until they came to the edge of the sown land, to the gates of Petchili or Transoxiana; there they gazed in stupefaction at the miracle of settled civilization, the abundant crops, the village barns swollen with grain, the luxury of the towns. This miracle, or rather the secret of this miracle, namely the patient labour needed to build up this civilization, the Hun could not understand. If he was attracted, it was as the wolf—his totem—is attracted when in time of snow he ventures near farms and catches sight of his prey on the other side of the fence. The nomad's instinctive reaction was the same: to break in by surprise, to pillage, and make off with his plunder.

The survival of pastoral and hunting peoples side by side with agricultural ones, the development of agricultural societies growing increasingly rich within sight of peoples still at the pastoral stage and suffering the terrible famine-crises which the life of the steppes involves in time of drought, thus added to a most striking economic contrast a social contrast which was often most cruel. This question of human geography became a social question. The feelings of the settler and of the nomad towards each other were, in Marxist parlance, respectively those of capitalists and proletarians enclosed within the same modern city. The agricultural societies which exploited the good yellow earth of north China, or the gardens of Persia, or the rich black earth of Kiev, were surrounded by a zone of poor pasture, in which climatic conditions were often forbidding, and where about every tenth year the oases dried up, the grass withered, and the beasts died—whereupon the nomads themselves died with them.

In these conditions, the nomads' periodical assault upon the cultivated lands was a law of nature. Moreover, the nomads, whether Turks or Mongols, were intelligent, sensible, practical people, disciplined by the hard realities of their environment, and naturally prepared to obey orders. When the sedentary societies, often already decadent, gave way before the shock of their attack, the nomad entered their cities and, as soon as the preliminary period of slaughter was over, easily took the place of the rulers he had overthrown. Unabashed, he seated himself upon the most venerable of thrones. Behold him Great Khan of China, King of Persia, Emperor of the Indies, Sultan of Roum. Then he adapts himself. At Pekin he becomes half-Chinese, at Ispahan or Rei half-Persian.

But was destiny fixed thereby, and conciliation assured between the steppe and the sown? Not at all. The inexorable laws of human geography continued to operate. If the Khan, however Chinese or Persian he had become, was not eliminated by some native reaction, then further famished hordes from the depths of the steppes appeared at the gates, and, seeing in their parvenu cousin simply a Tadjik or a Tobghatch—a Persian or a Chinese—would repeat the same process, this time at his expense.

Why did this adventure almost always succeed, and the same rhythm recur for thirteen centuries—for it was thirteen hundred years from the entry of the Huns into Lo-yang to the entry of the Manchus into Pekin? Because, throughout this time, the nomad, although very backward in material culture, possessed one enormous military advantage: he was the mounted archer. An incredibly mobile cavalry of archers formed the 'technical arm' which gave him a superiority over the settler almost equal to that given by artillery in modern times to Europe over the rest of the world. True, neither the Chinese nor the Persians were ignorant of this arm. From the third century B.C. the Chinese had modified their costume to adapt it to cavalry. As for Persia, it had known since Parthian days the power of a flight of arrows launched by a whirlwind charge of horsemen who then turned and galloped away. But neither Chinese nor Persians, nor Russians, nor Poles, nor Hungarians could match the Mongols in this. Trained from infancy to run down deer at full gallop in the vastness of the steppes; accustomed to lie in ambush patient and invisible; expert in all those ruses of the hunter upon which his food and therefore his life often depended, they were invincible. And this not because they often closed with their enemy, but on the contrary because, as soon as they had launched a surprise attack on him, they disappeared and then re-appeared, to hound him without letting him come to grips, to harass and exhaust him, and finally to overwhelm him when he was worn out, like an animal at bay. The mobility and bewildering ubiquity of that cavalry, when handled by a Djebe or a Subötei (the two famous strategists of Genghis Khan), made of it an almost scientific weapon. Plan Carpin and Rubrouck, who saw it manœuvre, noted particularly this decisive technical superiority.

The phalanx and the legion passed away because they depended on the political constitution of Macedonia or Rome and were the methodical products of states with which they were born, lived, and ceased to be. The mounted archer of the steppes, however, reigned over Eurasia for thirteen centuries, because he was the spontaneous creation of the landscape itself, the child of hunger and want, the nomads' sole means of rescue if they did not want to perish entirely of hunger in famine-years. Genghis Khan later succeeded in conquering the world because as an orphan he had been abandoned on the Kerulen prairie, and he and his young brother Djötchi the Tiger had managed to kill enough game each day to keep themselves from dying of starvation. The arrow of the mounted archer who appeared, opened fire, and disappeared again was in ancient times and in the Middle Ages a kind of 'indirect fire', almost as effective and demoralizing in its day as a modern artillery bombardment.

Why did that superiority come to an end? Why, after the sixteenth century, did the nomad no longer prevail against the settlers? Just because he was met by artillery. At one stroke, the settlers thus gained superiority which reversed their age-long relationship. The cannonade with which Ivan the Terrible scattered the last descendants of the Golden Horde, and the gunfire by which the Chinese Emperor K'ang-hi subdued the Kalmucks, marked the end of an era in world history. For the first time, but also for all time, the superiority in military technique had changed sides. Civilization had become stronger than Barbarism. In a few hours the nomad's traditional superiority vanished into a past that seemed like a dream, and the Kalmuck archers whom Alexander I, the romantic, still used against Napoleon on the battlefields of 1807, seemed as out-of-date as a phantom host of Magdalenian hunters.

The Direction of the Invasions

What directions did the invasions of the barbarians of Upper Asia take? From remotest antiquity to the eighteenth century, the movement of peoples in this region, in both invasions and migrations, took place almost always from north to south, from the steppe-zone to the zone of the cultivated lands. There was the invasion of the Cimmerians and Scythians to the south of the Caucasus, towards Asia Minor, Urartu and Media in the seventh century B.C., reported by Herodotus. There were the descents of the Indo-Scythians from the Gobi Desert into Bactria in the second century B.C., and then into India in the first century. Then the onslaught of the Hiong-nu—the Huns of the Chinese historians—and of the Sien-pei of the Gobi upon North China in the fourth century A.D. There was the invasion of the Tabghatch, from the same area and directed towards the same goal, in the fifth. The Hephthalite Huns' invasion of Bactria and then the Punjab in the same fifth century. Still in the fifth century, the invasion of the Balkans, of Gaul and Italy, by Attila's Huns. The descent of the Turks proper—the Tu-Kiu of Chinese inscriptions—from Mongolia into the country which they transformed into Western Turkestan in the sixth century, and their ceaseless inroads across the Chinese frontier in the seventh century. The establishment of the Khitaï, Mongolians by race, at Pekin in the tenth century. At the end of this tenth century, the occupation of Eastern Persia by the Ghaznavid Turks. The invasion of the Arab empire by the Seljukian Turks in the middle of the eleventh century. The conquest of North China by the Djurtchet or Kin, the 'Golden Kings' of the Tungus race, in the twelfth century. The conquest of China, Persia, and Russia by Genghis Khan's Mongols in the thirteenth century. The conquest of Persia by Tamerlane at the end of the fourteenth century, and of India by the Tamurids in the sixteenth. The conquest of China by the Manchus in the seventeenth. Such is the sum of the history of invasions which, throughout the course of some two thousand five hundred years, followed each other with impressive regularity in a North-South direction.

Were there any movements in the opposite direction in the same zone? Attempts, at least, in the shape of punitive and preventive expeditions, such as: the expedition of Darius into European Scythia, the Chinese expeditions into Mongolia, notably under Han Wu-ti at the end of the second century B.C., then under T'ai-tsong, of the T'and dynasty, at the beginning of the second century A.D., afterwards under the Ming Emperor Yung-lo at the beginning of the fifteenth, and finally under the Manchu emperors K'ang-hi and K'ien-lung at the end of the seventeenth and in the eighteenth centuries. Similarly, further West, we may add the repressive expeditions of the Abbasid Caliphs of Baghdad into Transoxania in the eighth century, of the Samanid emirs[1] to Chu and the Ili in the tenth, of Tamerlane to Mogholistan in the fourteenth, of the Persian kings Shah Abbas and Nadir Shah against the Uzbeks in the seventeenth and eighteenth. But all these expeditions from south to north had very markedly a preventive character. They were countermeasures comparable to the Roman campaigns in Cisalpine (and later Transalpine) Gaul. What emerges is the law of the 'descent' of invasions from North to South.

But turning to the south of the Mediterranean zone, we see exactly the opposite. Here the invasions started in the dry steppes of the Hedjaz and more generally in western Arabia or southern Morocco, and 'ascended' towards the north. Such were the invasions of Syria and Babylonia by the Amorites and Arameans in remote antiquity; the penetration by the Nabateans and afterwards the Ghassanid Arabs into Græco-Roman Syria, and by the Lakhmids into Sassanid Babylonia; such, too, was the invasion of Syria and Mesopotamia by the Islamic Arabs in the years 534–640. And such, finally, was the onrush of the Almoravids and afterwards the Almohades of the Maghreb upon Spain in the eleventh and twelfth centuries.

Can this double movement of invasions be attributed to ethnic reasons? Is there among the northern races on the one hand—that is, among the tall blond barbarians of the Teutonic

[1] Persian princes of Bokhara and Samarkand (903–990).

or Scythian zone in Europe, and the Turco-Mongols and Tunguses of the Altaïc zone in Asia—a 'bump' of conquest, something which marks them out and consecrates them for this rôle? The theories of Gobineau claimed this for the European barbarians; Léon Cahun came near believing it of his beloved Mongols, and perhaps some Japanese theorists have dreamt of creating a sort of neo-Genghis-Khanism of this kind! On the other hand, at least one contemporary archaeologist seems inclined to ascribe to the same 'virtue' the south–north invasions of the Arabs, and to see a mysterious, pre-ordained harmony uniting 'the Bedouin, those Vikings of the desert, with the Vikings, those Bedouin of the sea.'

This qualitative vision of history is not devoid of aesthetic charm. But the mere fact that the invasions were the work of races so different should put us on our guard against the racial explanation. In the zone of the northern steppes, who could be more unlike than the Scythians and the Huns? The Greek vases from the Crimea give us detailed anthropological documentation about the Scythians. They were the brawny Nordic warriors whom we meet again in Roman representations of the Gauls, Germans or Dacians. In contrast to this, the Chinese annalists and artists have left us portraits of the Hiong-nu which all resolve themselves into the portrait of Attila by Jornandès: the Hun-type. Moreover, linguists unanimously class the Hiong-nu among the Altaïc peoples, their language being either proto-Mongolian or more probably proto-Turkish, while the philologists tell us that the Scythians spoke a Persian dialect.

And yet, compare Herodotus with the Chinese historians: what the former says of Scythian life, the latter repeat almost word for word about the way of life of the Huns. These headhunters, with their chariots and their collapsible *yurts*, wandered with their flocks and herds, lived on meat and milk foods, took flight when attacked and attacked as soon as their enemies' vigilance relaxed; they thus appear to be, despite racial differences, at the same cultural stage, namely the pastoral. And the Arab invaders who came from the south belonged to the same pastoral stage. Such is the fact of human geography which in Asia governs the whole history of invasions.

Pastoral life, based on periodical movements of flocks, kept man at the nomad stage, a very inferior level, even though the races concerned might have been well endowed (as witness such figures as Genghis Khan or Kublai). Hence such practices as mass funeral sacrifices, abolished in Mesopotamia soon after the period of Queen Shubad of Ur (about 3000 B.C.), and in China shortly after the date of the royal tombs at Ngan-yang (about 1300–1200 B.C.), continued among the Scythians till the time of Herodotus, and among the Mongols until after the death of Genghis Khan (A.D. 1227). The cause of the invasions, as shown, is precisely the time-lag which placed in juxtaposition men who in some respects had remained in the third millenium B.C. and others who were relatively modern peoples—the steppes having preserved in Upper Asia the cultural conditions of the Neolithic Age while the southern lands had long since been at the most advanced level.

Does Climatic Rhythm govern Invasions?

Now, if the steppe can often feed passably well the nomad's flocks, and therefore the nomad himself, it also sometimes does not feed them well enough. For is there not a perpetual compromise between the good lands and the desert; is there not, speaking in terms of palæogeography, a transition from tropical to desert conditions? Dry years kill off the flocks, lead to famine, and force the nomad to seek his sustenance on the edge of the cultivated lands. Starting from this fact, Owen Lattimore, the American geographer, has attempted to discover beneath the periodical return of the Turco-Mongolian invasions of China the rhythm of the dry periods in the Mongolian lands. In that case the law of invasions would be a hygrometric law depending on rainfall. It is a tempting theory. But unfortunately, Chinese historians have been careful to show the political conditions at the court of China which have favoured, or one might say brought on, invasions. And it cannot be denied that these political conditions have frequently produced a kind of suction southwards of the nomads, disturbing the balance between their latent pressure and the normal resistance of the sedentary empires. The Tsin of the House of Sseu-ma at the beginning of the fourth century A.D., the Sung of the beginning of the twelfth, the Ming of 1644 were dynasties in decay, sometimes (as with the Tsin and the Ming) in decomposition, shoddy replicas of Honorius and Arcadius, who collapsed miserably before the flick of the nomad's finger. With men who were still living at the level of the third millenium B.C. prowling to the north of the Great Wall, and with the ultra-civilized denizens of the Sung court in 1125 (to quote only that one example) to the south, it only needed a momentary weakening of the defences for the Wall to give way. If, as Owen Lattimore claims, the climatic rhythm has here influenced history, it has done so only when conditions permitted it—just as the river banks may be flooded when the watch on the Yellow River relaxes its vigilance.

The Régime of Periodical Inroads and the Accident of Conquest

Nomadism, then, gave the Turco-Mongols clear superiority over the settled folk. The nomad, in the shape of the mounted archer, had in his favour mobility and almost ubiquity. His defeats did not matter, because he simply escaped; to turn them into disaster the Chinese legions would have had to chase him from the other side of the Gobi Desert to the Orkhon and the Kerulen where he had left his wealth, that is, his flocks and herds. In the eighth century a Turkish khan had been tempted to build on the Orkhon a fine walled capital, after the Chinese fashion. 'Do nothing of the kind,' said his old counsellor Tonuquq, 'As things are, the possibility of retreating indefinitely before the Chinese renders you immune from capture. If you shut yourself up behind walls, you are lost.' Conversely, in 1226 Genghis Khan's entourage were trying to persuade him to put off the war against the Tangut and employed the argument that the Tangut were pinned down by their urban way of life; the nomads would therefore always know where to find them when they wished to attack.

Because of this, a settled people was always vulnerable; and the system of raids was almost certain to succeed. Even if it was checked in the end, an incursion could open with a bout of joyous plundering. If, by chance, there happened to be some palace or barracks revolution in China, and the frontier was therefore thinly held, the conquest of a town, a province, or the whole empire would follow. This is the true law of Sino-

Mongolian relations. If the Chinese annals are examined closely, the Turco-Mongolian raids are a *leit-motiv* which, save at the zenith of the Han and T'ang periods, recurs almost every ten years. As long as the dynasty remained strong, these raids remained mere raids, pinpricks on the body of the immense empire. If the organism was sick, it meant death.

To sum up, the periodical raid (with corresponding counter-raids on the part of the settlers) was the norm of the relations between Turco-Mongols and Chinese. Real invasion and conquest were only an exceptional accident, about one chance in a hundred, often disconcerting the conquerors themselves. Such a case occurred in the tenth century, when the Khitaï Mongols, having seized the Chinese capital K'ai-fong by surprise, had no idea what to do with it and withdrew crestfallen.

Federates and Ripuarians

A special case was provided by the federate Tartars, established as settlers or as auxiliary troops along the line of the Great Wall on the Sino-Hunnish frontier. These Hunnish kinglets were vassals of China and possessed a smattering of Chinese culture; they had been provided with Chinese titles and set to govern their encampments on the Ordos, the Suei-yuan and the Chakhary, in Inner Mongolia proper, on behalf of the Empire. The evidence suggests that they were infinitely weaker than the Turco-Mongolian khans of Outer Mongolia who reigned over the Orkhon, the Tula, and the Kerulen. In reality, they often proved infinitely more dangerous, just because they had frequented the Chinese court, knew all its weaknesses, and had sources of information about conditions there, and because politicans, malcontents and traitors turned to them. The case of Lieu Sung, at the beginning of the fourth century A.D., is typical. It resembles that of so many Teutonic chiefs who about the same time had sojourned at the court of the Constantines or the Theodosii, and also that of so many Turkish chiefs who had lived at the court of Baghdad; just as the inroads of the federate Huns to the south of the Great Wall recall the growing encroachments of the Ghaznevids and Seljuks in Persia. When the federates did not themselves force the Great Wall of which they formed the outer guard, they opened its gates to the hordes of the North. Such was the case of the Ongut Turks (the White Tartars of the Chinese historians) who, after 1206, began to hand over the marches of Shan-si to Genghis Khan.

But Genghis Khan is an exception, since under his leadership the Mongols achieved a complete 'barbarian' conquest of Chinese soil, a thing which happened only twice all told, first with them and four centuries later with the Manchus. Usually the barbarian empires, masters of the vast steppes of the North, failed in their attempts to get possession of China; yet, where they had just failed, a few broken tribes succeeded. It was not the great Hiong-nu *chan yu*, masters of all Mongolia about the beginning of the Christian era, who overthrew the ancient Chinese Empire, but the federate Hun kinglets of whom we have just spoken. Likewise, the China of the T'ang in the tenth century was succeeded neither by the imperial T'u-kiu who were the terror of the land in the seventh century, nor by the Urigur Turks who had rather disdainfully protected it in the eighth, but by the petty tribe of the Cha-t'o Turks, established as frontier guards on the Ordos. Again, further west, the first conquest of eastern Persia by the Turkish race was not achieved by the Western T'u-kiu who had given so much trouble to Khosroes in the sixth century, but long afterwards, about the year 1000, by a little band of Ghaznavid mercenaries, who had formerly been praetorians in the service of the Emirs of Saman. Finally, the lasting occupation of the whole of Persia by the Turks, which was to stretch over four hundred and fifty years (1050–1500), was the achievement of the little Oghuz clan of the Seljuks, whom these same Ghaznavids had admitted into Transoxania as auxiliaries.

The second law at work here is undoubtedly indicated by the fact that the federate Tartars, placed at the geographical meeting-point of steppe and ploughland—thus at the cultural meeting-point of pastoral and of settled life—enjoyed unforeseen advantages. The barbarian at the city-gates soon became, whenever circumstances favoured him, the barbarian within the city; and there was no city, ancient or modern, which could for long resist him.

The Herdsmen of the Steppes and the Forest-Dwellers

Against the nomad herdsmen of the steppes, the settled farmers could have recourse to the trappers of the forests, who dwelt in the Siberian *taïga* or the Manchurian forest beyond the Mongolian steppe. Raschid-ed-Din has recorded that just as the Chinaman and the Persian despised the Turco-Mongolian herdsman as a barbarian so did the herdsman in his turn despise the forest-dweller as a savage. The farmer's appeal to the hunter could therefore make use of the forest-dweller's rancour against his hereditary enemy and immediate neighbour, the nomad. And sometimes this diversion succeeded. Thus in 840 the powerful Urigur Turkish empire of the Orkhon was overthrown by the obscure Kirghiz of the upper Yenisei. But to call in these hunters remained dangerous. In order to cope with the Khitaï of the Chakhary, the Sung dynasty—perhaps the most refined of the Chinese imperial houses—appealed to the Djurtchet, that is to the Tungus trappers of the Manchurian forest. The Djurtchet, about 1120, soon shattered the Khitaï who had fallen victim to Chinese refinement; but less than ten years afterwards they conquered all north China from the unlucky Sung. In their turn, the descendants of the Djurtchet, now known as the Kin, called in the half-nomad, half-forest Mongols of Mount Kenteï against the Tartars of the Eastern Gobi. The result, after twenty years, was the conquest of Pekin by the Mongol chief—Genghis Khan—in 1215.

The Steppe and the Sown

What were the consequences of the conquest of the plough-lands by the nomads? From the economic point of view, they are immediately obvious. In fourth-century North China, under the domination of the Huns, the ploughlands reverted to heathlands. About the middle of the century, the lower valley of the Wei, that is, the district around the former capital Sin-gan-fu, was so depopulated and cultivation so far abandoned that the villages were a prey to tigers and wolf-packs. To get rid of these unwelcome guests, the peasants appealed to the Hun chief who had taken the place of the Son of Heaven. He refused to intervene, since the invasion by weeds and heaths and by the animals of the steppe or the bush probably seemed to him the very proof of his own triumph.

The suppression, or at least the systematic withdrawal, of agriculture through the shrinkage of the ploughlands and the massacre or expulsion of the peasants was, moreover, one of the aims which the nomad conqueror pursued fairly methodically. It resembled the systematic devastation of Khorassan and Afghanistan by Genghis Khan and Tolui, in 1220–1221, reported by Djuwaynî and Raschid-ed-Din; and the destruction of Seistan by Tamerlane in 1384, reported by Sherif-ed-Din or Arabshah. Towns razed to the ground; rural populations systematically exterminated; and all carried out with a patience and a thoroughness that had nothing in common with the fury of a sudden sack. Trees sawn off. Canals blocked up or diverted into marshes. Wells filled in as completely as possible or permanently poisoned. Granaries and stocks of seed set on fire. The earth had been slaughtered and the waterways put to death. To understand the sometimes irreparable results of that work, one should see Sar-otar, a town in Seistan which was destroyed by Tamerlane in 1384. Where once a fertile oasis stretched, nothing was left but dismantled walls, upon which the sand-dunes were steadily closing in. It was a landscape of the moon. This 'death of the earth' is a poignant chapter to which the Mongol invasions contributed most effectively in the dry steppe lands.

Whole provinces of China ran great danger of suffering a similar fate. When Genghis Khan conquered Kan-su his generals pointed out to him that they did not know what to do with all these cultivated lands; that in these circumstances the conquest was useless. It would be best, they said, to massacre all the peasant population, as in Eastern Persia, so that the fields, left fallow, could revert to the steppe and to the dignity of pasturage. This proposal, however disastrous it may seem to us, was inspired only by considerations of a wise economy—a nomad economy, of course—and directed to the greatest benefit of the Mongol flocks. The project, we are told, was abandoned only because of the opposition of the wise counsellor Ye-liu Ch'ou T'sai; but it had almost been put into effect. Yet the Mongols deserve no more blame than the redskins who, having by a surprise attack become masters of some English settlement or Canadian village, could do nothing with it but set it on fire, in order that the clearing on which it stood might once again become part of their forest. The Mongol destroyed because he had no conception of rural economy, still less of forest economy. The case becomes striking when it is a question of a statesman as self-possessed, as balanced, and as full of common-sense as Genghis Khan. Yet, he was willing to listen to Ye-liu Ch'ou T'sai's explanation of the value of agriculture when his empire also included farming communities. Again, he listened with no less interest to the Moslem Mahmoûd Yalawatch when this scholar revealed to him, as the *Secret History* naively put it, 'the manner of governing towns'.

The lesson was grasped especially by the Great Khan's grand-son Kublai, whose reign (1259–1294) was occupied in rebuild-ing or maintaining what his great ancestor had or would have destroyed. It was also understood by the greatest of the Genghis-Khanids of Persia, the Ilkhan Ghazan (1295–1304), the friend and protector of the historian Raschid-ed-Din. Together they strove to restore the land of Persia, which had been destroyed by the crushing blows of 1221. Raschid-ed-Din, though he was a court writer and the official Genghis-Khanid annalist, could not refrain from drawing a frightful picture of the situation against which his master attempted to struggle. To the reader, the impoverishment of Mongolian Persia seems irremediable. The Tadjik peasants, decimated by the first waves of invasion, and afterwards mercilessly ground down by the Mongolian lords, had deserted the land, which lay fallow. No more settlers could be found willing to risk the loss of all their possessions at the first change of governor. Raschid-ed-Din hoped that the measures of restoration commanded by Ghazan would repopulate the countryside. Little did he foresee the coming of Tamerlane a century later, who by himself was worse than all the Genghis-Khanids. The traveller through the Persian countryside to-day still hears it cry out aloud against the cruelty of men.

After the 'Great Invasions of the Far East,' the Sino-Hun society of the fourth century in North China offered a sorry spectacle. Atrocious habits, a series of parricides and fratricides, a riot of treasons and refinements of perfidy—nothing was lacking to remind us of the darkest tales of Merovingian times. Admittedly, the same could not be said of the Sino-Mongolian society of the thirteenth century, presided over by the great Kublai and described to us by Western travellers like Marco Polo and Odoric de Pordonone. But as for the Sino-Mongolian or Yuan dynasty itself, it must be confessed that (with the exception of Kublai) no imperial Chinese dynasty has been more insignificant. Its last princes, ruined by debauchery and utterly lacking in will-power, sought to redeem their vices by a bigotry worthy of the Lamas; official Chinese history makes this an additional count against them. Above all, they quarrelled incessantly among themselves, ruining in a few years the imposing administrative façade which, under Kublai, had aroused the admiration of Marco Polo.

The fundamental trouble in China, as in the Khanate of Djagataï (i.e. Turkestan in the Mongol period), the Qiptchaq (or Golden Horde, then in South Russia), and even Persia, was that the Genghis-Khanids had not managed to rise to the Chinese or Persian notion of the State, that is, of the undivided State. Cousin fought with cousin, and brother with brother, to partition the kingdoms which had fallen into their hands, just as their ancestors had partitioned their family patch of meadowland. As a result of regarding the Chinese or Persian State as a collective family property, to a share of which each member of the family was entitled, and ruthlessly destroying one another to get it, the grandsons of Kublai ended in 1368 by being driven from China; and in 1335 the descendants of Hulagu disappeared from Persia,—yet another dynasty that had thus committed suicide.

Among other damage wrought by the nomad conquest was the arrest of the normal development of the peasant countries. According to Serge Elisséeff, even when China had been delivered from the Mongols it did not recover its creative spontaneity for a long time. After the shock of nomad rule, it showed under the Ming a distrust of itself and of the outside world, a timidity, a withdrawal, a kind of weariness which for five centuries did not allow more than mere imitation of times past. As for Russia, the rule of the Mongols led to Tsarism and to the adoption of Asiatic features of which it had not yet been cured by 1914 or 1917.

The Mongol Unification

With this damage done by the invading nomads went certain advantages. The unification of almost the whole of Asia by the Mongols re-opened the great transcontinental roads, put China and Persia in contact with each other, and also Christianity with the Far East. Chinese and Persian painting met and influenced one another. Marco Polo learnt the name of Buddha Çâkyamouni—Sagramoni Borcan; and there were Catholic archbishops at Pekin. The storm, when it broke down the walls which surrounded the enclosed gardens and uprooted the trees, also carried the seed of flowers from one garden to the other. The *orbis Mongolicus* offered in this respect something of the same advantages as the *orbis Romanus*. And it took the discovery of the Cape of Good Hope and of America to give the world an age worthy in this respect of the age of Marco Polo.

Across the ruins made by the Mongols, there passed the Mongol road. Unhappily, at the end of about sixty years, this road was closed again for nearly five centuries when Tamerlane appeared as the living antithesis of men like Hulagu and Kublai, These last had in a few decades, and thanks above all to their Buddhist or Christian sympathies, raised themselves out of their native barbarism to complete civilization. Tamerlane, on the other hand, was the civilized man turned by religious fanaticism and murderous nationalism into an utter barbarian. It was a return to barbarism masked by the pretext of Moslem piety; frightful massacres ordered in obedience to an abstract ideology, and in the name of a sacred mission; a mental deformity whose equivalent we have known in our own century, and which by comparison almost makes primitive savagery seem attractive.

Migrations or Invasions?

Hitherto we have not distinguished between migrations and invasions. Nevertheless the distinction is called for. Of migrations, properly so called, Upper Asia has sent forth fewer than is generally believed. The Hun invasions of the fourth century

A.D. did not transform the racial and linguistic appearance of
North China because they were affairs of petty broken tribes,
of ripuarian Huns and frontier-guards, of raiders numerically
of little importance and soon absorbed by the seething Chinese
masses. It is a fact no less significant that the Genghis-Khanid
conquest itself did not succeed in turning into Mongols the
inhabitants of Shen-si, Chan-si, and Ho-pei, despite the establishment of the ancestors of the Ordos and the Chakar on the
northern border of these three provinces. In fact, the conquests
of the Genghis-Khanids were too immense to have had lasting
or at least visible demographic consequences. The Mongolian
tribes, which had always been rather thinly scattered because
of the poverty of the steppes, were so overtaxed by the sudden
necessity of furnishing political and military rulers for China
and Persia, Turkestan and Russia, that they disappeared in the
process. On the testimony of Raschid-ed-Din, it is clear that
Mongolian Russia, the Khanate of Qiptchaq, received in the
thirteenth century only about 4000 authentic Mongols, all the
rest of the armies of Baty and Berké[1] being formed of Turkish
soldiers. Even in 'Mogholistan', the former Kara-Khitaï empire
which had become the *oulous* of Djagatai (or Turkestan), the
racial basis remained Turkish.

Similarly in Persia, the successive Turkish conquests had not
been able to rob the country of its character, and this despite
its comparative sparsity of population; the conquerors never
represented more than petty Turcoman clans. In the eleventh
century, the Seljukian Turks had been almost absorbed there
by the indigenous element or at least had become very profoundly Persian. If there was a partial acceptance of Turkish
habits in certain districts, e.g. in Azerbeidjan, it was because
the prairie-steppes of that region lent themselves better than the
gardens of Reï Ispahan or Shiraz to the pasturing of flocks. In
fact, it was in Azerbeidjan that the last Seljuks established themselves in the twelfth century and the Genghis-Khanid *ilkhans* in
the thirteenth. The partial acceptance of Turkish civilization
there was doubtless due less to political conquest by the great
Turco-Mongolian dynasties than to the slow, insensible, and
for long almost invisible penetration by obscure and often
anonymous clans, a creeping advance of the 'black tents' which

---

[1] Grandsons of Genghis Khan and founders of the Mongol Khanite of South
Russia. T.P.

may still be seen to-day as they follow the flocks throughout that region.

Of the conquests which the Seljuk Turks prized most, not one eventually turned Turk. Persia remained Persian and Syria Arab. On the other hand, beyond the bridge which Persia afforded, it was—quite unpredictably—the old Greek or Græco-Armenian land of Anatolia [Asia Minor] which became Turcoman. Here may be seen the difference between conquest and settlement. But perhaps the Turkish settlement in Anatolia succeeded only because the plateau, in all its central part, was already a steppe and thus naturally inclined towards Turkestan.

The migrations properly so-called which took place in Upper Asia must be thought of as movements which modified the ethnic and linguistic aspect of the country. Surely then they did not include the invasions of farm lands by the nomads, but only the movements of the nomads among themselves? An example occurred from the thirteenth century onwards in the region of the Orkhon and the district of Kobdo in Outer Mongolia, as well as in Inner Mongolia proper. All these territories were throughout the peak of the Middle Ages specifically Turkish, but became Mongol in character. Nearer to us, there was the migration of the Kalmucks from Zungaria to the Volga in the seventeenth century, with the extraordinary odyssey of their return from the Volga to Zungaria in the eighteenth. In such fashion the mutual relationship of the Turkish and Mongolian peoples changed ceaselessly in the course of history. Their common relation to the settled empires did not change on that account.

These examples show that we must look further than the flag, sometimes Turkish and sometimes Mongolian, which was planted upon the ancient empire of the steppes. The empire of the Hiong-nu or Asiatic Huns seems to have been a proto-Turkish empire at the beginning of the Christian era. It swallowed up many proto-Mongols, just as the empire of the European Huns, that of Attila, swallowed up many Finno-Ugrians, Sarmatians, Alans, Slavs and Teutons. Conversely, the Avar empire of the fifth century, in the Gobi Desert, was doubtless a proto-Mongol empire swallowing up the majority of the proto-Turkish nations. The 'T'u-kiu' empires of the sixth to eighth centuries and the Uigur empire of the eighth to ninth in

Mongolia were certainly Turkish dominations, ruling proto-Mongol tribes. In its turn, the empire of Genghis Khan was an empire under the Mongol flag, grouping together three-quarters of the Turkish or Turcoman and Tungus nations.

In sum, it is a matter, in these cases, of the substitution of one political power for another; the coming of a ruling tribe which is sometimes Turkish, sometimes Mongolian, rather than of what one could properly call a mass displacement of populations. For most of the time, territorial modification seems to have been limited to the occupation, by the dominant clan, of the territory of the upper Orkhon, around Karabalgasun and Karakorum, in the heart of Outer Mongolia proper, a territory which was the imperial region *par excellence* where camped the majority of the Hun *chan-yu*, as well as of the T'u-kiu, Uigur and Genghis-khanid *kaghans*.

The Resettlement of the Devastated Areas

Does that mean that the political upheavals of Upper Asia led to no modification in the settlement of North China, Turkestan and Hither Asia? Such a claim would be a travesty of fact. Fustel de Coulanges, while maintaining that the great Teutonic invasions had not noticeably modified the course of Gallo-Roman evolution, never denied that the fifth century saw the penetration of north-east Gaul by Teutonic settlement. It is equally certain that on several occasions, even at the zenith of their power and particulatly in periods of civil war, the Chinese emperors established in the northern provinces, Shen-si and Ho-pei, great numbers of Turco-Mongolian settlers to fill the gaps created by internal struggles or foreign raids. This was especially the case in the fifth and sixth centuries A.D., when the Tabghatch or T'o-pa, who were doubtless of Turkish race, first of all dominated the country as far as the Yellow River, and afterwards as far as the approaches of the Yang-tse, and became so rooted there that, unlike the Genghis-Khanjds and the Manchus, they were never thrown out, but ended by becoming entirely Chinese. They were absorbed by the Chinese masses. The case of these Franks of the Far East, as they have been nicknamed, recalls that of the Franks in Gaul. After Charlemagne's day, there was clearly no longer any difference in Neustria between a Gallo-Roman and a Frank. Likewise, in T'ang China, it is only when we see the name of an officer preceded for example by the patronymic Mu-jong, characteristic of the old Mongol clan of the Sien-pei, that we can conjecture that this Chinese officer has a Tartar ancestry.

In the West, the great invasions of the fifth century had at least appreciably modified—notably by the establishment of the Flemings—the dividing-line between languages. In China, nothing of the kind appears to have taken place. The division along the line of the Great Wall between the Chinese and Altaïc languages was no doubt largely the same as existed in the Han period. But this did not prevent the physical appearance of the northern Chinese being more or less modified by the continual absorption of these Turco-Mongolian and Tungus elements. In the same way in Normandy, the Neustrian was modified by Nordic settlements, although to-day there is no question of any but French-speaking populations here.

One of the reasons why, in China, the Turco-Mongolian invaders were definitely assimilated was that they settled. Now, the nomad who has settled down never reverts to nomadism. A typical example is that of the Uighur Turks. They had possessed the empire of the steppes (centering about the region of Karabalgasun on the upper Orkhon, in Outer Mongolia) from the middle of the eighth century to the middle of the ninth. At this date they were driven out by the Khirghiz and established themselves in the Chinese province of Kan-su, then in the rich oases of the central Gobi, at Bechbaligh (Dzimsa), Karachahr and Koutcha, where they adopted the settler's way of life. In the tenth century the Khitaï, having driven the Kirghiz from the Orkhon, suggested to the Uighur that they should return to occupy Outer Mongolia; but the Uighur refused this offer. Having settled down in their oases where the caravans of the silk traders called, they had no further desire to lead the adventurous life of the great northern steppes. The Kubilaïds, after their expulsion from China by the Ming at the end of the fourteenth century, for the same reason proved pitiably at sea in a kind of life which they no longer understood. Incapable of re-adapting themselves to their ancestral steppes, they only recovered a little under I ayan and Altan Khan at the end of the fifteenth century and the beginning of the sixteenth, and in Ordos and Chakar under the guidance and in the neighbourhood of that China for which they still felt nostalgia.

When the nomads become settlers on the invaded land, the steppe can produce farmers; but a settled peasant country can never turn them back into nomads. There can only be transformation in one direction, without possibility of return.

The Counter-Invasion of the Prairie by the Farmer

So far we have been concerned with the invasion of farm-land by the man from the steppe, who brought the steppe with him. The opposite movement equally exists, in the shape, e.g. of Chinese colonization of the grasslands, with its corollary, advancing tillage and retreating prairie. From the Han period about the beginning of the Christian era, the Chinese government applied itself to establishing military colonies north of the Great Wall in the Alachan, the Ordos, the Seui-yuan, and the Chakar. These became centres of soldier-farmers who created islets of cultivated land all the way across the ocean of the steppes. It was an achievement as praiseworthy as that of the Roman military colonies, from the Rhine to the Atlas Mountains; but it took much longer, since it has lasted to our own day.

The definitive conquest of the Mongols by the imperial dynasty of the T'sing in the seventeenth century led the Chinese peasants to drive back the Mongolian prairie and the Manchurian forest, to cut down trees there, clear the forest here, and to set up everywhere in the midst of the islets of tillage thus created the characteristic little Chinese farm. It was a silent and peaceful invasion before which the Mongolian herdsman or the Tungus forester continually gave ground, retreating all the time · northwards, just as the redskin perpetually withdrew before the American farmer, farther and farther towards the West.

The advance of cultivation in a south-north direction is still going on in Inner Mongolia before our very eyes. At the same time, working from north to south, there is proceeding in Outer Mongolia the methodical transformation by the Soviet rulers of the inhabitants of the Mongolian Republic into settled farmers. Attacked simultaneously on two fronts, on the Chinese side and on the Soviet side, the last nomads will soon have disappeared. A phase of world history is drawing to a close.

VI.

PASCAL'S PROBLEM—AND OUR OWN

ONE day history will end, because mankind will be extinct. It matters little that it may be in a future so distant that we have no interest in it. For the mind that poses the problem, that future has already come. It matters little whether the end will come as the result of some new glacial onslaught or after a final cooling of the earth, as a consequence of the ageing of our sun, which will turn from a yellow star into a red star; or, according to the 'anticipation' of J. H. Rosny, by the fact that our earth may turn into a desert, the soil erode, the waters disappear and the atmosphere evaporate—(the example of Mars and above all that of our satellite, the Moon, proclaim our destiny in this respect). Nor would it matter if, more dramatically, there should occur some cosmic collision, some conflagration in which our poor little earth was pulverized in an instant: *solvent saeclum in favilla.* It matters little that the death of the species may come only after a succession of scientific discoveries which, for a time, might make men seem like gods. Even though he should come to possess the most mysterious secrets of the atom and the cosmos, that human demi-god will perish.   And all his material work will have been in vain. Made only the more desperate by his complete knowledge of things and his mastery over them, he will have to surrender that ludicrous 'omnipotence'. Then he will see 'the eternal silence of infinite space' as it really is: as the sole problem. Can one imagine the final meditation upon the theme of 'infinite space' of the last thinking being on the last night of this planet?

But stay. . . . That meditation is already known to us. Pascal has recorded it in terms which need not be changed one iota:—
'Looking out upon the silent universe and upon Man left without light, abandoned to himself and, as it were, lost in this corner of the universe, without knowing who put him there, why he is there, what will become of him after death, incapable of all knowledge, I am stricken with terror like one carried off

in sleep to some frightful island rock, who wakes without knowing where he is and without being able to escape. And thereupon I marvel that man does not fall into despair at his miserable state.'

To this cry of anguish there is a modern echo:[1] 'Whether or not earthly man is the only being of his kind in the universe; whether or not he has brethren scattered far off in space, makes little difference to his way of facing his destiny. A ludicrous speck lost in the static and immeasurable cosmos, he knows that his feverish activity counts but little, is but a local phenomenon, ephemeral, without significance or goal. He has therefore no other resource but to set himself to forget the sheer immensity which crushes and ignores him.' And in the same scholar's *Thoughts of a Biologist* there is this *dies irae*: 'The human species will pass, as the dinosaurs and the stegocephali have passed. Little by little, the petty star which serves us as a sun will lose its power of light and warmth. All life will then have ceased on the earth which, a dead star, will go on revolving in limitless space. Then, of all human or superhuman civilization, of all discoveries, philosophies, ideals, and religions, nothing will survive. There will not even remain as much of us as remains of the Neanderthal Man, some fragments of whom have at least found refuge in the museums of his successor. In this tiny corner of the universe there will be obliterated for ever the quaint adventure of the protoplasm, an adventure which, perhaps, has already come to an end in other worlds, and which in still others will perhaps be repeated. And everywhere sustained by the same illusions, life will everywhere create the same torments, everywhere as absurd, as vain, as inevitably doomed from the outset to ultimate defeat and darkness infinite.'

I have felt bound to quote in full this searing page which drives man to intellectual despair—or to faith. For the natural scientist it is only too true. Yet the evolution of the cosmos, from the intra-atomic structure to the Milky Ways, though it proceeds through space infinite or curved, and through time infinite or limited, positively outrages the human mind, should life indeed be but a passing accident. Before this abyss we recoil in protest, as, in some Campo Santo, horses and riders recoil

---

[1] The conclusion of M. Jean Rostand in his book on *Man*.

before the spectacle of the open tomb. The evolution of life, if it does not culminate in the ascent into heaven of an immortal Soul, will have been nothing but a nightmare. Murder is its profession. The peace of the forests is only the assassination of plant by plant in a struggle for humus, water and light, and of plant by animal. As for human history, what historian, judging from on high, would dare to look upon it without horror? Such an agony can find only one excuse: the hope which the page just quoted mercilessly refuse us.

But, perhaps, the progress of science before the death of the earth will allow mankind to escape in time to less threatened planets? Possibly; although astronomers cannot readily suggest that any of the celestial lands of our solar system, from dying Mars to Venus (shrouded in an atmosphere that cannot yet be breathed), are capable of being colonized. But suppose we admit the hypothesis for a moment: it only puts off the fatal hour. For can we see mankind afterwards escaping altogether from the solar system, to take refuge on the unknown satellites of the 'nearest' star, Alpha of the Centaur? And doubtless from thence to the most 'neighbourly' of the nebulous spirals, that of Andromeda? We must give up the idea. . . . The *dies irae* which the priest intones over the coffin, is proclaimed each night to mankind by the dead stars with which the sky—that cemetery of stars—is sown, by the dead stars whose posthumous light continues to reach us across space and time.

Perhaps our own human species is not the only one in time or space? Among the millions of universe-islands or 'cities of stars' already located (and our Milky Way alone numbers forty thousand million stars), it is probable that some have existed or do or will exist where chance has renewed on a certain number of planets the chemical conjuncture which created on ours 'the adventure of the protoplasm'. What does it matter, since in that case these races of men are, as Pascal foresaw, imprisoned in their own islands, destined to live and die on them without communication with one another; each condemned to begin human experience all over again, without profiting by the experience of the others, without being able to give the others the benefit of its own experience? For each of these races too, all their effort will have been in vain. If we admit thus the hypothesis of the plurality of inhabited worlds, then periodically throughout infinity (and we are dealing here with hundreds of millions of light-years) the cosmos creates life, thought, and love; and creates them only to hurl them back into nothingness! This is a nightmare still worse than if there were but one race of mankind. A cosmic nightmare eternally in vain !

This, of course, is close to the Hindu conception. Shivaism saw the vanity of the cosmic effort; periods of annihilation succeeding phases of creation throughout eternity; it perceived the cruelty of such a vision and took a savage pleasure in it. 'The ages during which several millions of gods of heaven shall succeed unto one another, after each has lived out his allotted span; the time during which several Brahmâ shall die; the time after which Vishnu shall cease to be; all that is less than an instant to Shiva! When the time shall come that the sea, the earth, the air, the fire, and the wind shall be destroyed, several millions of Vishnus shall perish, and several millions of Brahmâs shall die likewise. Then shall Shiva gather up the heads of all these gods; of these heads shall he make his necklace; and he will dance on one foot a matchless dance, wherein this necklace will rattle on his eight shoulders; and he will sing strange airs which none else can sing, and taste of pleasures which none else hath known.'

A Nietzschean demiurge, or rather a Neronian and Satanic one whose ferocity is justified only, if we dare claim so much, from the aesthetic standpoint, by its esctasy of destruction—so that is the position to which we are finally driven? But in spite of the inhumanity of such a conception, we are obliged to repeat (with Nietzsche) that it still seems to us very human, *all zu menschlich*, 'only too human'. The drama of the world preserves its aesthetic value only as long as there remains a spectator to enjoy its wild and funereal beauty. When the last spectator has disappeared, what does the dance of Shiva matter to us?

But the actor himself is in danger of disappearing also. Shiva is deceiving himself if he thinks he can survive the other dêvas. The disintegration of the atom, the loss of energy resulting from the expansion of the universe, as well as, in another category, the hypothesis of a universe coming to an end—do not these amount to the sounding of the knell of the cosmic god? In the spiritual confusion of our time, the most nihilistic hypotheses become possible. 'There exists to-day,' Paul Valéry remarked on the eve of his death, 'a kind of strange and infernal harmony between the general state of the world and that of the realm of possibilities and of untrammelled creations or transformations which is the universe of the speculative spirit.'

The Sum of History! The silent drama of palæontologic evolution—which is nothing but a charnel-house of defunct species: then, emerging from this, the drama of human evolution fraught with so many protests and tears, so much blood-shed. The calvary of the living world? Agreed, if it is to end in man-made-God. But if, at the end of so much agony, there is in fact nothing but the tomb? Ah, then indeed the last man, on the last night of mankind, were he without hope of resurrection, might well utter in his turn the most tragic cry that has ever rung across the ages: *Eli, Eli, lamma sabachthani?*

Christians know the response which, throughout all eternity, the Eternal One has made to that cry. They know that the martyrdom of God-made-man was intended only to bring Him back to the right hand of the Father and, with Him, all mankind by Him redeemed. Apart from the Christian solution, apart from the *spiritual* solution, there is henceforth no other—no solution, that is, acceptable to both the reason and the heart. If the world is merely what it seems, is merely halting at the point to which the science and the scientific thought of this age have brought it—with an honesty for which we owe them thanks—it both mocks at the reason and revolts the heart. Christianity represents to-day, against so monstrous a negation, this revolt of the reason and of the heart, the protest of the spirit. Were it not for this protest, all human hope would founder. But in our threatened shipwreck the mission of Christianity is more than ever Salvation.

O Crux, ave, spes unica.

INDEX

INDEX